DATE DUE			

red

ANS

ng
ture-centered English program

Teaching
a literature-center

JAMES KNAPTON / BERTRAND EV

Random House • *New York*

English program

University of California at Berkeley

Foreword

For years teachers of English have been awaiting a revolution in their profession comparable to that which has altered drastically the teaching of the sciences, mathematics, and foreign languages. These teachers and the general public have recognized that somehow the teaching of English in high school has produced unsatisfactory results—the small number of American adults who read "good" books, the low cultural level of most television programs and movies, the difficulty businessmen have finding secretaries who spell and punctuate well, the difficulty secretaries have in making sense of their bosses' jumbled ideas, the murky language used by Americans in arguing political and social issues, the thousands of college freshmen who must take remedial courses in English, the number of college graduates who cannot be described as truly literate. High school English teachers, in the main, have patiently labored to close the gaps in learning not properly filled in the lower schools, to prepare their students adequately for college work, to instill good taste and respect for great ideas that are too seldom present in the culture of the nation.

Currently, numerous attempts are being made to improve the quality of English instruction: advanced placement programs, summer institutes, NDEA support, and subsidized programs for the culturally deprived. Regrettably, these attempts have concentrated on two extremes—the gifted and the slow students. The average student and the curriculum for him have been slighted, and it is the purpose of this book to deal directly with the curriculum for the main body of English students, both those who will go on to college and those who will not.

Many attempts at revolution have been plotted, but none has yet prevailed. In the past thirty years teachers of English have conscientiously tried one nostrum after the other: the experience curriculum, the core curriculum, group dynamics, semantics, team teaching, investigations of alienation and existentialism, so many varieties of linguistics that few teachers can name them, much less teach them. Grammar, formal, functional, or other, has been in and out so often that many teachers have stopped trying to keep up with fashion. Most recently an intimidating array of machines and programmed texts has threatened to relegate the teacher to the role of button-pusher. The rapid shifts of material and method have at last produced the bewildered cry "What is English?"

The frantic search for salvation through novelty has been stimulated by two gnawing convictions: that whatever has been tried so far has failed and that somewhere there exists an approach that will succeed. Perhaps in no other country is so much faith placed in the efficacy of education, and the acknowledgment is universal that "good English," in whatever terms, is essential to success in school, and success in school has been associated with success in other areas—financial, social, personal. The danger in this thinking is that the teaching of English may be reduced to serving only those specific goals. This book reasserts what good teachers have never doubted: that a mastery of "good English" and a grasp of humane values derived from the study of literature are not mutually exclusive, but in fact are best achieved together. The split, where it exists, must be closed. This book represents an effort to close it.

High school English programs have traditionally been divided into three discrete parts: literature, grammar, and composition (more recently literature, language, and composition). By this division, each part has suffered. The study of language divorced from composition and literature is surely as wasteful as the older split, where the study of *Julius Caesar* was followed by an exercise in theme-writing on "What I Did During Summer Vacation." What is more, English programs of the past thirty years have not been limited to the discrete matters of literature, language, and composition, but have offered an ever-widening variety of experiences, as though to equip students not only with the skills and understandings proper to the subject of English but with virtually all the knowledge and attitudes they might be expected to need in life. In trying to cover too many aspects of what has been called "total preparation for life," the English program has lost its identity.

The synthesis proposed in this book is no panacea that will relieve either student or teacher of responsibility for hard work. But the hope is that this work will be both more pleasurable and more rewarding because the program is unified, the activities meaningful. We present here a rationale of the Why, the What, and the How of the English program. Our basic premise is that the proper center of this program is literature. We are unrelentingly concerned with principles, but interested also in specific applications of these principles. Traditional as are many of the literary selections we recommend, the book is nevertheless radical in its insistence on a reconsideration of the basic justifications for the study of English. It is designed to give practical help to teachers and future teachers drawn to the teaching of English by the combination of idealism and dedication that the profession requires if English study is to make its appropriate and long overdue contribution to a literate and humane society.

J.K.
B.E.

Berkeley, California
May 22, 1967

Contents

Teaching
a literature-centered English program

Chapter 1

Why teach literature at all?

Unfortunately, the very first question that we must consider is also the most difficult to answer satisfactorily: *Why teach literature at all?* The answer—and the primary thesis of this book—is that until we have defined the purpose of teaching literature we cannot possibly have a rational basis for answering subsequent questions:

Teach which works?
In what order?
With what introduction?
With what form of presentation?
Accompanied by what activities?

These questions embrace virtually all of the procedural details that incessantly concern English teachers. They are questions from which there is no escape. They are answered yearly, weekly, daily, hourly, by anthologists, English staffs and program committees, and harassed individual teachers. If they are not answered philosophically, they are answered haphazardly, often "on the spot," for class hours move forward inexorably. The teacher who is busily explaining the Shakespearean sonnet form just before assigning homework on "When in disgrace with fortune and men's eyes," to be discussed next day by a twelfth grade college prep class moving through English literature chronologically, *has* answered them all—whether or not he is aware of the fact.

He has answered the question of Selection, for he is using a sonnet by Shakespeare.
He has answered the question of Arrangement, for he is moving chronologically through a national literature.

He has answered the question of Introduction, for he is lecturing on the formal characteristics of sonnets before this one is read.

He has answered the question of Presentation, for he is assigning independent outside reading of the sonnet.

He has answered the question of Activities, for he has told students to prepare for oral discussion tomorrow.

Perhaps his answers are all "right" ones. But unless he has a clear sense of why he is teaching literature at all, he cannot possibly know whether they are right or wrong.

Across the hall, another twelfth grade college prep class is holding a panel discussion on a newspaper article as part of a large unit on "Detection of Propaganda in the Mass Media." Two doors down the hall, another twelfth grade college prep class is engaged in a sentence-by-sentence reading and discussion of Lardner's short story "Haircut."

Are these also equally "right" things to be doing? Is one choice of activity just as good as another, one way of doing it just as good as another? More importantly, how is the teacher to determine rationally whether his procedures are good or bad?

The argument of this book is that there is no reasonable place to go for answers to any of the questions, big and little, that incessantly confront and worry English teachers except back to the initial one: Why are we teaching literature at all? If we can answer that, we shall have a basis for answering all the questions about Selection, Arrangement, Introduction, Presentation, Activities. If we cannot, we have no basis.

In attempting to answer our basic question, let us first turn the question so that it involves students as well as literature: *What can literature do for students?* With this phrasing, in fact, we have already implied a special kind of answer to the question: "Why teach literature?" We have now made a beginning by saying, "Because it can do something for students." But what?

It can do many things. It can expand their vocabularies, improve their skills of expression, acquaint them with literary forms and the characteristics of literary periods. It can widen their knowledge of past and present, acquaint them with foreign lands, peoples, customs. It can introduce them to the world of ideas, broaden their vision of life, help shape their beliefs, clarify and define their attitudes and ideals. It can enhance their imaginative faculties. It can give them a better understanding of their universe, their society, their fellow men, and themselves. It can give them pleasure.

In various wordings, these and many more claims have appeared on lists of objectives for the study of literature. With no effort, we could expand the list to include thirty "standard" functions, all worthy ones, that we might reasonably insist can be served by literature. Together, they would constitute as solid an argument for the study of literature in high school as can be made for any other subject.

Unfortunately, however, thirty answers to our initial Why are little better than none at all when we consider their usefulness for our immediate purpose. Thirty answers are too many to solve the great questions of Selection, Arrangement, Introduction, Presentation, Activities. If we try to follow them all, we shall not have a program, but a mélange. The task of Selection, for example, is simply impossible if we attempt to choose books that will serve all thirty Whys at once. As for Arrangement, we could not possibly decide on a method that would fit all purposes. To serve the purpose of acquainting students with literary genres, we would presumably want a typological arrangement, so that we could concentrate first on short stories, then on essays, then on poems, then on novels, then on plays. To serve the purpose of acquainting students with literary periods and the development of literary history, we should certainly want a chronological arrangement. To acquaint them with foreign lands, peoples, customs, we should want a geographical arrangement that would enable the class to "tour" one country after another through the literature of each. To serve the purpose of vocabulary development, we would presumably want an arrangement that would allow subsequent books to build on the vocabularies of preceding ones. To serve the purpose of developing writing skills, we should want yet some other style of arrangement.

We have no choice, therefore, but to refine our initial question: not "What can literature do for students?" but "What is *the very best thing* that it can do for them?"

Perhaps this redefinition of our initial question requires no defense. It carries no implication that literature is to be taught so that it will serve *only* "the very best thing" that it can do for students; even if the teacher were so disposed, he would be unable to confine its service to that alone. But it appears no less than perfectly reasonable that in selecting works, arranging them, introducing them, presenting them, choosing activities to accompany them, we should be directed by the best thing that literature can do, and not by secondary or incidental purposes.

What, then, is "the very best thing" that literature can do for students?

We believe that the best thing a work of literature, or any other work of art, can do is to provide *the experience of itself as a work of art*. We shall call this an "aesthetic experience," though clearly the aesthetic is not the only element in the total experience afforded by a work of art.

Now, why is this good—why, indeed, do we name it "the very *best* thing" that literature can do? Why should we want students to have not merely the experience of a single work of art but steady exposure to this experience throughout their school years? The "good" that is done by expanding their vocabularies or improving their skills of expression is practical and obvious. What "good" will aesthetic experiences do them?

Critics, philosophers, poets, essayists, novelists, dramatists have expressed themselves on the subject for centuries. But the gist of all that they have said is that the experience of works of art exercises a salutary effect on the inner being. Sidney insisted that poetry (literature) excels history and philosophy in "moving":

> And that moving is of a higher degree than teaching, it may by this appear, that it is well-nigh the cause and the effect of teaching.

Without "moving" power, other subjects can teach us about such matters as justice, honor, compassion; but poetry can make us want "to do that which we know." To "learn about" admirable human values is good, but it is less good than being induced to internalize them. The business of art, said Tolstoy, is not instruction but infection. Arnold defined "culture" as "a study of perfection," and went on thus:

> If culture, then, is a study of perfection, and of harmonious perfection, general perfection, and perfection which consists in becoming something rather than in having something, in an inward condition of the mind and spirit, not in an outward set of circumstances,— it is clear that culture . . . has a very important function to fulfil for mankind.

The center of Arnold's culture is literature, and literature's means, by virtue of its art, is its power to "move," so that from it we not merely know but seek to be. This is the ultimate worth of the aesthetic experience.

But we need not rely exclusively on the testimonials of poets and philosophers here; faith in the power of art to get through and affect the inner being is intuitive and universal. The least philosophical modern parent, who perhaps never in his life gave a moment's thought to such nonsense as "aesthetic experience," is curiously pleased when Johnny loses himself in a good book or takes up the violin. Can this be only for some crass reason—that book or violin keeps him out of mischief? Or because books and violins are status symbols? No doubt these considerations play a part, but not the main one; the parent unphilosophically assumes that, in some mysterious way, book or violin does Johnny "good."

The philosopher's sober reflection on the point and the ordinary parent's intuitive assumption are thus basically in accord. But of course both may be quite mistaken, as we also may be. It may never be scientifically proved that steady exposure to aesthetic experiences does the slightest good in the sense we mean. Possibly the very idea is romantic nonsense, as, indeed, may be Wordsworth's faith in the power of Nature to transform the human spirit:

> *One impulse from a vernal wood*
> *May teach you more of man,*
> *Of moral evil and of good,*
> *Than all the sages can.*

Perhaps, in fact, we are claiming even more for the power of art than Wordsworth claims (at this point) for the power of Nature. He argues that Nature can potently teach of man, evil, and good, whereas we contend that art can make us want to be better men. A closer parallel to our view is Fra Lippo Lippi's justification of his theory of art in Browning's poem:

> *If you get simple beauty and naught else,*
> *You get about the best thing God invents.*

What we are saying is that if you get the aesthetic experience and naught else, you get the best thing literature has to give. Art has not yet, seemingly, made the mass of mankind notably better; it seems not, during the long ages past, to have enhanced the inner nature of mankind very significantly. But have we deliberately sought to give it its best chance to do so?

If there is so much as a chance that art can do even a little of what we hope, it would surely be absurd to aim the teaching of it at some lower purpose, such as expanding vocabularies or learning about lands, periods, genres. To aim the teaching of literature at any lesser purpose would be, in effect, to forgo the realization of its best potential. We do not mean, of course, that in teaching we should ignore the usefulness of literature for secondary purposes such as vocabulary development and improving students' skills of writing and speaking; we believe that literature affords the very best means of accomplishing such goals, and later chapters will make this point abundantly clear.

But in the chapters that follow we aim primarily to provide literature with its best chance to do the best thing it can for students. To that end, we shall recommend the selection of works that have within them a rich potential of artistic experience, and we shall recommend that these works be arranged, introduced, and presented in the ways best calculated to release this potential. Of course English teachers have no monopoly on the development of humane human beings; art, music, language, history teachers have means at their disposal also. But probably English teachers, through literature, have the best means of all, and they should not shirk their responsibility or waste the extraordinary opportunity that is theirs by settling for lesser goals. The Great Society, of which we hear much at this crucial point in human history, will simply never exist unless it is composed of humane human beings; if literature can help, be it ever so little, to create these, we cannot teach it to better advantage.

Chapter 2

Which works of literature?

Selection

If above all else we want literature to give students aesthetic experiences, we must choose those works that can provide these experiences in strong measure.

While we are selecting works, we should exclude all other considerations. We should not, for example, undertake to solve the problems of placement and arrangement at the same time we are making our choices. We should not worry about assigning due quotas to American, English, and foreign literatures. We should not be concerned to see that any particular century is duly "represented." We should not worry about balancing short stories, novels, poems, essays, and plays. Later we may need to consider these details. But while we are selecting we should not allow ourselves to be diverted from the task of choosing first-rate works.

Why first-rate? The preceding chapter has answered the question: because first-rate works can provide the most potent aesthetic experiences. That is why they are first-rate. But how do we identify the first-rate? Should each teacher choose what he personally prefers? Should a committee assemble the works that its members like best? Should we ask classes of students what works they enjoy?

Eventually, the judgments of individuals, committees, and high school students must play a part—but in final decisions, not initial ones. The initial list, from which individuals may choose, ought to be compiled according to the best judgment that we can get, and to get that judgment we must consult wide authority. This authority is not oneself, or a committee, or a high school class. It is, rather, a consensus that includes critics, scholars, literary historians, and literate general readers, not of one year or generation, but of many years and generations, the more the better. We can be most sure of the oldest works, less sure of the later, and not sure at all of the latest.

We can be sure about Homer and Virgil, Dante, Chaucer, Cervantes, Shakespeare, Milton. Among novelists, we can be sure of Fielding, Austen, the Brontés, Dickens, Thackeray, Hardy, Conrad, Hawthorne, Melville, Twain, James. In drama we can be sure of the Greeks, Shakespeare, Goldsmith, Sheridan, Ibsen, Shaw. In the short story we can be sure of the best of Hawthorne and Poe, de Maupassant, Balzac, Tolstoy, Chekhov.

Yet even among older works, about which we might expect to be positive, critical opinion shifts somewhat. Shelley has moved downward and Keats upward; Browning and Tennyson are now more valued for a few poems with a modern look than for the great bulk of their poems that were prized in 1900. Certain of Shakespeare's plays— *Measure for Measure, Troilus and Cressida*—are more highly valued in our time than they were in the nineteenth century, although, of course, they are not rated among the greatest tragedies and comedies. Is our time right about these plays, or does its special interest in them only reflect a contemporary aberration? Dr. Johnson, the soundest critic of his time, grossly undervalued Milton after a hundred years. *David Copperfield*, which long stood at the top of Dickens' novels, now rates below *Bleak House*. Is our time right about *Bleak House*, or were the preceding three generations right? Or is there no such thing as being right in such matters?

Perhaps there are not and cannot be absolutes in the identification of literary "bests." Looking backward as far as Homer, we are likely to prefer the *Odyssey* to the *Iliad*, not because it is artistically superior but because it is more to the taste of our time; those incessant bloody encounters on the plains of Troy and those interminable genealogies and lists of men, ships, and gods lack the appeal, in our time, of Odysseus' timeless journey. Looking far back, we are prone to elevate those works that have some specific applicability to our times, our problems, our temper, and to demote other works, even more highly prized by previous generations, because they lack particular "relevance." No doubt the spirit of Donne commends itself more to our temper than does that of Spenser—or, for that matter, of Milton. Our time's special preoccupations have led Shakespeareans to set *Measure for Measure* higher than the Victorians did. The greatness of *War and Peace* has always been evident, but the historical accident of Hitler's penetration deep into the heart of Russia and then his long, costly withdrawal, paralleling the Napoleonic experience so powerfully detailed in the novel, caused the reputation of Tolstoy's masterpiece to shoot upward. In the early 1940s, it seemed even greater—if that were possible—than it is.

If a given generation's estimate even of long-established works deviates, sometimes wildly, according to its specific temper, it is evident how inaccurate any generation is apt to be in judging its own products. Our generation is not peculiar in this respect. Chaucer's age preferred Gower to Chaucer. In his own time, only Milton fully appreciated the greatness of Milton. The prodigious social and political influence of *Uncle Tom's Cabin* in its own time made it seem a great novel; it is in fact a deplorable novel, artistically worthless. Whitman's *Leaves of Grass* passed unnoticed for twenty years. Every age has produced its authors who struck the fancy of the time and stole the show from one or two real masters whose prestige had to wait on time's correction. It is all but true that every period is likely to think its worst writers the best, and its best the worst.

Every age represents, in one direction or another, a distortion, an aberration. It has its special, flaring issues, social, philosophical, and other. Works that accommodate themselves peculiarly well to the time's aberration are likely to be overrated by contemporary readers and even by the best contemporary critics. When thereafter the issues that make them seem important, and even great, yield place to new issues, or pass away entirely, these works are often seen to be of value only as documents of their time.

Timely social documents are not necessarily great literary documents and may not be literary at all. It is often argued, as a reason for emphasizing contemporary works in English programs, that because these works deal with issues of immediate concern to students they are capable of giving an immediate and powerful experience and hence are preferable to older works that lack particular applicability to present issues. According to this reasoning, English teachers during the 1850s would have been right to teach *Uncle Tom's Cabin* in their classes rather than *King Lear*. We cannot dispute the likelihood that Uncle Tom would "get to" the students more readily and with more obvious effect than Lear; we may have to concede that he would reach them with twenty times the force. Further, by the same argument, teachers should then have taught *Uncle Tom's Cabin* rather than the similarly contemporary *The Scarlet Letter* and *Moby Dick*—works heavy with allegory and symbol, great artistic novels with no direct comment on the blazing main issues of the 1850s. Again, we cannot doubt that the effect on students of Stowe's social document would have been far more obvious than the effects of Hawthorne's and Melville's masterpieces.

But the experience of *Uncle Tom's Cabin* would have been a *social* experience, not an aesthetic one. This novel has little power to give an aesthetic experience; and in the 1850s what little aesthetic force it had would have been obliterated by its social force.

But is not a social experience just as good as an aesthetic one? Perhaps it is even better; but we need not place the two in competition. Our point is that they are *different* and should not be confused; and the primary business of the teacher of literature is with aesthetic experiences, which otherwise may not be represented at all in the education of most high school students. In the 1850s, since the teacher could not be expected to have had the wisdom to choose *The Scarlet Letter* or *Moby Dick* in preference to *Uncle Tom's Cabin*, he should have omitted all three and chosen *King Lear*, about which there was no question in his time, as there is none in ours.

We may now seem to have reasoned our way to two conclusions that we do not quite intend: (1) works that explicitly address themselves to contemporary problems automatically disqualify themselves as far as the power to provide aesthetic experience is concerned; and (2) every generation ought to exclude all contemporary works from the English program because no generation has the perspective needed to distinguish its great literary works from its mere social documents.

The first is of course completely false. Many, perhaps most, of the supremely great works in the world's literature had special relevance for their times. Even an isolate like Emily Dickinson, to take an extreme case, wrote poems that are intimately bound up with her age. The works of Dante, Cervantes, Chaucer, Spenser, Shakespeare, Milton are profoundly involved with their own times. The world's most powerful novelists—Dickens, Hugo, Zola, Dostoevsky, Tolstoy—have characteristically grappled with the urgent problems of their day. It is not because certain works concern themselves with the age's problems that they fail as literary works, nor is it because certain other works skirt their age's problems that they succeed: *Uncle Tom's Cabin* does not fail because it took up the issue of slavery, nor does *Moby Dick* succeed because it avoids it. *Huckleberry Finn* tackles the question of slavery and is Mark Twain's masterpiece; *Tom Sawyer* confronted no such national issue and is a pygmy beside the other. *Bleak House* addressed itself centrally to a specific abuse of its time and is, say our Dickensians, Dickens' masterpiece. But *Wuthering Heights*, set in the wild and isolated moors, treats no issues of its time and is no less a masterpiece. Whether or not a work takes up the special issues of its day has nothing to do with its greatness or lack of greatness as a literary work. But a work that takes up the crucial issues of its time is more likely to be overvalued in its time, and a work that skirts these issues is more likely to be ignored in its time.

Turning now to the second question, whether contemporary works ought simply to be excluded from English programs, we find a complex and vexing problem. To begin with, this much can be stated as fact: history of criticism amply proves the inability of any period to distinguish unerringly between the wheat and the chaff of its own products. If the English program is to include only the best—i.e., that which potentially offers the richest aesthetic experience—it must exclude everything produced by the current generation.

But now our logic has led us to a conclusion that is intolerable, if not monstrous. By this logic, planning a program in England in 1600, we would have had to forgo *Twelfth Night*, which was brand new, though we might have admitted *Gammer Gurton's Needle* and *Ralph Roister Doister*, which were forty years old. We must, surely, find some way to escape from our own logic.

We cannot abandon our basic principle, that only the best should be included, because there is simply no alternative; if we abandon that, we have nothing. If what we truly seek is literature that has the richest potential for aesthetic experience, we have no choice but to include only the best works that we can identify with assurance; and we cannot identify the contemporary with assurance.

Can we, then, cheat on our basic principle just a little, making an *exception* of the contemporary? We may say that we shall be sure to take only the best from *older* literature, where we can know what is best, and that we shall take from the contemporary the best that can be identified, knowing that we run two risks: (1) that we may not succeed in choosing the best of our time and may indeed choose very badly, and (2) that even if we manage to choose the best of our time it may not be as good as much in the past that we shall have to forgo in order to include it.

If we do so compromise, we are saying in effect that we are taking the best from the past because we know it is *best*, but that we are taking some of the contemporary just because it is *contemporary*. Evidently, then, what we really mean is that the contemporary should be represented, regardless. But if we proceed in this way we shall be wholly false to our principle. We have not chosen the *Odyssey* because we thought the ancient Greeks should be represented, or *Hamlet* in order to represent the Renaissance, or "Lycidas" in order to represent Milton and the seventeenth century, or *Gulliver's Travels* in order to represent the eighteenth century, or "Tintern Abbey" in order to represent the Romantic period, or "Dover Beach" in order to represent the Victorian Age, or *The Scarlet Letter* in order to represent the American novel. We have chosen all of these because they are all first-rate works, and for that reason alone. Why, then, should we choose any contemporary works on the grounds that the contemporary must be represented?

It appears that we cannot turn loose our basic principle just a little; we must either hold to it or abandon it altogether. Are the arguments for "representing" the contemporary sufficiently compelling to warrant abandoning our principle? Let us examine these arguments.

A leading one is that contemporary works, whether or not we know them to be first-rate, open a channel to the study of older literature. Since students live in the same present that envelops the author, are likely to be interested in the issues of their own time, and are at least partially familiar with the language and ideas in current works, some of the barriers to appreciation of older works are absent. We will deal with this argument more fully later in the book.

Another argument—now greatly fashionable—is that current works, even if they are not first-rate, can actually reach students with greater force than older great works just because they are contemporary and therefore contain live issues with which, perhaps, students are already involved. An English teacher in the 1850s would have had little trouble in motivating students to read *Uncle Tom's Cabin*, for its very immediacy would have done the job— Lincoln told Mrs. Stowe that the book had started a war. Just so, in our time, motivating students to read James Baldwin's *Go Tell It on the Mountain* is far easier than motivating them to read *Pride and Prejudice*.

What is more, there is every probability that Baldwin's novel will strike them with harder impact than Austen's will—even though *Pride and Prejudice* is a masterwork among masterworks, whereas the reputation of *Go Tell It on the Mountain* may or may not prove to have marked only an eccentricity of our time. If it were primarily for their gross weight of impact that we should choose literary works for students, then we should no doubt take *Go Tell*

It on the Mountain and omit *Pride and Prejudice.* In the 1930s *The Grapes of Wrath* would have hit students harder than *Les Misérables.* During the same period O'Neill's *The Hairy Ape* would have struck them harder than *King Lear.* And today—or at least a few years ago—*The Diary of Anne Frank* strikes students with an immediacy beside which the experience of *Romeo and Juliet* seems remote and pale. A mere newspaper or magazine account of the assassination of President Kennedy gives a jolt to students who lived through that shocking day beside which the effect of Shakespeare's account of Caesar's assassination is a vague tremor. Of course there are exceptions; but in general it is fair to say that any contemporary work that is reasonably well written and meets timely issues head on stands a good chance of outweighing Homer, Dante, Cervantes, Shakespeare, and Milton in terms of its immediate impact on students.

In the face of this fact, should we not summarily reduce the enormous problem of selection by limiting choices to the contemporary? Does it really make sense to try to involve students in the fate of an old mad king caught in a storm on an ancient British heath and speaking in Elizabethan English, when they can so much more easily be involved in any current book that treats the struggle for human rights? Does it really make sense to try to involve them in the subtle sensibilities of Jane Austen and her remote little circle of eighteenth-century English gentry, when they so naturally "dig" the sensibilities of Holden Caulfield? Is it not simply perverse to try to excite them with the tale of a legendary wanderer and his encounters with giants, sorceresses, waves, winds, rocks, and whirlpools, when their very environment, without a drop of motivational sweat from the teacher, has preconditioned them to respond to voyages of atomic submarines and spaceships? And is it not simple madness to try to involve them in experiences like "Oh to be in England, Now that April's there" and "I stood in Venice, on the Bridge of Sighs," when nothing, but *nothing*, in their living environment has preconditioned them for any such stuff?

Or, if we do bow to tradition and make a few token

selections from three thousand years of literature that preceded our generation's thirty, will it not be wise to confine
our choices to works that rather obviously have some message for our times? Of course no authors before our time
dealt with *exactly* our problems, but only, at best, with
problems similar to ours; they cannot, therefore, be expected to gain quite the immediate credit with students
that authors have who are here among us. But if teachers
make a special point of relating these select older works to
present problems, thus showing that they are, to a degree,
timely, surely some of the disadvantage of their antiquity
can be overcome and students may be willing to give them
a hearing. By this way of thinking, teachers should obviously avoid such Shakespeare as *A Midsummer Night's
Dream*, a mere fantasy of moon-mad youths in the woods
of legendary Athens that has absolutely no timely message
to give us; but they can safely take *Julius Caesar*, because
we have recognizably similar problems today with dictators,
demagogues, propaganda, and assassinations. They can risk
Romeo and Juliet, too, which makes a modern connection
through *West Side Story*. Students will see that it does
not fit the local scene very closely and that its lovers speak
an alien tongue, but if teachers stress its resemblances to
West Side Story, the reading may be tolerated. *Huckleberry Finn* is clearly usable because of its applicability to
present social concerns, but teachers should think twice
about including *The Scarlet Letter* and *Moby Dick*—brand-
ing sinners and grappling with whales not being major
problems of our time.

In groping for answers to the basic questions of selection
—answers necessary before we choose even one work in
the entire program—we have now reached two conclusions
that, alas, do not fit together:

1. We should select *no* contemporary works, because we
   cannot be positive that they are first-rate.
2. We should select *only* contemporary works (except
   for a few classics that can be made to seem timely),
   because students are easily involved in their issues.

The first of these positions is patently absurd; it makes no
sense to exclude living writers from English programs. But

the second is equally absurd; to read only the contemporary is to waste what is too precious to be wasted, to risk losing our perspective, to surrender entirely, in Eliot's phrase, to "the stranglehold of the present." Is there a solution?

The first necessity is to try seriously to identify the best of the contemporary and the near-contemporary. That means that teachers should consult something more than their individual tastes in recent works and that they should consult something more than publishers' blurbs, best-seller lists, and the opinions of a random critic or two. In the past thirty years the number of novels, plays, collections of stories and poems, and other works that have been greeted by someone or other with epithets like "Great!" "Superb!" "Magnificent!" "Incomparable!" is almost as large as the number of those that have received no such accolades. It is necessary, in short, to get the best evidence that is available if teachers are at least to minimize the probability that their contemporary choices will be bad. Teachers who seriously undertake to amass such evidence will quickly find how much harder it is to sift new works than old ones. They will also come to the sobering realization that it is impossible to be certain.

Assuming, then, that teachers will choose as wisely as they can, we can go a step or two further. First, we can include many short works—poems, stories, essays—no one of which takes long to teach. But long works are another matter. Thorough reading and discussion of a novel or a full-length play, from the time it is introduced until all activities are completed, may take between three and eight weeks. When so large a part of a semester's program is devoted to one long work, teachers should be sure that it is really first-rate. If they give this time to Pride and Prejudice or to King Lear, they can be sure. But if they give it to a novel or play of only ten or twenty years' standing, they can have no real assurance that they are spending these weeks economically.

But half a dozen short stories can be read as a weekend assignment and discussed in an hour. Even if the teacher should decide to give two whole class hours to the intensive reading and discussion of one short story—"Haircut," for example, or a new story in the latest issue of Harper's—and even if the next twenty years should consign these works to oblivion, the two hours are only two hours. But six weeks are six weeks, and to spend them on *Northwest Passage* instead of *The Scarlet Letter* is to risk squandering too much.

Much the same may be said of poems and essays. Perhaps we can be sure enough of Frost, Eliot, Robinson that we can award them as much time as Wordsworth, Keats, and Tennyson without serious risk. We may be less sure of e. e. cummings—but what of that? If half an hour is given to "what if a much of a which of a wind" and "next to of course god america i," and if time proves that these were only freakish excrescences, we have, after all, squandered only half an hour.

What is suggested, then, is that English programs can include many modern short stories, poems, and essays with less risk than if they included recent novels and full-length plays. It is harsh truth, but a truth nevertheless, that we cannot be sure enough even of Hemingway, Faulkner, O'Neill, Miller, and Tennessee Williams to use the time needed to study their works closely, let alone the great number of more strictly contemporary novelists and playwrights. To allot four weeks of close study to a single modern work is to play against heavy odds. But if teachers choose carefully among recent short works, out of the abundance that they choose they should manage to be right nearly half the time, and these are fair odds. With short stories, in particular, it is a safe bet that the twentieth century has produced hundreds as fine, judged as works of art, as the best of Poe, Hawthorne, de Maupassant, and Chekhov.

But does this acceptance of short works mean that we must absolutely exclude long modern works? It does not. Chapter 7 offers a suggestion, worked out in detail, that admits the use of many modern novels and plays. Very briefly, the suggestion is that while intensive study of unquestionable masterpieces is proceeding day by day *in class*, students are to be reading widely on their own, in works selected from lists drawn up to accompany the in-class study. Thus, for example, while a class is working its way line by line through *Antigone*, individuals on their own may be reading *The Skin of Our Teeth* and *Our Town*; while a class is studying *Moby Dick*, individuals may be reading *The Old Man and the Sea* and *Northwest Passage*; and while the class is studying *Macbeth*, individuals may be reading *The Emperor Jones* and *Death of a Salesman*. By this plan, longer works studied in class are always, or nearly always, older, whereas outside lists should include both older and more recent works, the latter even predominating in some cases.

We should return, finally, to the second of our two mutually contradictory propositions, namely, that contemporary literature should be preferred to older works in the English program. The main argument for this, as earlier stated, is that contemporary works, just because they are contemporary, will take quicker hold on students' minds and provide more potent experiences than older masterpieces.

The gist of the most often repeated opposing argument is expressed by the term "cultural heritage." English teachers are often reminded, and steadily remind themselves, that they are obligated to pass this heritage on. We dare not waste the riches of the past, on which the continuing civilization builds. If we did so, we would soon revert to barbarism. The cultural heritage is not simply inherited; it must be learned. And if it is to be learned, it must be taught. Of course English teachers are not solely responsible for the transmission of this heritage; the total responsibility is shared by all education. But that literature, from Homer to Eliot, contains a solid core of the great heritage is indisputable, and that English teachers bear a major share in the total responsibility is indisputable.

In reasserting this standard argument for teaching two thousand years of literature, we have again brought two guiding principles into collision. The argument holds that older literature must be taught *because the cultural heritage must be preserved*, but we have earlier argued that contemporary literature should be preferred because its timeliness assumes the ready involvement of students in potent experiences. Which of these arguments should prevail? Or should we compromise—teaching older works in order to preserve the heritage, but contemporary ones in order to provide experiences? As a matter of fact, compromise has been our usual solution.

But we also said earlier that the thing to be valued most in literature is the experience of the work as a work of art and that our choice in selection, as in approach, arrangement, and presentation, should be guided by this idea. We should therefore choose those works that have the greatest potential for giving this unique experience. How does this earlier conclusion bear on our new dilemma? Does our purpose of providing aesthetic experiences accord better with the argument that the cultural heritage must be preserved or with the argument that contemporary works most nearly guarantee students' genuine involvement?

In reasserting the standard argument that we must teach older works so as to preserve the cultural heritage, have we not introduced an idea that conflicts with our insistence on aesthetic experience as the most precious commodity to be derived from them? If we say that we must, above all, preserve the heritage, do we not assert that what we value most is *knowledge* of over two thousand years of literature —knowledge of individual works, authors, periods, transitions, genres, currents, themes, ideas, and all else that goes to make up cultural history? And in saying this, do we not admit that we really care only secondarily about aesthetic experience? Is it, ultimately, *knowledge of* or *experience of* that we really care most about? This is a question about which every teacher should try to be perfectly honest, for everything depends on the answer.

Do we mean that we should teach Homer, Virgil, Dante, Cervantes, Shakespeare, Milton, and the rest so that the new generation will "know about them," and about the periods, genres, ideas, historical evolutions that they represent? Is this what "passing on the cultural heritage" means?

If it is, then surely we should forget about those two thousand years of literary history and teach, instead, none but contemporary works for the experience they render. We can, after all, count on history to give students such awareness of the past as is needed for perspective in the present; probably history does the job even better than literature. We can thus spare the English teacher and the school time allotted to literature for what literature can do better than history: *give students the experience of art.*

Again we seem to have concluded that the English program should be composed of contemporary works chosen because these involve students immediately and seriously. These we can teach, not for their historical value, as we teach older works in "passing on the cultural heritage," but for their experiential value. We thus remain faithful to our insistence that the finest value of works of art is experience rather than knowledge. Better to teach *The Glass Menagerie* for its experience than *Antigone* for its knowledge of the Greeks. Better *Go Tell It on the Mountain* for its experience than *The Scarlet Letter* for its knowledge of Puritan New England. Better half a dozen poems from a collection of tributes to President Kennedy for the experience than "Lycidas," "Adonais," and "Thyrsis" for the acquaintance they give us with elegiac tradition.

But the real question is whether the experience of *The Glass Menagerie* is better than the experience of *Antigone,* whether the experience of *Go Tell It on the Mountain* is better than the experience of *The Scarlet Letter,* whether the experience of an elegy for President Kennedy is better than the experience of "Lycidas." We have agreed that the experience of contemporary works is more readily accessible than the experience of older works because students are already motivated by their involvement in the present. Great concerns such as today's concern for civil rights predispose readers to become involved in *Go Tell It on the Mountain.* They are "ready" for the experience of the book; they will fairly devour it. They will not eat up *The Scarlet Letter* with half such relish. The experience of the recent novel will seem immediate, will excite them visibly, stir them to hot discussion and perhaps even to animated writing. The experience of the older work will seem comparatively remote, "literary," and unreal; the response may appear more like dispassionate attention than like excitement. Which is the better experience?

Rather, which is the "righter" experience for a teacher

of literature to aim at? Which experience is more purely aesthetic? In contemporary works—except those that have no special relevance for contemporary issues, for example, "Stopping by Woods"—the aesthetic experience is often overwhelmed by the social one. For example, if we read *The Grapes of Wrath* in the mid-1930s, our experience was more social than aesthetic. On the other hand—supposing that the book truly has an aesthetic experience to give—we can read it in 1966 with a better chance of experiencing it as a work of art. In 2066, the aesthetic experience should come through in still purer form.

What is suggested here is that an experience of a work as a work of art is markedly different from an experience of a work (even though it be a perfectly good work of art) as a document of our time. To become concerned in the 1960s for Dido, left behind so many ages ago and so far away from our own shores, is to have one kind of experience; to be concerned in the 1960s for the plight of a racial minority is to have another.

What is further suggested is that, supposing for just a moment that Baldwin's artistic power were equal to Virgil's and that the *potentiality* of aesthetic experience were equal in the two works, it will be more difficult for the contemporary reader to derive this experience from *Go Tell It on the Mountain* than from the *Aeneid*; in fact, this experience may be denied students who have a normal amount of social awareness.

And, finally, quite aside from the question whether the aesthetic experience is in any sense "better" than the social experience, it is in any event the special concern of the teacher of literature because it is the unique thing that literature, as an artistic phenomenon, has to offer. The experience of art is to be involved not with what we are already involved with, but with what except for the artist we would *not* be involved with.

The implications of these attitudes for the practical task of selecting works for an English program are clear: except for short pieces that take little time, we should use few contemporary works for intensive study and discussion in the classroom—though we can make much use of longer modern works for independent reading. Among both recent and older works we should seek not those that have an obvious relevance for our time and its special issues, but those that are least "timely." In choosing among works, we should prefer "Stopping by Woods" to a poem, perhaps equally fine, directed to the issue of civil rights—for what we are primarily after is aesthetic experience, not social instruction. But the social studies teacher might well use the civil rights poem in presenting the issue. The job of the teacher of literature is to develop students' capacities to care about Dido and Hecuba.

We can afford to be less careful about relevance to "timely" issues in choosing works from the past, but we should not disregard them entirely. We should certainly teach both The Merchant of Venice and As You Like It. But if we can teach only one, in a semester in which racial issues are feverish, we should omit The Merchant of Venice because it relates to these issues and teach As You Like It because it does not relate to them. We should certainly teach both Julius Caesar and Romeo and Juliet. But in these years we should not choose the former just because it dramatizes an assassination. Neither should we choose the latter just because it is like West Side Story. We should probably not teach Antony and Cleopatra in high school at all; but in any event we should not choose it just because of Liz and Dick's Cleopatra—as, in fact, many teachers have done. We should certainly teach Huckleberry Finn, but not because Huck's experience is socially relevant now; and we should not teach Uncle Tom's Cabin for two reasons: it does relate closely to the present, and all its "art" exists to promote a social rather than an aesthetic experience.

We may apply this principle geographically as well as temporally. We should probably teach "The Celebrated Jumping Frog of Calaveras County" everywhere; but we should most insist on teaching it in Vermont and least in California, particularly in Calaveras County. In Calaveras County we should rather choose "The Legend of Sleepy Hollow." We should teach Ethan Frome everywhere, but we should care least to teach it in New England and most to teach it in New Mexico. We should teach, or be sure that students read, *Life on the Mississippi* everywhere but on the Mississippi. We should teach "The Village Blacksmith" in New York City and "Chicago" in Hayfork, California. We should teach *Moby Dick* everywhere, but we should teach it especially in Kansas, and not especially in Nantucket; but we should especially teach *O Pioneers* in Nantucket.

These drastic instances illustrate what may be called the principle of reverse proximity in the selection of literary works. This principle represents a categorical repudiation of ideas that have guided the making of reading programs for a generation or more and that particularly direct the efforts of most program makers today. Though recent years have seen a dramatic upturn in the search for literature of genuine quality to replace the "reading materials" of the '30s, '40s, and '50s, this upturn has been accompanied by a false kind of justification—namely, that the classics, as well as contemporary works, really do "have something to say to our time." A regrettable effect of this justification has been the pronounced tendency of program makers to emphasize works that make ready connections with contemporary interests, attitudes, problems; a particularly gross example is the reintroduction of a book or two from *Paradise Lost* because Satan's habit of flying about the cosmos relates to present space travel. This is no reason for teaching *Paradise Lost*.

For many years a certain state college offered a famous English course with the title "Books That Make Up Your Mind." The reading list was composed exclusively of works that bore directly on twentieth-century issues. The value of such a course is not in question here. But though it posed as a course in literature, it missed the point of literature. It may very possibly have been a better course than any course in literature ever was; but it was not a course in literature. The object of a course in literature is not to "make up your mind" about present or specific issues; the influence of aesthetic experience is subtler, deeper, more pervasive, non-specific. What *Uncle Tom's Cabin* did for people's minds in the 1850s represents one kind of thing;

what becoming involved with the silent figures on a Grecian urn or becoming concerned for Hecuba does for the inner being is quite another. Our very first responsibility in selecting literary works for students is to the latter kind of experience.

We have not yet touched all aspects of the problem of selection; others are more appropriately discussed later. It is to the question of placement that we now turn.

Placement

We should begin by making a distinction between "placement" and "arrangement." "Placement" refers to the assignment of works by years; we shall have in mind grades 9, 10, 11, and 12. "Arrangement" refers to the order in which works are taken up within each year; it is discussed in Chapters 3 and 4.

The problem of placement has become critical for individual teachers and departments in recent years because the availability of inexpensive paperbacks has freed English programs from the straitjacket imposed by traditional anthologies. Ninth grade teachers formerly taught from the ninth grade anthology, tenth grade teachers from the tenth, and so on. Teachers might or might not supplement the anthology's offerings with poems, essays, and stories of their own choice, but for the most part the problem of placement was solved by the anthologies. With adoption of a four-year series, a school's English department automatically provided for degree of progression, avoided accidental repetition of readings, and ensured that teachers of the upper years knew, or could easily discover, what their classes had read earlier.

Whatever their other faults, the anthologies performed invaluable service for placement. Anthologists unquestionably committed errors of judgment, and they did not consistently agree with one another; a particular short story might appear in the volume for grade 9 in one series, in grade 10 of another, in grade 11 of another, and in grade 12 of yet another. But these are minor discrepancies, and the fact is that every anthologist of a major series gave much more judicious thought to the problem of placement than the individual teacher finds time or is competent to give, and more judicious thought than a departmental committee, meeting in a limited time, can possibly give.

The abrupt decline of dependence on the anthology series has thus placed an appalling responsibility on departments and teachers. It has created a necessity for members of departments to agree on the works to be assigned to each year; the alternative is a chaos of repetition, lack of progression, lack of direction. Though many works of literature might be taught almost equally well in any one of the four years and though many of these works could be taught profitably not once but repeatedly during two, three, or even four years, it is also clear that certain works are more appropriate for certain years than for others, and it is inevitable, unless concerted thought is given to the problem, that some works will be badly misplaced. If the ninth grade teacher, simply because he is mad about *King Lear*, seizes on that play for his class, and the twelfth grade teacher, similarly wild about *Julius Caesar*, lays claim to it, a double evil has been committed. And though any Shakespearean play would repay study each year for four years, it would make poor sense to use it repeatedly and to find time for no others.

Confronted, thus, by an incredible variety of paperback literature, including collections of short stories and poems, individual volumes of novels and plays, all available, all good, all inexpensive and attractive—but *no* volumes explicitly labeled *Ninth Grade*, *Tenth Grade*, *Eleventh Grade*, *Twelfth Grade*—teachers can avoid chaos only by (1) turning their backs on the whole lot and reverting to the old tried-and-true anthology, or (2) buckling down to the task of working out and adhering to a reasonable plan of placement. The objections to the first solution are obvious: the ponderous traditional anthologies lack the attractiveness of new, neat paperback volumes that offer ably edited long works and fine collections of short works; the anthologies have become crowded with materials of little or no literary quality; and they have become overloaded with editorial paraphernalia of a quality, kind, and quantity to make the study of even fine literary pieces distasteful. They do indeed offer a solution to the practical problem of placement, but they offer little else.*

What is more, though there is much to commend, even the placement of works in the typical anthology series suffers from one ruinous fault: eleventh grade volumes are regularly confined to American and twelfth grade volumes to English literature. This is mainly a problem of "arrangement," which we shall discuss in the next chapter. But "arrangement" dictates some practices of "placement" that are disastrous. Because Poe, for example, is American, most of his writing is always reserved for the eleventh grade volume—when as a matter of fact his stories and poems alike are best suited for the ninth grade. Similarly, and even more absurdly, the eleventh grade volume always includes much Longfellow—when truly there is nothing of Longfellow's that needs placement later than the ninth grade. These are only random examples; typical eleventh grade volumes include many poems and stories that have been placed in that year not because they belong there from the point of view of relative difficulty, but only because they are American. Similarly, the twelfth grade volume monopolizes much that should have been placed in either the ninth or tenth grade volume: the simple, lovely short poems of Wordsworth, for example. Shakespeare's sonnets, which ought to be distributed throughout four years, are regularly restricted to the twelfth grade volume. A little, even, of Milton could be brought into the ninth grade, but is not because it must be saved for the "English Literature" volume. We need add here only that limitation of the eleventh grade volume to American literature outlaws the inclusion of a Shakespearean play in that year; but with this gross absurdity we must deal later. Finally, because the cream of American and English literature must be saved for the eleventh and twelfth grades, ninth and tenth grade anthologies are necessarily filled out with inferior works, and worse.

There seems to be no choice for individual teachers and

* See James J. Lynch and Bertrand Evans, *High School English Textbooks: A Critical Examination* (Boston: Little, Brown and Company, 1963).

departments but to grapple seriously with the job of place-ment. The lists presented in the Appendix to the present volume may be useful, but of course they are not final. For few of the listed works is there an absolute right or wrong of placement. Many could go in either the ninth or the tenth grade, many in either the eleventh or the twelfth; some might do as well, or nearly, at any level. Our under-lying principle has been to place each work as *early as it can be profitably undertaken*, though we know that the same work might be more deeply probed and appreciated in a later year. In placing *Huckleberry Finn*, for example, in the ninth grade, we do not deny that twelfth graders would gain much more from this novel than ninth graders will; we mean, rather, that ninth graders can get much from it, and in any event enough to make teaching it at that level practicable. On the other hand, in placing Henry James' *Portrait of a Lady* in the twelfth grade, we mean, while not denying that students might earlier get *something* from it, that teaching this novel is not a paying proposition before grade 12. In short, our principle has been to place each work as far down as it could reasonably be placed, saving the upper years for works that cannot reasonably be placed lower. Still, many of these works, such as Shake-speare's sonnets, could be taught in any of the four years. To have followed our rule here of placing works as far down as they could reasonably be placed would have meant placing all these in the ninth and tenth grades. But we have distributed the sonnets throughout the four years; we have treated poems of other major poets similarly, for ex-ample, Browning, Wordsworth, and Shelley. So, also, Ba-con's essays. At the extremes, however, are authors who most properly belong to the ninth grade (Poe, Longfellow) and to the twelfth (James, Eliot, Yeats).

A further principle of placement needs comment, and this can be illustrated by references to Shakespeare's plays. Our assignments of these are, with few variations, tradi-tional, for this placement seems eminently reasonable. But the year in which a given play is best studied should be determined by the number of plays that have previously been studied. If a ninth grade class reads only one play,

Julius Caesar, then in the tenth grade it should read *As You Like It* or *The Merchant of Venice*. But if a ninth grade class reads two plays, it should go, in the tenth grade, to a play usually given to the eleventh grade, such as *Romeo and Juliet*. If a ninth grade class reads three plays—*Julius Caesar*, *As You Like It*, and *The Merchant of Venice*—in the tenth grade that class might read *Romeo and Juliet* and *Macbeth*. Then, in the eleventh grade, it would be ready for plays usually left until the twelfth grade, such as *Twelfth Night* and *Hamlet*, and in the twelfth grade it should certainly reach to *King Lear* and *The Tempest*. If a class is to read only four Shakespearean plays in four years, a good order is *Julius Caesar*, *As You Like It*, *Romeo and Juliet*, and *Macbeth*. If in all four years only two Shakespearean plays are to be read, one in the tenth and one in the twelfth grade, *Julius Caesar* should go to the tenth and *As You Like It*, *The Merchant of Venice*, or *Macbeth* to the twelfth.

Let us summarize it this way: a school that includes three of Shakespeare's plays in each of the first two years can take Shakespeare's hardest and most complex plays in the eleventh and twelfth grades; but the school that teaches only one play a year, or one play every other year, should keep to the easiest plays and should never attempt *Hamlet*, *Twelfth Night*, *Lear*, or *The Tempest*. The same principle applies to novels and to such major poets as Milton and Wordsworth; depending on what it reads in the ninth grade, a class might get to "L'Allegro" in the tenth grade, but, lacking preparation, it might not get there until the twelfth.

Finally, readers of this book should reserve judgment on both the choice and placement of works listed in the Appendix until they have read the remaining chapters, especially that on Presentation. Whether *The Portrait of a Lady* can be profitably included in a twelfth grade reading list or whether nothing more demanding than *Northwest Passage* can be included depends finally, and more heavily than on anything else, on the method of Presentation that is used. Our selection of works implies the use of a method of Presentation that will make their use feasible.

Chapter 3

What kind of arrangement?

The basic question for Arrangement is not *how to arrange* works within a semester or year, but how to decide this question. The possible ways of arranging a large number of works in a reading program are numerous almost to infinity. Given a hundred pieces in a year's program, we could go on shuffling them forever, like a double deck of cards, without exhausting the possible combinations. How are we to decide that one way is better or worse than another?

In treating the placement of works over four years, we have simply assumed that there is sense in moving from the less to the more difficult from year to year, and we can similarly assume that in the course of each year there should be a comparable progression. Without making a fetish of difficulty—as we would indeed be doing if we tried to arrange one hundred works in their precise order of difficulty—we can recognize the good sense of beginning the ninth grade with the generally less difficult works and ending it with those that are generally more difficult.

As is well known, the traditional arrangements in most common use for the eleventh and twelfth grades are the chronological and the geographical or national combined: the literature of America (or, sometimes, "of the Americas") arranged chronologically in the eleventh, and the literature of England (or, more recently, of Europe) arranged chronologically in the twelfth. Regularly, too, these outer frames are complemented by inner frames consisting if literary genres and sub-genres. Thus, for example, when the chronological survey of English literature reaches the Age of Elizabeth, the class may first study a group of Elizabethan lyrics—which group may itself be divided into sub-groups like Sonnets, Songs from Plays, and Other Lyric Forms—and then proceed to Elizabethan Drama. Occasionally there may be a third group, Elizabethan Prose Literature—and this, too, may be broken into Essays, Prose Fiction, Travel Narratives, etc.

On the other hand, ninth and tenth grade anthologies are likely to include examples of every kind of grouping principle. In a single volume a number of pieces may be grouped because they are all short stories; others because they have to do with sports; others because they are characterized by adventure, suspense, or humor; others because they are about war, others about occupations, others about the space age, others about Christmas. The most common ways of grouping works in high school programs are these: by chronology, by genre, by nationality, by topic, by theme, by occasion, by mode, by mood, or by technique (satire, humor, suspense). Groups that include numerous works also usually require sub-groups: a group of short stories (genre) may have sub-groups by nationality, and these sub-groups may be arranged chronologically. Is one of these ways right while the rest are wrong? Is one way better than another?

Much earlier, we insisted that without a clear idea of why he is teaching literature, that is, of what it is, above all, that literature can do for students, a teacher has no sound basis for deciding any of the subsequent questions —of selection, arrangement, approach, presentation. Accordingly, we now assert that works should be arranged in whatever way or ways will give each work its best chance to do the best thing it can for students. Unfortunately, to state the principle is not to solve the practical problems of arrangement. But it gives us a start by suggesting how we should go about solving them.

Should "Dover Beach" be placed in a group with poems by Tennyson and Browning because (1) all are English, (2) all are Victorian, and (3) all are poems—i.e., should it be set in the three frames of geography, chronology, and genre? Or should it be placed in a group with *Romeo and Juliet,* Bacon's essay "Of Love," Suckling's "Why so pale and wan," Elizabeth Browning's sonnet "How Do I Love

Thee," Emily Brontë's *Wuthering Heights*, Chekhov's short story, "The Tryst," Salinger's short story "For Esmé —with Love and Squalor"? In the latter group, we have not cared about (1) nationality, for these works are English, American, and Russian; we have not cared about (2) chronology, for two works are Victorian, one is Cavalier, two are Elizabethan, one is Romantic, one is Contemporary; and we have not cared about (3) genre, for the group includes poems, short stories, a novel, a play, and an essay. We have cared about only one thing: that all these works have to do with Love.

Should Poe's "The Masque of the Red Death" be set in a group with other stories by Poe and stories by Hawthorne because (1) all are American, (2) all are of a single historical period, and (3) all are short stories? Or should we set it in a group with Coleridge's "Christabel," Shakespeare's *Julius Caesar*, and Bacon's "Of Superstition," not caring about nationality, age, or genre, but only about the supernatural element common to all the pieces?

Should Keats' "Ode on a Grecian Urn" be set with other poems by Keats and with poems by Wordsworth, Coleridge, Byron, and Shelley because all are English, Romantic, and poetic? Or should it be set with Bacon's "Of Beauty," Shakespeare's "Not marble nor the gilded monuments," Poe's "To Helen," Millay's "Euclid alone has looked on beauty bare," Oliver Wendell Holmes' "The Deacon's Masterpiece" and Aiken's "Bread and Music," all having to do with beauty and its battle with impermanence?

Should we group Twain's "Jumping Frog" with Holmes' "Ballad of the Oysterman," Thurber's "Walter Mitty," Shakespeare's *Midsummer Night's Dream*, Benchley's "My Face," and Burns' "To a Louse," because all are comic? Or should we assign each according to its time, place, and genre? Or should we attempt to identify a specific *theme* in each of these works and then place it with others of similar theme? Or should we merely group the story with other stories, the poem with other poems, the essay with other essays, the play with other plays?

We have earlier said that the best thing an artistic work

can do is to affect the reader as an artistic work, i.e., afford him an aesthetic experience which, joined with many similar experiences over a long period, may hopefully have a salutary effect on him as a human being. Now which plan of arrangement will give each work its best chance to affect students in this way? Let us evaluate each of the main systems of arrangement according to this criterion.

Chronological

It is argued for the chronological order that works are in fact *written* in chronological order and that since every literary work is a product of its time, bearing characteristic marks of its time, we can best understand and appreciate it by studying it in its historical context. The best way to ensure that works in a school program will be seen in their historical context is, without question, to arrange and teach them in historical order, keeping knowledge of historical and literary conditions, movements, transitions abreast of the reading. This is a persuasive argument for the chronological, and its general truth seems beyond dispute.

But the study of works in chronological order is subject to a fault so grave that we may question whether it is at all compatible with our avowed aim of enabling artistic works to strike students with their best artistic force. What happens is that literary study in a chronological program becomes the study of history and literary history. What becomes all-important is not that the individual poem or drama shall reach students with its full artistic force, but that students shall perceive how it expresses and represents its time. Instead of coming home to students' bosoms, it stands as a specimen of Renaissance, Romantic, or Victorian thought, attitude, feeling, form. Whatever may be argued to the contrary, the object of the study of works arranged chronologically comes to be to "learn about" them and their historical context. But our main object of reading literary works is not to "learn about" them but to be affected by them. These purposes are at opposite poles.

It is often argued that this reversal of the true purpose

is the result of an *abuse* of the chronological arrangement, and that the abuse can be avoided if teachers are constantly on guard—if they take pains to see that historical context is used to make the literary works understandable and is not used as means and excuse for teaching history. There seems no cause to doubt that the wary teacher can do much, by fighting against the tendency of the chronological arrangement to subvert the very purpose of reading the works arranged, to minimize the harm.

But if a teacher must steadily fight against his plan of arrangement in order to prevent it from destroying his purpose, why cling to that plan? Why add a handicap to what is already hard? Why not abandon it for a plan that furthers, not obstructs, his purpose?

Arranging chronologically does offer advantages—for the arranger. He does not have to think, but only to follow the years; and the finished course itself is tidy. There is no denying that the orderly commends itself to students better than the disorderly, and there is no surer way to be orderly than to proceed chronologically. A chronological course has beginning, middle, and end; students and teacher know where they have been, where they are, and where they are going. These are tangible virtues. But good reasons should give place to better. The fact is that the chronological arrangement of a program of literature thwarts the best reason for teaching literature and bends the whole course to its own purpose, which is knowledge of literary history, despite the teacher's efforts. Finally, it is a regrettable truth that teachers who prefer to teach literature chronologically, faithfully following the outline of American literature from Cotton Mather to Norman Vincent Peale and the outline of English literature from a twenty-line excerpt of the Beowulf to Auden's "Musée," do value literary history, and very probably they eventually set it above the experience of the works themselves. They do *not*, in fact, make strenuous effort to prevent the acquisition of historical knowledge from usurping experience as the primary purpose. Rather, they characteristically lecture on backgrounds to supplement the anthology's pages—already heavy with facts about age, author, and genre—and they tend to discuss individual works mainly in terms of the historical context. Their quizzes, tests, and final examinations are loaded with questions that require students to exhibit their knowledge of works as specimens of the times that produced them. Such teachers are disappointed most of all when students mistakenly date Dryden after Pope or make Swift a contemporary of Dr. Johnson. Such teachers, like the anthologies they teach from—which offer one half-page from "The Rape of the Lock" hemmed in by eight pages about the age, satire, rationalism, Pope, and mock-heroic—diminish the works of literature to the role of incidental illustrations for what is really important, literary history.

If "the best thing that a work of art can do" manages to fight its way through the frames with which the chronological arrangement surrounds the poem or the play and succeeds in reaching the students, it does so in spite of the arrangement. But what we seek is an arrangement that will help, not hinder, in getting the experience of the work home to the bosoms of students. If it is truly this experience that we value most, we must reject the chronological arrangement.

Here the devout chronologist will explode: Is the student to learn nothing about literary history? Is he to be kept ignorant, at all cost, of periods, influences, backgrounds, developments? Is he not even to know that Browning is Victorian and Keats Romantic, that "Death Be Not Proud" is seventeenth century and "The Deserted Village" eighteenth? If literary works are products of their times, how can they be understood by students who are ignorant of those times? And can students have this "aesthetic experience," this "best thing that a work of art can do," if they do not even understand the work?

This inevitable outburst of the history-oriented teacher does in fact betray his real position: he does mainly want students to "learn about" a body of works and their content, and is at most secondarily concerned to have them experience the force of individual works of art. If he had to choose between "knowledge of" and "experience of," there is no doubt which he would choose.

We must agree that there is no deep experience of literature without understanding of literature, and we must concede that for many works understanding depends on the reader's having a knowledge of relevant historical facts. But it is not necessary to *arrange* and *teach* works of literature chronologically in order to equip students with the particular historical facts needed for understanding. Obviously, the student who knew nothing of the contemporary political situation in England would be lost in Dryden's "Absalom and Achitophel," though possibly even in that eminently political poem he can get "the best thing the work has to give" without elaborate knowledge of the situation on which it comments. The point, in any event, is that such historical information as is needed in order to clarify a poem or other work can be presented (1) just before the poem is read, (2) during the actual reading aloud in class, and (3) during the analysis and discussion that follow reading. We shall examine these occasions in later chapters. But to insist that a whole program be arranged historically so that the facts of history will be available for understanding individual works is to rationalize: what one *really* wants, in that case, is to have students acquire knowledge of history and literary history.

If the unrelenting chronologist looks honestly into his own motives, he may discover some impure elements among them. He may find that he is unwilling to surrender his favorite arrangement because it provides a body of facts to talk about and to give tests on. It is easier to talk about the historical context of a literary work than about the work itself. It is easier to devise an examination on historical aspects than on artistic qualities. It is easier to feel satisfied that one has really done something when one's students have acquired a body of knowledge than when they have only, one hopes, "experienced." But none of these is an acceptable reason for proceeding chronologically.

Geographical

Much that has been said above against the chronological arrangement is equally applicable to the geographical, or national, arrangement. The basic reason for opposing both is the same: these arrangements, whatever their advantages, miss the main point of teaching literature.

In part, our objection to geographical arrangement is directed against the nearly universal practice, of many years' standing throughout the United States, of teaching American literature as a body of national documents in the eleventh grade and English literature similarly in the twelfth. Is it really the experience of individual works that we are seeking to give students when we restrict the reading program of an entire year to the products of one nation? If it is, why should we care, in the eleventh grade, whether the literature from which this experience is derived is American, Russian, French, or Greek? If it is, why should we care, in the twelfth grade, whether it is derived from an English poem or an American poem? Can we really believe that by including in a year's reading only the literature of one nation we increase the likelihood that individual works will affect students as works of art? Or are we, really, concerned rather to teach a body of national literature so that students will "know about" it?

As is well known, the programs for ninth and tenth grades are rarely organized by nation or by chronology, and the various styles of arranging works in those years are often justified on the grounds that we want students to sample widely, to get acquainted with all sorts of literature, and to learn to enjoy what they read. But then, the same argument continues, in the eleventh and twelfth grades students ought to study a body of literature systematically, and the best way to do so is to take a national literature, chronologically ordered, in each year. But why ought they? Why should we assume that it is right for ninth and tenth graders to enjoy, but that eleventh and twelfth graders must settle down to "learn about" a national literature laid out historically?

We are concerned, of course, for "cultural heritage," and more particularly for American cultural heritage. It would seem un-American to graduate students who are ignorant of the body of their country's literature, together with the traditions and ideals bound up with it. Not know about the Puritan and Colonial period? The Westward Movement? The Passing of the Frontier? Agrarianism and Commercial Capitalism? Bret Harte and Local Color? The Rise of Realism? Yet though we find ourselves shocked at the thought that high school graduates should be left ignorant of these matters, what has all this to do with the experience of literary works as works of art? If some of this knowledge, specifically applied, is necessary in order to extract the aesthetic experience from a given work, then obviously students must have it. But it is evident that when we limit a reading program to the documents of one national literature, we are not thinking first about the experience of works as works of literature. We are thinking about teaching students the history of literature in our country, illustrated with literary examples.

Some of the faults that attend the practice of limiting the eleventh grade program to American and the twelfth to English works have been suggested earlier. The basic fault is that this arrangement simply misses the point of teaching literature. But before we leave the subject we must name certain specific absurdities of this abuse.

First of these, which applies especially to American literature in the eleventh grade, is the inclusion in the program of many documents that are not works of literature in any true sense, because they are not works of art. They have claimed space in the program only because they have value as national documents. The typical eleventh grade anthology of American "literature" gives as much as one-third of its pages to such documents, as does the school program that is based on such an anthology. Perhaps no single piece of evidence shows more conclusively that when we lay out a body of national works for study, we are not thinking of literature first, or the experience of literature first, but of national documents and of having students "learn about" them. If not, why have we included a sample from George

Percy's A Discourse of the Plantation of the Southern Colony in Virginia in a program of literature? Or Roger Williams' "Letter to the Town of Providence, January, 1655, on the Limits of Freedom"? Or William Bradford's "The Mayflower Compact"? Or the inaugural addresses of several Presidents? Or selections about the Virginia Colony by John Smith and William Byrd? Or Winthrop's "Speech to the General Court"? Or Patrick Henry's "Speech in the Virginia Convention"? Or, for that matter, even the Declaration of Independence? We may easily agree that all these, and many more that clutter the eleventh grade "literature" program, should be known to American students as students of American history, and perhaps the salient passages of some should even be memorized. But their presence in a program of literature merely demonstrates that literature and the experience of literature are not our first considerations when we restrict a program to one national literature.

It must be added that besides many documents of historical rather than literary significance, the eleventh grade program also includes many grossly inferior stories, essays, and poems chosen not for artistic qualities but for their illustration of reactions to events of national significance. Hardly an anthology of American literature exists that does not include Emerson's "Concord Hymn," which countless children have memorized and recited; yet, surely, this poem does not deserve, on literary grounds, to displace other poems by Emerson of which some are very fine. Because it has a good, ringing clarity, it should go into a sixth or seventh grade program, but not an eleventh. Can Whittier's "Barbara Frietchie" really belong there? Joaquin Miller's "Westward Ho!"? Longfellow's "The Republic"? Lindsay's "The Santa Fe Trail"? Can such Americana as "Whoopee Ti Yi Yo, Git Along Little Dogies," which merely illustrates "Pioneer Life in the West," deserve space in an eleventh grade volume of selections chosen for their distinction as works of art?

It is a regrettable fact that the eleventh grade anthology and program is often the poorest of the four years, meagerest in its offerings of first-rate literature, because selection has been based on nationalistic rather than artistic principles. The eleventh grade volume should stand next to the twelfth in the character of the artistic works it offers to students; as a matter of fact, because of the number of merely illustrative pieces it groups around headings like "How the West Was Won," "War Between the States," "Independence," "The Virginia Colony," "The American Dream," and "Literature of the Prairie," its total character is inferior to that of a good ninth grade volume.

We turn now to the second major absurdity that results from restricting eleventh and twelfth grade programs to national literatures. We have broached this absurdity earlier, in discussing Placement. It is very briefly this: restriction of eleventh and twelfth grade programs to American and English literature inevitably brings many works into these years that could and should be taught earlier. Before discussing this grave fault, we should mention the third absurdity here also, because it is closely related: the restriction of eleventh and twelfth grade programs to national literature forces omission of certain international masterpieces that could be taught in these years and should not be taught earlier. We shall return to this problem in just a moment.

As was stated earlier, much of American and English literature is "saved" for the eleventh and twelfth grades in order to fill out the historical surveys that are traditionally taught in these years. So long as the final two years undertake to survey national literary history, works of Poe, Longfellow, Holmes, Harte, Twain, Bryant, Irving, Whitman, Dickinson, and others in American literature *must* be included in them—for how could the history of American literature be represented without them?—and similarly all the standard authors of English literature are needed to fill in the historical outline of the twelfth grade. Thus it is that in an eleventh grade program we find such works as "Barbara Frietchie," "Paul Bunyan's Big Ox," "Concord Hymn," "Rip Van Winkle," "Thanatopsis," "The Pit and the Pendulum," "The Great Stone Face," "Oh Captain My Captain," "The Outcasts of Poker Flat," "To Build a Fire," "Richard Cory," "Stopping by Woods," and so on and on—when all these and many more of similar difficulty could and should be taught in the ninth grade. It is not unusual to find Holmes' "The Chambered Nautilus" in the eleventh grade program; there is always much of O. Henry, to illustrate the evolution of the short story form in America. Clearly, these works would not be included at this grade level if they were not needed for the survey of American literary history.

Much the same can be said of the misplacement of English works as the result of their being needed to illustrate literary history in the twelfth grade. Random pieces by Wordsworth, Coleridge, Byron, Shelley, Keats, Browning, and Tennyson do occasionally find their way into ninth and tenth grade programs—but the standard, frequently anthologized poems by these authors are always found in the twelfth grade, where, en masse, they are needed to represent the Romantic and Victorian Periods. But Wordsworth's brief and lovely Lucy poems should be taught in the ninth grade; so should Shelley's "The Cloud" and "Ozymandias," among others; so should a sonnet or two by Keats; so should almost all of Byron's short poems, particularly the short narratives like "The Prisoner of Chillon" and "The Destruction of Sennacherib"; so should much of Tennyson and some of Browning. As for the giant Shakespeare, from eighty to one hundred of the sonnets could and should be spread over four years, beginning in the ninth grade with the great "open" ones like "When in Disgrace" and ending in the knottier ones like "The Expense of Spirit." But it is a rare ninth, tenth, or eleventh grade volume or program that includes a sonnet by Shakespeare: the sonnets are saved until the twelfth grade survey of English literature, when not more than six or eight are used, along with sundry other Elizabethan Lyric Poems to represent this genre in this age. This is truly "a waste of shame."

It is, then, absurd to come upon Wordsworth's "We Are Seven" and "My Heart Leaps Up" in a twelfth grade program, along with Tennyson's "Break, Break, Break" and "Crossing the Bar"; upon Blake's "Lamb" and "Tiger"; upon Coleridge's "Ancient Mariner" and "Christabel"; upon Scott's "Lochinvar," Burns' "To a Louse" and "To a Mouse," and Kipling's "Recessional." To say that it is absurd is not to suggest that these, and many more like them, are somehow inferior and do not deserve study in the twelfth grade; as a matter of fact, all are fine enough to deserve teaching in all four years. The point—following a principle earlier established—is that they could all be taught earlier, would enormously enrich ninth and tenth grade programs, and could thus simultaneously form a basis for "harder" works to be undertaken in the eleventh and twelfth grades and, by not taking up space in those grades themselves, make room for complex works.

The last observation brings us directly to our third absurdity, namely, that restriction of the eleventh and twelfth grades to American and English literature forces the omission, or the misplacement, of works that should certainly be included in those years because they cannot properly be placed earlier.

Let us begin with an example. The omission of a Shakespearean play from the eleventh grade program for the simple reason that only American literature can be included in that year is perhaps the most glaring single absurdity in the whole four-year reading program. If there were no other reason to think ill of the practice of restricting the eleventh grade program to American literature, the fact that this arrangement excludes Shakespeare should be sufficient to damn it. It is a fact, of course, that many teachers slyly smuggle Shakespeare into the eleventh grade program, where he marks a highly conspicuous period of "time out" from the survey of American literature. But the very fact that Shakespeare must be smuggled into a program the laws of which exclude him is enough to condemn the principle on which the program was designed.

Excluding Shakespeare from the eleventh grade means that, in many schools, students get only two of his plays in four years, one in the tenth grade and one in the twelfth, most commonly *Julius Caesar* and *Macbeth*. The Shakespeare gap between the tenth and twelfth grades is clearly indefensible. There is not, in American literature, a single play worthy of replacing any one of the twelve to fourteen plays of Shakespeare that make reasonable choices for high school use. In anthologies and programs the choice often falls to Wilder's *Our Town*, Anderson's *Winterset*, Van Druten's *I Remember Mama*, Miller's *Death of a Salesman* or *The Crucible*, Williams' *The Glass Menagerie*, or an O'Neill play. It sometimes falls, more unfortunately, to a radio or television script or to a Broadway musical such as *The King and I*. And the chosen full-length play is often supplemented by one, two, three, or a small group of one-act plays (American, of course) such as O'Neill's *Ile*, Susan Glaspell's *Trifles*, Hall and Middlemass' *The Valiant*. It is not necessary to deprecate the quality of any of these plays in order to insist that none is a worthy replacement for a Shakespearean play; the fact is that there *is* no wholly adequate replacement for a Shakespearean play, even if we were to break geographical bounds and include the Greeks and Shaw. But in fact the very best of American drama does not stand up in world competition; and much drama taught in the eleventh grade has as its sole qualification the fact that it *is* American. This is not qualification enough, either for drama or any other genre.

O'Neill has long held the name of greatest American playwright; yet O'Neill's plays have "dated" more in a little over a generation than Shakespeare's have in four hundred years. Viewed in a world perspective, O'Neill seems never to have got beyond being an amateur; he is local rather than universal, and his art is experimental, overdrawn, gimmicky, and crude. At his worst, as in *Ile*—a favorite item for representing American drama in the eleventh grade—his melodramatics are ludicrous. Wilder's *Our Town*, perhaps the most frequent American substitute for a *Twelfth Night* or a *Romeo and Juliet*, is an extended colloquialism with little to offer except its small-town folksiness, "whereof a little more than a little is by much too much." It is good as hot dogs and peanuts are good, but not great as dramatic masterpieces are great. Maxwell Anderson's three or four widely used plays are dramatically superior to Wilder's; but how can we justify reading Anderson's blank verse when we could read Shakespeare's if the eleventh grade were not all-American? Williams' *Glass Menagerie* merely depresses, and Van Druten's *I Remember Mama* has neither more nor less claim to the distinction of being studied in the eleventh grade than any other popular success from any Broadway season since 1920; we might as well use *The Goose Hangs High*, *The Road to Yesterday*, *The Passing of the Third Floor Back*, or *Dulcy*. There is nothing wrong with any of these plays; but there is nothing right with them as replacements for *Twelfth Night* or any of a dozen other Shakespearean plays that go unread because of them.

From the gross example of the exclusion of Shakespeare because he is not American, we turn to the example of *Moby Dick*, now often included in the eleventh grade because it is American. For many years, until recently, *Moby Dick* was considered too difficult at any high school level. It was taught by a few bold and unreconstructed teachers who also thought nothing of tackling *The Brothers Karamazov* while other English teachers, who took seriously the professional injunction never to try anything difficult, were using *Johnny Tremaine* and *Little Britches*. But in recent years *Moby Dick* has come to be much used, its rise to favor marking a widespread rebellion against the prevailing philosophy of giving students only what they can read unaided and without effort. The change is, of course, as admirable as it has been dramatic. Yet *Moby Dick*, a full, rich, complex, and even profound work, like *King Lear*, *The Brothers Karamazov*, and works of comparable complexity, should go into the twelfth grade if it is to be used at all. However, it cannot be fitted into a twelfth grade survey of English literature; it is American, and must go into the eleventh grade survey of American literature. On the other hand, *Pride and Prejudice*, probably the briefest and clearest of the world's supremely great novels, which might, if it were not English, be used effectively in the eleventh grade, goes instead into the twelfth. If the principle of allotment by nationality did not prevent, these novels should obviously be reversed.

We come finally to a more general problem that results from restriction of eleventh and twelfth grade programs to American and English works. This is the problem of a half-dozen masterpieces that hold extraordinary place in the world's literature. They are Homer's *Iliad* and *Odyssey*,

Virgil's *Aeneid*, Dante's *Divine Comedy*, Cervantes' *Don Quixote*, and Goethe's *Faust*. These are works that, if they are used at all—and why should they not be used?—cannot reasonably be placed anywhere but in the eleventh and twelfth grades: Homer and Cervantes in the eleventh, the other three in the twelfth. But none of them can go into either of these years, because they are neither American nor English.

Because they cannot legitimately go into these years, one of three fates befalls them: (1) they are not used at all; (2) one or another is smuggled into these years; (3) they are brutally abbreviated or adapted and packed into the ninth or tenth grade.

The first of these alternatives—if we truly mean what we said about selecting works that have greatest potential—is indefensible, and no further comment is possible. If we do not use some or all of these works, we simply cannot really mean what we have said.

The second exposes once more the fault of the "national" arrangement and placement of literary works. The eleventh and twelfth grades are the first in which high school students, with reading abilities well developed by the first two high school years, can do justice to works of these immense dimensions. But to smuggle them into American literature, where they must look only alien and odd in the company of Poe, Longfellow, Bret Harte, and "Get Along Little Dogies," or into English literary history, where they can seem only like chronological and geographical aberrations, is surely absurd. They should not have to apologize for their *entrée* anywhere. But apologize they must, when one of them intrudes upon Bret Harte and the development of Local Color.

The third alternative, as a matter of fact, is the only one in more than occasional use, and it extends to only two of these consummately great works. The *Odyssey* and *Don Quixote*, in some kind of diminished form—adapted, abbreviated, or "retold"—are sometimes included in the ninth grade. The others—except for the rarest kind of program and the rarest of unreconstructed teachers—go unplaced and unread. Until about thirty years ago, the *Odys-*

sey was often included in ninth grade programs and *Don Quixote* in either the ninth or tenth grade. But our point is that whenever even two of these world masterpieces have been used, it has been in the ninth or tenth grade. Yet it can make little sense to place them in the lower grades and to have Bret Harte, Poe, and Longfellow abundantly present in the eleventh grade, and to have the simpler poems of the great Romantics and Victorians in the twelfth grade. But for the restriction of the upper years to American and English literary history, some of these six monumental works could be studied in those years.

There they could be studied complete and in depth, not in excerpts or modern summaries. In recent years, bright new translations of these works have appeared and are available in inexpensive, attractive paperbacks. Homer's works, the *Aeneid*, and the *Divine Comedy* can be read in either prose or verse translations. In either prose or verse, they are no more difficult than *King Lear*, so that teaching them in the upper years is entirely as feasible as teaching *King Lear* or *Moby Dick*. To omit them, or to consign them to the lower years, where they are represented only by excerpts and retellings, is a monumental waste.

Other classical works also are forced from their appropriate place by the national limitation of the last two years. A recent anthology series, commendably seeking space for great works, includes *Antigone* in the volume for the ninth grade. More recently, another series, attempting a large unit on "The Trojan War," includes bits from the *Iliad*, the *Aeneid*, Euripides' *Trojan Women*, and Ovid's *Metamorphoses*—all in the ninth grade volume. Both series give the eleventh and twelfth grades exclusively to American and English literature. It is not uncommon at present, with the return to favor of a belief in the English program as a place for the study of first-rate works, to find teachers undertaking *Antigone*, *Oedipus Rex*, *Agamemnon*, *Prometheus Bound*, or *Medea* in the ninth grade or the tenth— undertaking them there because they cannot be included in the upper years because of the national limitation. But not one of these is a satisfactory choice for ninth or tenth grade. They should be read in the eleventh and twelfth grades.

Before we leave the subject of geographical arrangement, which we have discussed only in terms of the traditional restrictions that afflict the eleventh and twelfth grades, we should mention one kind of movement made in recent years to break the strict boundaries of America and England. This is the development, for the eleventh grade, of a program called "Literature of the Americas," and, for the twelfth, of a program that includes works from England, continental European countries, and Africa. These programs are obviously in accord with the spirit of our times in their wish to escape the narrowly nationalistic bounds of the traditional arrangement; in that, they have succeeded.

But they have succeeded at the heavy cost of perverting even more flagrantly the primary purpose of teaching literature. They offer literature not for the artistic force of each work, but for its usefulness in acquainting students with the writings of many countries and peoples. Though still dominated by the literatures of the United States and England, these programs attempt a comprehensive geographical tour. Included in the eleventh grade program besides works from the United States are representative writings from Canada, Central American countries, and each of the South American countries. All countries are somehow represented; but if, for example, no suitable piece of Colombian literature is available, Colombia is represented by a brief article written about Colombia by an American who has traveled there; and so also Ecuador, Guatemala— every country is "somehow" included in the tour. The program for the twelfth grade visits the countries of continental Europe and Africa in similar fashion.

That we need to break the pattern of the exclusively American and British in the two upper years, there can be little doubt. But to break it by a means that further abuses the primary purpose of studying literature is to miss the point of breaking it at all. Actually, even the purpose of "acquainting students with foreign lands, peoples, customs, cultures" is not even partially served by a tour that represents Mexico through one short narrative sketch, two brief poems, and an article about Mexico. We would give students of other lands a feeble and distorted view of the

United States if we tried to represent our country through one short story by Bret Harte, a poem by Longfellow, and one article about America written by a tourist. But of course this is not the point. Even if, miraculously, through a rapid literary tour of all the Americas, we were able to give students a comprehensive and accurate picture of every single country, we should, in doing so, still miss the point of teaching literature. Experience of each work as a work of art has nothing to do with geographical tours.

Typological

Although genre often figures as a subordinate principle of arrangement within the geographical-chronological frames used in the eleventh and twelfth grade programs, its real home is in the ninth and tenth grades, especially the latter, where it dominates all other plans. Tenth grade anthologies are often identified by titles like "Types of Literature" and "Literary Types." In these, and in the programs based on them, geography and chronology also figure, but as the subordinates of genre, just as genre is their subordinate in the upper years. To judge from the prevailing traditional arrangements used in the four years, we find that in the ninth grade the main purpose is to introduce students to literature as "Adventure," "Enjoyment," etc.; in the tenth, to introduce them to all the genres and sub-genres; and in the eleventh and twelfth, to survey the histories of two national literatures. Our problem here, as with the chronological and geographical arrangements, is to determine whether arrangement by genre is more likely to increase or to decrease the chance of the individual work to affect students as a work of art rather than as an illustration of genre.

Like the chronological, the typological order has notable virtues. First, as with the chronological, arranging by type requires neither thought nor understanding of what the works to be arranged are "about"; anyone who can distinguish a short story from an essay, an ode from a sonnet, a novel from a play can assemble a program without making gross mistakes. Second, again like the chronological, this is a solid kind of order, which allows students and teachers to know precisely where they have been, where they are, and where they are going. A typical practice is to begin the year with short stories, move to non-fiction prose (including essays, excerpts from biographies, accounts of travels, etc.), to the novel, to poetry in a catalogue of many forms, and finally to drama, including one-act and full-length examples. Third, arrangement by genre excels other arrangements for the purposes of classifying and comparing not only one major genre with another, but sub-genres with one another (as sonnet with ode, informal essay with formal essay, short story of plot with short story of character). In fact, there is hardly any limit to the extent of classification and comparison that this arrangement makes possible. The large unit on short stories, for example, can be subdivided geographically and chronologically. Thus the class may begin with a group of American short stories, arranged historically so as to trace the development from Poe and Hawthorne up to contemporary *New Yorker* stories, and from there it can go to English stories, Russian stories, French stories; indeed, the recent deluge of inexpensive and excellent paperbacks now makes it possible to go on with Irish stories, Spanish stories, German stories. There is no doubt that for the purpose of studying the characteristics of literary forms, comparatively and otherwise, arrangement by type is the right way.

But is it right for our purpose? Arrangement by type will best serve the purpose of studying literary types, just as chronological arrangement will best serve the study of literary history and just as national arrangement will best serve the study of national bodies of literature. But will it also best promote the chances of individual works to affect students as works of art?

If we could use the genres merely as convenient frames, without allowing the manner of arrangement to influence the great purpose of reading, then the typological arrangement might actually be as good as any. But what happens in actual practice?

Inevitably, arrangement by type introduces certain emphases that profoundly affect or actually determine the purpose of reading. A group of short stories, for example, though brought together ostensibly only for convenience, turns out in practice to be truly "Unit on the Short Story." In the course of studying this unit, teacher and class become increasingly concerned with certain knowledges, with *knowing about* "The Short Story": its origins, its development in various countries, its structural elements, its special techniques, modifications devised by particular authors. Examination of any anthology of "Types of Literature" will quickly support this observation, as will examination of any school syllabus that is sufficiently detailed to betray specific emphases of study. So also will observation of classroom discussion while study of "A Unit on the Short Story" is underway; but most significant as evidence of what the true purpose of such a unit tends to become are the questions asked on written examinations covering the unit. These invariably ask what Bret Harte contributed to the Short Story, how the typical nineteenth-century story differs from the twentieth-century story, how Chekhov's stories differ from O. Henry's, how the Short Short Story differs from the Short Story. Often, as a major activity used to supplement the fixed list of stories in the unit, teachers have students investigate contemporary magazines and newspapers to find which ones include stories, of what kinds and qualities: How do *New Yorker* stories differ from *Saturday Evening Post* stories? Which syndicated magazine sections of newspapers print short or short short stories? How do the stories printed in contemporary issues of periodicals compare with the "classics" used for class study? Are they more like the stories of Hawthorne, Chekhov, de Maupassant, O. Henry, or Mansfield?

Perhaps it is not quite inevitable, but the evidence of actual practice shows that when we put ballads together because they are ballads, sonnets because they are sonnets, familiar essays because they are familiar essays, Russian stories because they are Russian stories, one-act plays because they are one-act plays, we become preoccupied with the study of group characteristics and with individual works as examples to be discussed in terms of the group rather than as works of art, the force of which is to be experienced.

This criticism of the typological arrangement is not meant to suggest that we should teach literature so as to keep students ignorant of the characteristics of the various genres. There is no sin in knowing about the form of the sonnet, Bret Harte's use of Local Color, the differences between familiar and formal essays. It would be preposterous to have students read a short story without becoming aware that it was a short story, or a sonnet without knowing that it was a sonnet. But our objection is to a system of arrangement which so strongly directs the emphases of study that "knowing about" these matters becomes the great purpose. We must seek some other system of arrangement, which will keep the main purpose from being lost.

Topical

The favorite grades for arranging works according to topic are the ninth and tenth, and especially the ninth. In the tenth grade, topics are often used to subdivide genres—so that we may find one group of short stories about sports, another about dogs, another about adventures. Less frequently, historical units in the eleventh and twelfth grades are similarly divided; there, however, the topical subdivisions hardly do more than rename historical groupings—thus, "The Puritans," "The Civil War," etc.

One advantage of topical arrangement is that, unlike arrangements we have already discussed, it does not threaten to make concern with chronology, genre, or nationality take over as purpose. In the "purest" sorts of topical groupings, there is no evidence that any thought at all is given to these matters. In a unit on "The Family," for example, there may be two or three poems, two or three short stories, a play (even *Romeo and Juliet*), half a dozen articles or familiar essays, an excerpt or two from biography or autobiography, and, perhaps, a family scene from a novel; some of these works may be contemporary, some nineteenth century, some Elizabethan; and some may be American, some English, some French, some Russian. What is of central concern is that all the readings must have to do with "The Family," and in assembling them the arranger has not cared for genre, country, or time. It is almost impossible, thus, for the reading of literature to turn into comparative studies of genres, national bodies, or literary history. And for avoiding these false ends, if for no other reason, the topical arrangement does not preclude the teacher's introducing such information about genre, history, and country as seems desirable, so that topical arrangement need not mean that students will read many works yet never know a sonnet from a short story or whether Shakespeare was an eighteenth-century American or a pre-revolutionary Russian.

Is the topical arrangement, then, what we want? As it is generally practiced, at least, it is not. In actual use it has two gross faults, the second of which is largely a result of the first.

First, the evidence of anthologies and school programs shows that the use of topics as devices for grouping works particularly invites inclusion of non-literary pieces and inferior literary pieces. One notable virtue of the chronological and typological arrangements is that these have just the opposite effect (a partial exception is the historical American literature program, which includes much that has national but not literary importance); in particular, when an anthologist or program-maker selects pieces for a typological program, he has a strong incentive to include first-rate stories, sonnets, etc., because he wants "good examples" of these genres. But the topical arranger's only need is to find pieces that fit his chosen topics, and works that fit nicely but have no artistic character take precedence over masterpieces that, unfortunately, fit badly. Non-literary works have a curious way of fitting more neatly into topical frames than literary works, the finest of which never seem to fit at all. Under what topic, for example, could one include *A Midsummer Night's Dream?* Yet an excerpt from *Life with Father* seems made for inclusion in a topic on "The Family."

Hence teachers may examine the contents of topically

arranged anthologies without finding any pieces that, as students of literature, they recognize or have heard of: contemporary articles about astronauts, fitted together in a unit called "Man and Space"; biographical sketches of baseball players and how they won their place with the Giants, along with real or fictitious accounts of swimmers, jumpers, racing horses in a unit on "Sports"; a hike up Everest, a moment with Byrd at the South Pole, a battle with an enormous bear in the frozen North, a scuba diver's encounter with a wing-flapping monster of the deep, all in a unit of "Great Adventures"; one of Walt Whitman's worst poems, an article on modern freeways, an excerpt from a speech by Franklin D. Roosevelt, portions of "Yankee Doodle" and "Git Along Little Dogies," together with an incident in which school children of sundry backgrounds learn to "get along together" in a unit named "This Is America!" or "Getting Along Together." These are typical topics, and these are typical "literary works" that are included when topical arrangement directs a program. If, occasionally, we encounter a Lucy poem, Burns' "To a Mountain Daisy," or Emerson's "The Rhodora" or "Forbearance" tucked into a unit on "Nature," it looks merely odd among the better-fitting sketches about beavers building dams and ants getting ready for winter.

Second, although topical grouping avoids the faulty emphases of learning about different genres and literary periods that direct purposes when works are grouped typologically and chronologically, the fact is not necessarily an improvement. Most topical units appear designed for students to "learn about" the particular topics within which the readings are grouped. Especially when the readings themselves are no more than readings, rather than literary works of artistic quality, the effect of the unit is that of merely reading about astronauts, reading about the ways of wildlife, reading about life in America, reading about our neighbors in other lands, reading about family life, reading about transportation and communication, reading about the sea. The evident purpose of the total unit is to "learn more about" space, animals, American life, other lands, family relations, transportation, the sea. The experience of works of literature as works of literature is a very different thing from "learning about" specific topics and is unlikely to take place in these circumstances.

In a curious way, too, any fine little poem or similar work of art that is fitted into a topical arrangement actually suffers by comparison with the more ordinary articles and sketches that obviously address the topic more directly. Thus, for example, Emily Dickinson's small masterpiece "I Like to See It Lap the Miles," placed amid articles about freeways, railroads, and telephone wire stringers in a unit on "Transportation and Communication" looks foolish because it has so little information to offer. Arnold's "Dover Beach," set among articles on algae, whaling, coral reefs, and tropical fish in a unit on "The Encircling Sea" looks like something to be skipped over quickly in order to get on with the real meat of the unit. In such units, which give to reading a predominantly social science tone and purpose, the individual work of art is placed in the least advantageous light, and the experience of it as a work of art will not take place except by miracle. Hawthorne's superb "Dr. Heidegger's Experiment," set among informative articles on scientists and scientific projects in a unit on "The Challenge of Science" has the look of a queer relative who had to be invited to the party.

Is it possible to devise a topically arranged program that does not grossly discriminate against literary works and the experience of them as works of art? On the evidence of existing practice, we shall have to conclude that the likelihood is remote. But if the attempt is to be made, we should bear in mind an injunction expressed in the preceding chapter on Selection. The injunction is that works for the entire program must all be selected before any thought is given to the particular way in which they are to be arranged. Otherwise, "Selection" becomes a mere hunt, not for first-rate works of literature, but for pieces that "will fit." If all the works in a topical program are artistically first-rate, the entire group will stand a much better chance of being read for the experience they have to offer rather than for mere information on the topic.

But this is only the first step, and the second one is

much harder. Perhaps, even, it is impossible. Suppose that
we have chosen one hundred fine works, long and short, to
be read in the tenth grade. These include *As You Like It*,
The Merchant of Venice, six or eight of Shakespeare's
sonnets, *Les Misérables*, half a dozen poems by Dickinson,
two or three each by Wordsworth, Coleridge, Byron, Shelley, Keats, Browning, Tennyson, Arnold, numerous poems
by American poets, two or three of Bacon's essays, other
essays by Chesterton, Emerson, and H. M. Tomlinson, a
dozen short stories by Hawthorne, Chekhov, Cather, Crane,
Galsworthy, de Maupassant, Maugham, and Hardy. Next
we examine our list for topical affinities. The very first thing
we shall become aware of is that, except absurdly, none of
these works will fit into such familiar units as "Man and
Space," "Family Life," "Man at Work," "The Encircling
Sea," "Sports," "The Challenge of Science," "Getting
along with Others," "Transportation and Communication."
If we want to use any such units, we shall have to scrap our
whole list of selections.

We might, of course, place Tennyson's little "Flower in
the Crannied Wall" under the "Challenge of Science,"
since it was indeed the challenge of science that prompted
the poem; but the poem is not "about" science in the way
in which an account of the operation of the first atomic
reactor is. It is not at all a scientific document, but an artistic work which records a moment of personal perturbation:

> I hold you here, root and all, in my hand,
> Little flower—but if I could understand
> What you are, root and all, and all in all,
> I should know what God and man is.

Perhaps nothing makes clearer the essential distinction between science and social science purposes, on the one hand,
and artistic purposes, on the other, than the attempt to set
an artistic work within a science or social science frame or
topic without destroying the work. Probably Tennyson's
little poem comes as near as any artistic work ever written
to "belonging" in such a unit; yet to suppose that it really
does belong there is to fail to distinguish one order of
things from a totally different order. Literature is not sci-

ence or social science; its purpose is not a science or social science purpose; it is not "about" science or social science. It may draw inspiration or imagery from these, but, having done so, it parts company with them.

We may perhaps be able to fit a number of our tenth grade selections into an enormous topic like "Nature"— for in a sense all things, literary and other, are covered by that gigantic canopy. Wordsworth's Lucy poems, Emerson's "The Rhodora," Burns' "To a Mountain Daisy," Shelley's "Lines Written in the Euganean Hills," Dickinson's little verse about the bird that spied a worm and "ate the fellow raw"—all these, surely, are clear cases and ought to fit under "Nature" if any literary works do. But even these—though they take place in "nature," use natural images, describe natural scenery, and generally praise the goodness of natural things—are not *about* "Nature," in the sense in which an article on railroading is about railroading or an account of an ant colony is about "The Animal Community." Could Wordsworth's "My Heart Leaps Up" really belong beside a short scientific treatise on what causes rainbows, in a unit on either "Nature" or "The World of Science"? As for Lucy, though she lived amid rural nature, among untrodden ways, beside bubbling springs, and is compared to a violet half hidden by a mossy stone and to a lone star in the sky—is hers a poem about "Nature"? Is it "about Nature" at all? Or is it about a deep loss, once violently felt and now recollected "in tranquility"? Can Lucy be set in a unit on "Nature" and no harm done to what the poem is?

When we consider the larger works of our list, like Shakespeare's two plays and Hugo's novel, the impossibility of setting them within any topical frame is instantly apparent, and the effect of placing them there will prove grotesque. *As You Like It*, or most of it, takes place in woods and fields, with forest, shepherds and shepherdesses, running brooks, snakes, lionesses, deer; "Nature" is perhaps more prominent in it than in any other Shakespearean play. Yet can we place it in a unit on "Nature"? To do so would misrepresent it as badly as if we placed *The Merchant of Venice* in a unit on "Getting along with People" or Hugo's monumental work under "Our Daily Bread," commemorating the start of Jean Valjean's difficulties.

Of all the literary types, only the essay can be accommodated reasonably well in topical frames. Bacon's "Of Parents and Children" will go into a unit on "The Family" and Emerson's "Self-Reliance" will go into one on "Growing Up." Even so, the great essays characteristically treat ideas, and are not content with giving mere information on topics. Topics call for information chiefly, and therefore a first-rate essay, set among articles in a topical unit, is condemned to look nearly as uncomfortable as a poem in the same place.

What we are forced to conclude at last is that literature does not primarily treat topics, or it does not treat them as informative articles do. When it is set in topical units, it looks as if it were placed there so that students can "learn about" the topic. Students will, of course, from most literature, learn at least a little about topics. But in learning the little that literature has to teach about topics, they will miss the best thing that literature has to offer and at the same time learn less about topics than they would from informative pieces. Placed in topical units, literature looks inferior to informative articles that plainly discuss the topic and make an obvious contribution to the students' knowledge of it; and in fact, for this purpose, literature is inferior to informational articles. "I Like to See It Lap the Miles" is a silly choice if what we want is to have students learn about "Transportation and Communication." We must, somehow, if we are to group literary works within any kind of frames or units, find what will not diminish them, but enable them to look their best, be their best, and do their best.

Chapter 4

. . . Thematic arrangement?

The terms "topical" and "thematic" are often confused. In most anthologies and school programs, they are used as if they were interchangeable. A program that labels its way of grouping works "thematic" may include units on "America," "Nature," "Other Lands," "The Great Outdoors," "People Worth Knowing," "About Dogs"—but in another program or anthology these very units are called "topics." Further, in the same anthology units may be called "topics" in one paragraph, "themes" in the next, and "topics" again in the third.

If "topics" and "themes" are indeed synonymous, we shall waste time by discussing thematic arrangement, for we shall have to say the same things about it that we have said about topical arrangement. But let us see whether we can make a usable distinction.

We may begin by suggesting that "topic" implies *no point of view* and that "theme" not only implies a point of view but in a vital way *is* a point of view—*the* point of view that shapes the material of an artistic work. It may act strongly, as a positive assertion, or more subtly and pervasively, as an unobtrusive but controlling attitude. Second, it may be useful to think of "topic" as something quite *outside* a work, or group of works, but of "theme" as something *inside* the individual work. But here a problem immediately arises that may be the source of the confusion that appears in anthologies and programs. When the themes of several works are represented by a single unit-heading that stands for a whole group, this collective title resembles a topic rather than a theme, and in that case the arrangement of a whole reading program made up of such titles appears more topical than thematic. Though we can distinguish the themes of individual works, it is difficult to give them a collective title, for grouping purposes, without having them turn topical before our very eyes.

The crucial distinction is that "topic" as a device for classifying or grouping, seems only to identify a category in impersonal, non-committal terms, whereas "theme" seems regularly to involve personal attitudes, emotions, qualities. This distinction can be clarified with some illustrations.

If we take extreme cases, we can distinguish easily between the topical and the thematic. The unit-heading "About Dogs" is unmistakably topical. It says only that ten or twelve stories, poems, sketches, articles thus grouped will all pertain to dogs. It merely names a unit in which students will read about dogs and expresses nothing about the *theme* of any one work or about the themes collectively—and indeed the actual themes of a dozen works "about dogs" may be so different that these works could not possibly be brought together in a thematic unit. Similarly, a unit-heading such as "Other People, Other Lands" is unmistakably topical. In it one expects just what one in fact finds: works of various genres, set in several countries, representing various social levels, customs, values, occupations, all illustrating similarities and differences among peoples, and tending, as a group, to acquaint readers with "Other People, Other Lands." But if we sorted out these works by their *themes*, we might find that no two would fit together in a thematic group. Or take "In Time of War," again a clearly topical unit which implies only that every work included has to do with war: here we might find an account of shipbuilding in the early years of World War II, a poem like Hardy's "The Man He Killed," a short story like Bierce's "The Horseman in the Sky," a skirmish from Homer's *Iliad*, Crane's *The Red Badge of Courage*, Tennyson's "Charge of the Light Brigade." But "War," as a topic, suggests no *thematic* affinities among these works, and if we were to treat them thematically we might not put any two together. So too with a unit on "Nature"—a great favorite of anthologists, for obvious reasons. A unit on "Nature" might include an essay by Beebe, a descriptive piece by John Muir, an account of Audubon's life and work, some poems by Wordsworth, Bryant's "To a Waterfowl," Emerson's "The Rhodora," Shelley's "West Wind," Burns' "To a Mountain Daisy," Kilmer's "Trees," Shakespeare's *As You Like It*, Frost's "Stopping by Woods," Tennyson's "The Brook," London's "To Build a Fire," Arnold's "Dover Beach." These share outdoor settings and various details of "Nature"—trees, birds, flowers, brooks, the sea, wind, mountains, bitter cold. "Nature" is a proper topic for all of these but it is the *theme* of few or none. The fact that Shelley's poem has a wind, leaves, and prominently mentions Spring is sufficient justification for placing it under "Nature" as topic, but not for placing it under "Nature" as theme, for its theme more nearly resembles "We Shall Overcome." The poem is not *about* Nature, but only uses its trappings. So too with "Dover Beach," which describes a real sea and a figurative sea, the sound of waters coming and going across the shingle, a still night, a moon; these are enough to place it in a topical unit on "Nature"—but it is not a "Nature" poem and is not about Nature, but about the dependence of one person on another, and its theme is expressed in "let us be true to one another." Thematically, then, it would go not with other works that have a setting in Nature—as it does go with them topically—but with other works that express the need of one person for another.

In illustrating what is obviously "topical," we have also moved toward defining "thematic." But now the task grows harder. It is easy to clarify "topical," and just as easy to classify works under topical headings and to show how topical groupings differ from thematic groupings. But it is hard to identify themes of individual works, and it is harder still to assemble a number of works that have thematic affinities under a common designation that is reasonably accurate—and that does not turn out to be topical. Let us first see whether we can name some headings that are as certainly thematic as "About Dogs," "Other People, Other Lands," "In Time of War," and "Nature" are topical. A favorite theme of twentieth-century literature is

"The Individual and Society," or, perhaps more precisely, "The Alienation of the Individual in Modern Society." A recurrent theme of literature since time immemorial is "Man's Inhumanity to Man." Countless works have been written that express "Courage in the Face of Adversity." Romantic novels, poems, plays, stories in great number make a common assertion to which Shakespeare gave the definitive expression: "The Course of True Love Never Did Run Smooth." In abbreviated form, without the full thesis statement, the concepts of Honor, Loyalty, Love, Heroism, Justice, Mercy, Fidelity, Patriotism, the Indomitable Spirit, Faith, Hope, Charity are embodied in many works. All these clearly represent an essentially different order from "About Dogs." For grouping works of literature, thematic affinity appears truer and more meaningful than topical affinity.

Though we have barely touched the problems of devising a thematic arrangement, we have now gone far enough to differentiate "thematic" and "topical," and before going further we should pause to consider what advantages, if any, there may be in arranging works by themes.

We have shown that arranging by genres leads to a study of genres, that arranging by chronology leads to a study of literary history, that arranging by topic leads to pursuit of knowledge about the topic, and that all three arrangements, accordingly, impede rather than further the reading of works for their effects as works of art. What reason is there to suppose that arranging by themes will better serve the latter purpose? The key, perhaps, is that the theme of a work is what a work is *about*, whereas type, chronology, and topic are not. In arranging works on the same or similar themes—in arranging them, that is, according to what they are *about*—we would undoubtedly be giving prominence to a more significant affinity than if we grouped them in any other way. Even a group composed exclusively of short stories will have—unless the themes merely happen to be the same—a less vital bond than a group of works that are bound by theme, even though these latter works may represent every variety of genre. And certainly a thematic group will have a truer affinity than a chronological group, and a more intimate relationship than a topical group or a national group. Given a common theme, a Greek play, a Russian short story, an English poem, and an American novel, ranging over a period of two thousand years—hence having neither time, place, nor genre in common—are closer together in a significant sense than four Greek plays, or four nineteenth-century Russian short stories, or four Victorian poems, or four twentieth-century American novels on different themes. What is most important, their thematic affinity, because it is an *inner* affinity, is more likely than any other kind of affinity to keep the experience of the individual works as works of art central and not to emphasize some external consideration—country, genre, topic, period.

Potentially, then, thematic arrangement seems the most desirable of the arrangements we have considered. It alone is consonant with our purpose of reading works of literature primarily for the experience that, as works of art, they can give; the others substitute peripheral purposes for the main one. A poem in a thematic group can be read for the aesthetic experience it has power to give, and at the same time—and this is a principal reason for *having* "groups" at all—something of the force of all the other works accrues to it. The artistic impact of three fine works related by theme should prove greater than that of three works otherwise related or not related at all.

Who can ask for anything better? May we not now consider our search for the best possible arrangement at an end?

Unfortunately, we have had to say that the thematic arrangement is *potentially* best; and potentially is here an enormous word.

What stands in the way of calling thematic arrangement *actually* the best kind are the practical difficulties, first, of identifying the themes of individual works of literature, and, second, of grouping these works accurately and usefully according to the themes they share. It is easy to deal theoretically with theme, as we have done in differentiating it from topic and in describing it in terms of feeling, attitude, point of view, personal qualities. But it is not at all easy to deal practically with theme—that is, to identify the themes of specific works and to group works by theme so as to make a usable program of reading.

We need not run through an extensive list of the world's poems, stories, novels, plays in order to show the magnitude of the problem. We can suggest it with just a few works. Take, for example, Shakespeare's plays. Earlier, we blithely suggested that the romantic comedies, along with other romantic works, share a theme that is neatly stated by Lysander in A Midsummer Night's Dream: "The path of true love never did run smooth." But, then, we can hardly read a page of As You Like It criticism without being advised that this play is Shakespeare's great effort on "the pastoral theme." The theme of The Two Gentlemen of Verona and of The Merchant of Venice we will find identified as "Friendship versus Love." The theme of the late romances, Cymbeline, The Winter's Tale, and The Tempest, we will find, is "Separation and Reconciliation," or "Regeneration and Renewal." If we leave the comedies and turn to the tragedies, what do we find? Who will presume to state categorically the theme of Hamlet? Is it "Revenge," and should it go in a group of works, along with Poe's "Cask of Amontillado," for example, in which someone wreaks vengeance on his enemy? (Here, of course, we encounter another sort of problem: "Amontillado" is assuredly a ninth grade work; Hamlet is a twelfth grade one. Should the happy coincidence of theme tempt us to do violence to both by placing them in the same year so that we can teach them as a thematic unit?) But what a vast deal of Hamlet is left out if we summarily deposit it under "Revenge"! Coleridge, if he planned the reading program, would presumably put it under "The Evils of Procrastination." Olivier, if he did the arranging, would put it with stories of "Men Who Could Not Make Up Their Minds." But honor is an enormous thing with Hamlet, and others would put the play with Lovelace's little poem "To Lucasta, On Going to the Wars," and other works under the thematic head of "Honor." Shall Macbeth go under "Ambition," along with Bacon's "Of Ambition" and Hawthorne's "The Ambitious Guest," among others? Or is *Macbeth* not really so much about ambition as it is about "Right and Wrong," so that it should be placed with works in which men decide between conscience and expedience? And whatever shall we do with *King Lear*? Is its theme "Ingratitude"? Or "Redemption through Suffering," "Parents and Children"? Or what?

The works of Shakespeare are the most intensively studied of all the world's literature. But after four centuries no critic who ventures to state the "theme" of any play can have the least confidence that another critic will agree with him. And who would have it otherwise? If we should ever agree absolutely about *Hamlet*, to take the obvious case, something would be lost to the world, like Everest, which has been climbed.

Though it is critically customary to insist that even the most complex literary works are unified by a single theme, however many subordinate themes each may have, the practical fact, when we soberly attempt to pinpoint the theme and cold-bloodedly name it, appears to be that no single thematic statement is adequate to describe any large and complex work.

But even this fact would not necessarily discourage us if only we could have better luck in identifying the themes of small works. We could then argue that large works might be allowed to stand unclassified in school programs, to be read "whole" for whatever theme or themes they contain, and could proceed with the task of classifying all the shorter things—poems, stories, essays. It is true that many short works are fairly easily classified by theme. Poets write of unrequited love, of the transitory nature of earthly things, in praise of beauty, of the importance of striving, of the effects of melancholy, of the goodness of life, of personal inspiration, of the joyous spirit, of the healing power of nature, of personal loss, of triumph over adversity, of the perversity of things, of man's eternal hope, of the indomitable human spirit, and so on. Short stories often have similarly identifiable themes. Bacon's essays, one by one, run a gamut of literary themes, ready-named by the titles. So far the task looks easy.

Yet one who sets out to work his way through a large

collection of poems, stories, and essays with the deliberate purpose of identifying themes and formulating collective titles for thematic groups soon finds that he is in for a jarring and frustrating experience. If he attempts to organize three hundred separate titles according to theme, he will find himself discouraged after an hour or so, ready to quit after half a day, and therefore too much intimidated ever to try again. If, fighting off frustration with the steely resolve that his "indomitable human spirit" shall prevail, he finally makes his way through to the end of the list, he will know only too well how wretchedly imperfect his accomplishment really is. He will feel little confidence in the rightness of his decisions—however warmly he may defend them to others—because he will remember that in more than half the cases he was uncertain, and resolved his dilemma by assigning works only "tentatively" to their respective groups—where, of course, he let them stay. He will be tormented by recollection of specific cases: Should "Lycidas" *really* have been placed in that particular one of half a dozen possible groups? Did he put any of Emily Dickinson's poems in the right place? Was he even right about Coleridge's "Ancient Mariner"? Can it really make sense that Twain's "Jumping Frog" finally landed in the same thematic group as one of Hardy's short poems? Is it not likely that half of his thematic headings are, after all, really topical? Do all literary works really have themes? Do any of them? Is there really such a thing as theme, or is it only a bit of professional jargon, useful for intimidating students? Was his whole undertaking basically preposterous and hopeless to begin with, like Crane's man pursuing the universe around and around?

In the end he may feel that there was nothing absolute or even accurate about any one of his placements except Scott's "Breathes There the Man," leading a group headed "Love of Country." And, finally, still left over after all the other leftovers from three volumes have been "tentatively" placed, remains "Kubla Khan," like an odd nickel after the accounts have been balanced.

We noted much earlier that classifying literature chronologically, typologically, geographically, or topically has the advantage of being easy and foolproof. Even the hardest of these—the topical—requires only a passing glance at the content of any given piece. But to classify thematically requires intimate acquaintance with every work, and even then the accurate identification of "the" theme is a problem for criticism; criticism, as everyone knows, involves interpretation; interpretation is ultimately a personal thing: hence if one should succeed in classifying a great many works thematically to his own satisfaction, he could not be sure of satisfying any other person or justified in insisting that any other person follow his program.

It is from these preliminary difficulties of identifying and classifying themes accurately that the major faults in the use of a thematic arrangement stem. If at first we ask why it matters so very much whether the arranger succeeds in identifying the theme of a work and accurately classifying it with other works, we discover the answer soon enough in the actual teaching. The "slant" given to a work by its placement in a thematic group is subtly powerful, and if the slant is wrong, the work will be distorted in the reading. If the theme with which it is *primarily* associated in grouping is in fact only a secondary theme, representing but a fraction of the work, the result, in teaching and reading, is a faulty emphasis that does violence to the whole—which is, of course, what matters most. When the primary theme of a complex work has been correctly identified, it serves as a valuable focal point for reading and discussion; much of the art of the work can be made apparent by discussion which is aimed to reveal how subordinate themes contribute to the main one, as tributaries run into a river, and how details of setting, action, character, and other elements have been selected and assembled by the author to support the main theme. But if the teacher uses this sort of structural mapping when a minor theme has mistakenly been identified as the main one, the result is disaster, and it would be better if theme had never been chosen as the grouping principle or used as a focal point for discussion. It is no doubt better to teach chronologically, typologically, or even topically than to teach thematically when themes have been identified wrongly and works set in false thematic groups. We began by asserting that thematic arrangement is potentially the best of all kinds; perhaps we must now acknowledge that it is also potentially the worst.

Even when themes have been correctly identified and works appropriately grouped, the method involves risks. One is the overemphasis of theme to the exclusion of other elements, as though "theme" were all that matters in the study of a poem, play, or novel. It is, of course, *the whole work* that matters, and the study of theme must be used as a means of getting at the whole work but kept subordinate to it. Another is overemphasis of the group theme to the extent that individual works that make up the group are reduced to the role of materials used to teach the theme itself, as though the works were of secondary importance and learning about the group theme of main importance. Here the effect is comparable to that of using individual short stories in a typological unit for the main purpose of teaching "the short story, its characteristics, techniques, evolution," or using the works in a topical unit to teach "knowledge of" the topic. The effect is comparable, but worse, because theme involves feeling, attitude, point of view; to assemble and teach a dozen works for the purpose of getting students to adopt a particular point of view, to inculcate a particular attitude in their beings, is to abuse literature, regardless of whether this attitude is a desirable or an undesirable one. This, of course, is not to suggest that literature should be so taught as to have no effect on students' attitudes, feelings, habits of thought, ideals; if it has no effect on these, there is surely no very compelling reason for teaching it at all. But the effect of art on our beings is, at its best, more indirect than, or, in any event, different from, that of head-on instruction designed to make us take a particular point of view toward specific matters.

To illustrate, let us assume that we make a unit of a dozen works with a pronounced "anti-war" theme. We take Wilfred Owen's powerfully ugly "Dulce et Decorum Est," his "Strange Meeting," and his "Anthem for Doomed Youth," Hardy's "The Man He Killed," Sandburg's "Grass," Crane's *The Red Badge of Courage* and his ironic "War Is

Kind"; lift Falstaff's disquisition on "Honor" from its context in *Henry IV*, Part 1; add Siegfried Sassoon's bitter "Does It Matter?" and Richard Eberhart's "The Fury of Aerial Bombardment," and top the unit off with the horrors of *Hiroshima*.

Now we have a real dilemma on our hands. From the start, we have insisted that chronological, typological, and topical arrangements are undesirable because they tempt teachers and students to make knowledge of chronology, type, and topic, rather than experience, the primary purpose of reading literary works. And next we have argued that thematic arrangement is potentially best because it gives us the best chance to keep experience of the work primary. But here we have framed a thematic unit with which, it appears, we are trying to sell students on a specific point of view, get them to adopt an "anti-war" attitude. Even if we agree that this is a desirable attitude for students to have, the fact is beside the point; the point is that if we *use* the works in this unit in order to get across to students *the message of the entire unit*, we are "teaching a theme" rather than teaching individual works for the experience of them as works of art. We have taught these works for less than the best thing they have to offer, and therefore we have abused them.

Is it possible to teach the works arranged in such a unit and yet manage to keep the experience of each work primary, not secondary to the force of the total unit's message? If it is not possible, then surely we should include no such thematic unit; we should use some other kind of unit, if any at all, that is preferably innocuous, leaving each work free to be itself and do what it can best do by itself. There should be a best reason for bringing works together. They should, we have said, have in common the most important thing that it is possible for works to have in common.

And this something, we insisted earlier, is *theme*. We have argued on behalf of thematic arrangement that when works are brought together by this bond, something of the force of the whole group accrues to each work and enhances its single power: three works with the theme of

"Man's Inhumanity to Man" will individually strike harder and, hopefully, penetrate students' beings more deeply than if they were not components of a group. All this looks proper enough.

But now, having twelve works that are united by an anti-war theme, we intuitively rebel—not because we do not think an anti-war theme desirable but because we perceive that when these works are taught as a group it will be the group message that we seem really to be teaching. We find that we have suddenly become not dealers in artistic experiences, but advocates of specific social attitudes.

Can we solve the problem by balancing our anti-war group off against a group with a bellicose theme—poems, plays, stories that stress the joys of combat, the glory of dying in battle for one's country? We could start this unit off with an excerpt from *Henry V*, the King's incredibly moving Crispin's Day battle oration that stirs the heart like a trumpet; we could use Homer's *Iliad* here, Tennyson's "Charge of the Light Brigade," Alan Seeger's "I Have a Rendezvous with Death," John McCrae's "In Flanders Field," Rupert Brooke's "The Soldier," Collins' "How Sleep the Brave," the ever-potent two lines of "Thermopylae," *The Song of Roland*, and we could wind up the unit with Longfellow's "Morituri Salutamus" and with Horace's own original that Wilfred Owen balked at, "Dulce et decorum est/ Pro patria mori."

To solve the problem thus would have the good democratic virtue of giving equal time to opposing points of view. *But the same basic objection would still hold:* we would still be missing the main point of teaching literature. In fact, we would be compounding our error by teaching one group of works for its group message and then teaching another for its contrasting message and thus doubly emphasizing the importance of "message," as opposed to aesthetic experience, in works of art.

"In his hands," wrote Wordsworth about Milton's use of the sonnet, "the thing became a trumpet." It is nothing against Milton's sonnets that he sometimes used them so. But it is something against us as teachers of literature if we frame thematic groups and use them so. If we deliberately did so—deliberately framed thematic groups so that they would inculcate in students the specific attitudes that we want inculcated in them—we could be charged with conducting a vicious practice. But even that is not the point: the point is that if we did so we would be misusing individual works by subordinating aesthetic experience, which is the best thing each has to give, to the collective instruction.

The necessity, then, if we are really going to use thematic groups, is to keep the experience of individual works in the place of first importance and to subordinate the group message, though not the group experience. How can we do so?

First, we must reverse one practice that is regularly used by teachers of thematic groups. This practice consists of directing students' attention explicitly to the fact that there is a group and to its nature. It is not uncommon for teachers to distribute dittoed sheets listing works under thematic group headings written in capital letters at the top of the page and underlined. At the very worst, having distributed such sheets, teachers may then proceed: "Now, students, you will see that we are next going to read a dozen works on LOVE. We will start off, as you see, with Shelley's 'Indian Serenade,' to see what it has to say about LOVE; then we will read Browning's 'Love among the Ruins' and get its view, Bacon's 'Of Love,' and so on. By the time we get to *Romeo and Juliet*, which, as you see, ends the list, we should all have a much clearer idea of LOVE." So introduced, the unit becomes machinery for studying LOVE; and when the introduction is followed by repeated references to the group theme while individual works are being read and discussed, it is inevitable that consciousness of the unit itself should overwhelm the experience of individual works. What is here emphatically urged is that teachers avoid listing works under thematic titles, avoid announcing the fact that there is a group title, and avoid stressing the relationship of individual works to the group title. Most students are not so obtuse but that they will soon enough recognize thematic affinities among works they are reading, and that is as it should be, for thus their awareness comes about by induction rather than imposition.

Second—and with this we shall be concerned in later chapters—we must manage to treat each work of a group not as though it were one of a group, but alone, an entity, whole in itself—as in fact a work of art is. A familiar analogy may be useful here: a string of pearls is a more impressive thing than a single pearl, and it is very easy for the perfection of a single pearl to be lost in a necklace of pearls. Our problem is to make the necklace, and yet somehow to preserve the identity of each separate pearl. In short, what we want is to have each pearl *gain*, rather than lose, by being part of a necklace; we want it to have the advantage of being one of a group, and not the disadvantage. With this problem, among others, we shall be concerned in the chapter on Presentation.

Before we make a final assessment of thematic arrangement, we should acknowledge one further objection that is often made to it. This is the tedium, for students and teacher alike, of reading work after work on "the same old theme." It is vain to deny that the prospect of reading through a whole semester's list of works under the heading LOVE is uninviting. The twentieth work on the list, even if it is *Romeo and Juliet*, is likely to cloy, and by the end of the semester LOVE will be something to gag at; the last works on the list, however exquisite, will be wasted from loss of appetite. Not all themes are as perishable as LOVE, but even masculine themes like honor, justice, courage reach a point beyond which we want to hear no more. Teachers must stop short of this point; to go beyond it is to risk losing everything.

But the danger of surfeiting from too long exposure to works of a common theme is one that can be avoided. If every work *is read for itself*, as it should be, if the teacher refrains from laboring the relation of work after work to the group theme, and if the number of works in any one thematic unit is kept small—sometimes only three or four, never more than ten or a dozen—the problem should be eased. A four-year program, carefully worked out, makes it possible to return to the same theme year after year; there is no need to pack every poem, story, play, novel, and essay that bears on LOVE into one massive unit in the sophomore year. And if works are both *selected* and *placed* by year before they are arranged in thematic groups, there should be no occasion to overload any unit in any year. Let us suppose, for a moment, that forty of the works selected for a four-year program have a love theme. If we place them according to comparative difficulty, as best we can determine that, the chances are good that some will be found appropriate for each year, though the numbers will hardly turn out an even ten each.

What is to be concluded, now, about thematic arrangement? We asserted that it is potentially the best arrangement, chiefly because it joins works by a significant bond, perhaps the most significant. And because they have this important relationship, we argued, the impact of each will gain: it will have power beyond itself by being one of a group. But over against these virtues we have set such formidable ills as to raise doubt whether thematic arrangement ought ever to be used. Abused, it can distort and misrepresent works, subordinate experience to message, become a propaganda device for anthologists, program arrangers, or teachers who want to inculcate their pet attitudes in students. Stretched too long, and overstressed, it can become intolerable for everyone; at its worst, too, it can be simply silly.

To aim at a thematic arrangement for a full four-year program of exclusively first-rate works set in exactly the right places and viewed in the right perspective is to aim at the ideal. Probably there is nothing better for anthologists, program arrangers, and teachers to do than work toward this ideal. We have earlier labeled it unfortunate that thematic arrangement is much harder to work out satisfactorily than typological or chronological arrangement. But the disadvantage can also be seen as advantage. To arrange works thematically, teachers must study them long and seriously; they must probe them to the heart, as good criticism tries to do. It is impossible to compose a satisfactory thematic unit of even three works without knowing intimately what they are "about." The honest efforts of English teachers to create impeccable thematic arrangements—little groups of three, six, ten works—can alone make the difference between first-rate and second-rate teachers. We may never completely translate protentiality to actuality by achieving a definitive thematic arrangement, but serious, sustained efforts toward that goal are as valuable as the achievement.

Meanwhile, the practical, day-to-day business of teaching literature must of course go on; it cannot stand still until the perfect four-year thematic program has been devised. Since that is so, the wisest solution may be to use a variety of arrangements—not even excluding the chronological, typological, and topical, as well as others that are shortly to be described. And as individual thematic groups are perfected, or seem to be, more and more of them can be worked into the program; ultimately we should produce a four-year program deserving of general approval.

Other ways

What we have been leading up to suggesting is that— though we still insist that the thematic way is potentially the best *single* way—a four-year program can reasonably accommodate several arrangements. It is thought by many teachers that there really *ought* to be variety, for the sake of variety; we have pointed out that thematic arrangement, for example, can be monotonous. On the other hand, it is a fact that an anthology, or a school program, that is a hodge-podge of group units has a random look and seems to make no "whole" sense. The program opens, let us say, with "The Short Story" (genre); next it has "Classical Myths" (history, geography, and genre); then "The Challenge of Science" (topic); then "The Darker Side" and "The Lighter Side" (mood, attitude); then "Satire" (mode, purpose); then "Our Contemporaries" (history, topic); then "America the Beautiful" (geography, theme); and it may end with "The Novel" (genre) and "A Shakespearean Play" (author, genre). Here is indeed variety, but variety that betrays a sad fact: that the arranger had no consistent principles but was guided only by expediency.

If a program is to employ a variety of group arrangements, the least we can do is require that there be a better reason than variety for the sake of variety. For the moment, let us hypothesize that we have been mistaken in arguing that some one kind of arrangement—thematic—if it could be accomplished perfectly, would be best for all works in a four-year program. (And *best* here, as elsewhere, means that this arrangement will give each individual work its best chance to do the best thing it can do for students— i.e., get to them as a work of art.) Let us consider the possibility that certain works, because of their nature, will best get through to students if they are set in one kind of arrangement, and that others, because of their nature, will best get through if they are set in another. Is it not possible, for example, that some works will even perform best in a topical group—the least defensible kind of arrangement? And that certain others may do best if placed chronologically? Or by genre?

Devising a program in this way is essentially different from devising a program of various arrangements merely for the sake of variety and at the whim of expediency. It means that before placing Hawthorne's "Great Stone Face" in a group of allegorical works rather than in a typological or thematic group, one would take into account the nature of the story and weigh the advantages of placing it in that kind of unit. What is suggested here is that *theme*—which we earlier identified as the most important single element that works of literature can have in common—may not in fact be most important for *all* works. The intrinsic nature of certain works might conceivably be more accurately reflected if, for example, they formed a "horror" group than if they were grouped by theme. In works in which *theme* is the dominant element—as in Wilfred Owen's "Dulce et Decorum Est," for example—there can be little doubt: theme is the most important element; and such works should be placed together accordingly. But in works in which theme is not clearly identifiable, and in any event is unemphatic, is it not possible that something else, such as allegory (mode) or horror (effect) is a more vital bond than theme? The theme of Browning's "Love among the Ruins" is emphatic and unmistakable: "Love Is Best." But is the theme of "Pictor Ignotus," or "My Last Duchess," or "Fra Lippo Lippi" similarly pronounced? According to the possibility we are now suggesting, "Love among the Ruins" should clearly be placed in a thematic group with other works that affirm the value of love; but the three dramatic monologues might perform better if they were set in a group of dramatic monologues than if they were separated and placed each according to its theme—as best we can determine that—with works of similar theme. Which is better, which is worse—to place these monologues together with others and run the risk of teaching "the dramatic monologue, its characteristics and techniques," or to risk forcing them into thematic units in which they uncertainly belong?

Perhaps we have here a workable solution to the problem discussed in connection with thematic arrangement, that of identifying themes and classifying works accurately according to thematic affinities. We might devise a program in which all works *that have strong and unmistakable themes* are grouped thematically, but in which other works are grouped in a variety of ways, according to their most important affinities. Let us look at some problem cases.

Many a Ph.D. candidate has faltered on being asked to state the theme of "Lycidas," and many an examiner, no doubt, has asked the question hoping to find an answer for himself. Is it "bereavement," and should the poem be grouped with other works that express loss? *Is* "Lycidas" primarily an expression of Milton's grief at loss of King, or is that only the *occasion* of the poem—which is a very different thing from theme? Remembering the question posed early in the poem, "Were it not better done, as others use,/ To sport with Amaryllis in the shade," and remembering Milton's answer at the end:

> At last he rose, and twitched his mantle blue;
> To-morrow to fresh woods, and pastures new—

remembering this, and remembering also how Milton turned from the pagan Renaissance and its beauty to shoulder the burden of the Puritan cause, can we really suppose that we have represented the poem faithfully in placing it with poems of bereavement? Should it rather go with Herbert's "The Collar"—

> *Methought I heard one calling,* Child!
> *And I replied,* My Lord—

and with Wordsworth's "Ode to Duty," and with Frost's "Stopping by Woods"—and, indeed, perhaps with *Hamlet* —as works in which poet and protagonist hear and heed the call to duty?

Or, to take a very different case: Keats' four great odes (Melancholy, Grecian Urn, Nightingale, Autumn) all have sufficiently different themes that if we were to put them into thematic groups according to theme, we would have to separate them. What is more, though the themes are discernible, they are subtle, diffuse, all but unnamable, and we could not count on having anyone agree if we placed them under precisely named thematic headings. We could classify them readily enough by topics, but the absurdity of doing so is easily illustrated: "Ode to a Nightingale" would go under "Birds" or "Wild Creatures"; "Autumn" would go under "The Four Seasons" or "Nature." But the first is not "about" birds, and the second, though the occasion is Autumn, is not "about" it. But in this case—which is not unique but provides a striking example—would it not be preferable to keep the odes together, in a group of their own? We would not keep them together just because they are all by Keats or because they are all odes or because they are all from the Romantic Period, or because they are all English, but because, being all these, they cohere more closely with one another than any one would cohere with a thematic group. Their cohesion is pervasive and goes beyond affinity; we might more aptly describe it as homogeneity.

AUTHORSHIP

If we made such a unit, we would be conceding that *authorship* sometimes makes for a closer relationship than theme or any other element that works have in common. We might even conclude that authorship is *always* the most important relationship of works, and if we did so, we should base whole programs on arrangements by author. At each grade level, then, all the poems we used by Wordsworth would make up a unit; the poems, stories, and novels by Hardy would be kept together; we might have a group of Frost poems in each year. If we made a program of this kind, we would have only one practical problem, which is not very difficult to solve. We would have to decide the order in which to take up our author-units in each year. In the ninth grade we could have small groups of works by Whitman, Hawthorne, Poe, Longfellow, Wordsworth, de Maupassant, Frost, Bacon, Dickinson, Tomlinson, Byron, Chekhov, Crane, Lord Dunsany, Saki, Bryant, Thurber, Shakespeare, Twain, and others. Which should we use first and which next? We might simply go alphabetically—which would mean that we evaded our responsibility to make any kind of rational decision. We might go chronologically—but what possible justification would there be for doing so? But the sanest way, surely, would be to start off with the less difficult authors and move along to the most difficult; in this event we would no doubt start with Longfellow, Poe, and Bryant, and end with a couple of essays by Bacon, some poems by Emily Dickinson, and some sonnets and a play by Shakespeare.

But besides this minor problem of order, we would meet two other problems not so easily solved. The first is the problem of maintaining a sense of "program" throughout the year. The second is the problem of avoiding "teaching authors—their characteristics, techniques, forms, attitudes." As for the first problem, we should acknowledge that it exists also with thematic groups, topical groups, and typological groups, though not at all with a chronological arrangement: the sense of "program" is strongest of all when a class is studying the history of a literature, for one age grows into the next and there is always a clear sense of where one has been and where one is going. But the problem that arises with author groups is more severe than that with thematic, topical, or typological groups because the author groups are usually much smaller. In the ninth grade we might use only two or three poems by Wordsworth, not more than two essays by Bacon, not more than two stories by de Maupassant, whereas in a thematic unit we might consistently have between six and a dozen works, and in a typological unit we might have twenty short stories and fifty poems. Further, the purpose in moving from one large theme to another or from one major genre to another is more readily apparent than that of moving from one author to the next on the list. Indeed, except that we expect to find the second slightly more difficult than the first, what possible purpose could there be for moving from two stories by de Maupassant to two poems by Whitman to two essays by Tomlinson?

That some sense of program is necessary is hardly debatable. Even dull students recognize and react against evident aimlessness. To go from author to author without apparent reason is not much different from going from one work to the next without apparent reason. The problem seems to have no satisfactory solution.

The second problem is as difficult and even more serious. Organization by author inevitably focuses attention on *author*. It would be hard to present, say, five poems by Bryant without in effect "making a little study" of Bryant: who he was, when and where he lived, how his poems are characteristic of him. Try as the teacher might and should to prevent the shift of emphasis, the three poems must appear as examples or as devices used in order to "learn about" Bryant—after which the class would move on to Poe to "learn about" him, and so on throughout the year. There is, of course, nothing wrong with "learning about" Bryant or any other author, and few works will yield their best fruit unless something is learned about the author; but this is not the main reason for studying any literary work, and any style of arrangement that makes it seem to be so is a faulty one. Our principal objection to arrangements by chronology, type, or country is that they tend to become principal subject matters, substituting knowledge of history, genre, and country for experience of artistic works as the main "why" of teaching and studying literature. Arrangement by author puts "knowledge of authors" first. We must therefore reject arrangement by author on the same grounds for which we rejected the other systems. In fact, remembering our first serious objection above, we have an additional reason for rejecting it: the other systems, whatever their faults, do convey to students a strong sense of "program," whereas arrangement by author carries none.

But even if it is not suitable as a basis for a whole program, arrangement by author can perform yeoman's service in supplementing the main system. The odes of Keats very possibly should go together, not for the purpose of "learning about" Keats but for the massive impact of the group. More often, probably, several poems or other works by a single author will go appropriately into a thematic unit that contains works of various authors—as, for an obvious example, Shakespeare's sonnets that protest the ravages of Time might be kept together, not because they are by Shakespeare but because they share a theme. Should Keats' "Grecian Urn," which, like these sonnets celebrates a triumph over Time, be separated from the other great odes and placed with the sonnets, after all? In this case we would say no, because the relationship of the odes together is stronger than the thematic relationship.

OCCASION

We must now, but briefly, mention other possible arrangements, none of which would serve for an entire program but may, like arrangement by author, supplement the main plan. First, let us consider arrangement by *occasion*. Elementary school teachers often present, at Christmas time, a range of activities befitting the season; among others, these activities include the reading of Christmas poems, short plays, stories, and other pieces. Similarly, literary pieces relating to Lincoln are used with other activities on or around Lincoln's birthday. A unit involving Puritans, turkeys, Indians, and the first Thanksgiving gives occasion for similarly appropriate pieces in November. What virtue would there be in an "occasional" arrangement at the high school level?

Its deficiencies as a general plan are obvious. First, too many fine works of literature, eminently suited for study in high school, would have to be omitted simply because they suit no particular occasion. Second, few really good works that associate themselves with a particular occasion are in fact "about" that occasion, and to place them in an occasional group would be to misrepresent them and possibly to miss the real point that, as artistic works, they exist to make. There are additional shortcomings, but these will suffice to show the unsuitability of occasional arrangement as a general plan. But to say so much is not to deny its advantages as a special variation.

The seasons of the year, along with the great holidays and birthdays, provide occasions that can take up many of the leftovers from the main idea of arrangement. In some cases, too, there may be positive gain in seizing the opportunity given by occasion. An unannounced reading of Whitman's "When Lilacs Last in the Dooryard Bloom'd" on Lincoln's birthday may gain a better hearing for that rather tedious poem than it could gain in any other circumstance. The first bright day of Spring may be the best possible time to read Browning's "O To Be in England." And Surrey's fresh sonnet, "The soote season that bud and bloom forth brings," will reach students who study it on March 21 with far more force than if it were read in a group of sonnets on "Unrequited Love" (theme). Proceeding chronologically in the twelfth grade, teachers reach the Canterbury "Prologue" in mid-September or early October; but the spirit of the pilgrimage will communicate more eloquently to students if this great opening is read precisely

> *Whan that Aprille with his shoures soote*
> *The droghte of March hath perced to the roote* . . .

Herrick's "Corinna's Gone A-Maying" is not a poem to be read in the dead of winter, as it would be in a chronological tour of English literature, but on the first day of May; and "Loveliest of Trees" is rightest when cherry trees are blooming.

A year-long program so devised as to exploit whatever is in season would clearly be intolerable; students would emerge from it with a ludicrous notion of what literature is. Further, in making such a program, teachers would be tempted to pad out skimpy "occasional" units with whatever pieces were timely, whether artistic or not. The seasons, the great holidays, and the great birthdays have called forth much mawkish, artistically worthless writing which, unfortunately, by association with its occasion, can be made to look better than it is; the emotions of Christmas will tolerate almost anything. But as a *deviation* from the general plan of arrangement, the "occasional" group has great merit.

MODE, MOOD, TECHNIQUE

We should not end this discussion of possible arrangements without mentioning *mode*, *mood*, and *technique*, which together account for many units in anthologies and school programs. If we put together the morality play of *Everyman*, Spenser's *The Faerie Queene*, Bunyan's *Pilgrim's Progress*, we are evidently relating allegorical works; to such major works as these we could add shorter works of strongly allegorical bent, like Hawthorne's "The Great Stone Face," Poe's "The Raven," and Tennyson's "Crossing the Bar." The emphasis of our unit would thus be on the *mode* of allegory. We could similarly fashion a unit on the mode of satire. We could set up a unit of heavily descriptive works, also, or of works that make use of pastoral elements. A poem like "Lycidas" could fit into a variety of groups, depending on which affinities of this poem with other works we wish to stress: (1) pastoral— in which event we would set it with other works that use pastoral machinery; (2) thematic—with other works that have a similar theme (if we can determine what its main theme is); (3) genre and sub-genre—with other elegies; (4) author—with other works by Milton; (5) chronology —with other seventeenth-century works.

But, to keep to the case of "Lycidas," we might also set it with works grouped by *mood*. Probably the most frequent mood-group in actual use brings together various humorous pieces under a title like "The Lighter Side," or, perhaps, just "Humor." The mood of "Lycidas" is profoundly sober; we could place it with Milton's own "Il Penseroso," Tennyson's "Break, Break, Break," and Arnold's "Dover Beach" under "The Darker Side" as a general heading, or more specifically under "The Melancholy Tone." Other mood groupings include works that produce effects of suspense, terror, exhilaration.

Or, finally, we might group "Lycidas" with works that exhibit similar *technique*. Grouping by technique is widely used as a sub-arrangement, often within the enveloping frame of genre grouping. A unit on the "Short Story," for example, may be broken down into "Stories with a Surprise Twist," "Stories That Develop Character," "Stories with a Single Tone." But most often it is used inside poetry units, and sometimes it furnishes the organizing principle for an entire year's work with poetry. One way is to begin with a set of poems that exhibit pronounced rhythm and strong rhyme, then move to a group with prominent alliteration, then to a group notable for visual imagery, to a next group rich in simile and metaphor, then to poems notable for their use of onomatopoeia. One purpose of such grouping is obvious: the introduction of students to the devices of poetry through an ordered series of illustrations, moving from the more obvious characteristics such as rhythm and rhyme toward, ultimately, the subtlest and most sophisticated devices of highly complex poetry. "Lycidas," presumably, would be assigned to a group near the end of the series, representing perhaps "The High Style," in which the elements of sound and imagery are woven into a rich symphony; "Lycidas" would take its place beside Spenser's "Epithalamion" and "Prothalamion," Dryden's "Song for St. Cecilia's Day," Keats' "Ode on a Grecian Urn," Tennyson's "Ulysses," and perhaps Milton's own "Il Penseroso" and "L'Allegro"—all poems of rich texture and magnificent harmony.

Perhaps in a four-year program there *should* be space for groups of works brought together because they share similar techniques, mood, or mode. But clearly such groups should serve only as deviations from the main scheme of arrangement, and perhaps only as a means of using works that defy placement otherwise. Probably the least objectionable of these three ways of grouping is mood. But on the other hand what can be said positively even for it? What is gained by bringing together humorous works, or satirical works, or grief-filled works, or suspense-filled works? If what we truly seek is an arrangement that will assure each work in the group its best chance to reach students with full force, what relevance has grouping by mood? Grouping by mood would mean, for example, that we must separate "Il Penseroso" and "L'Allegro," perhaps letting them stand at the head of contrasting groups. But is there not something basically wrong with a system that forces the separation of these poems?

As for grouping by either mode or technique, the main objection is more serious. We have insisted from the start that the main objective is to have individual works reach students with their utmost force as works of art. But now let us say that we have set up groups of poems according to their technical aspects: one group has much alliteration, another has strong rhythm and rhyme, another has onomatopoeia, and so on. Try as we may to enable each poem to communicate its whole artistic force to students, it will be a miracle if we do more than teach students to identify poetic devices; our unit as a whole will turn into a lesson in poetic techniques. In effect, we shall be using Poe's "The Bells" to have students learn about onomatopoeia (though indeed in this case it is questionable whether there is a better reason). By the time we have worked our way through a series of such lessons up to a complex symphony like "Lycidas," students will have become expert in detecting the individual elements that have been woven together to make up the full harmony. They will have come to "know about" techniques. But the primary object of teaching poetry is not to have students "know about" techniques, but to have them affected by the artistic force of poetry. Similarly, if we fashion groups according to mode, our arrangement will influence or even usurp our deeper purpose; if we bring together a number of satires, we shall be "learning about" satire.

This is not to say that students need know nothing about poetic techniques, or about the characteristic devices of satire, in order to experience the artistic force of certain works; and it is certainly not to say that knowing about them will *prevent* us from experiencing this force. On the contrary, there are times when, if we are ignorant of the artistic devices of a work, we miss its force entirely; but the relation of "knowing about" an author's artistic devices to experiencing the effects of his art is a subject for discussion in a later chapter.

We have now surveyed the main possibilities for arranging works. Obviously there are additional ways of more informal and perhaps even impromptu nature, and it may be that some of these are as right for a given moment in a program and a small body of particular pieces as any of the major ways that are commonly used. Although we have found the thematic arrangement to be potentially most promising, the main argument of the foregoing discussion is that there is, or seems to be, no such thing as a single right kind of arrangement that should be used invariably. The main purpose in teaching literature will be best served by one kind of arrangement for some works and by another for others. With the problem of arrangement, therefore, as with the problems of approach and presentation, which are next to be discussed, probably the most reasonable course is always to take our cue *from the work itself* and to place it in whatever sort of group will do most for its chances of getting through to students as an artistic experience. Though it seems likely that for the greater number of works the main purpose of teaching will be best served by thematic grouping, it is also likely that certain works— and we named, for example, the great odes of Keats—will come through most potently if they are grouped on some other principle.

To demonstrate how a thematic unit can be worked out, some sample groups for the tenth grade are appended to this chapter. One advantage of thematic grouping is that it offers individual teachers considerable freedom in ordering the work of the semester. The following groups could obviously be arranged in other ways, and we do not mean to suggest that the arrangement given here is the best possible one. It is merely suggestive. The works to be read outside of class which are listed in the right-hand column

A Sample Thematic Unit for the Tenth Grade

INTENSIVE ANALYSIS IN CLASS

OUTSIDE READING

HONOR AND COURAGE

Anonymous	Sir Patrick Spens
Bacon	Of Honor
Anonymous	Gawain and the Green Knight
Lovelace	To Lucasta, on Going to the Wars
Shakespeare	Henry IV, Part 1
Bierce	A Horseman in the Sky
Crane	The Red Badge of Courage
Hemingway	The Snows of Kilimanjaro

Forbes	Johnny Tremaine
Hemingway	The Old Man and the Sea
Kennedy	Profiles in Courage
Faulkner	The Bear
Mitchell	Gone with the Wind

TRUE AND FALSE VALUES

Hardy	The Man He Killed	Lee	To Kill a Mockingbird
Gogol	The Cloak	Masters	Spoon River Anthology
Maupassant	The Necklace	Anderson	Winesburg, Ohio
Wordsworth	The World Is Too Much with Us	Wilder	Our Town
Robinson	Richard Cory	Steinbeck	The Pearl
Lardner	Haircut	Lewis	Main Street
Hawthorne	Rappacini's Daughter	Salinger	Catcher in the Rye
Bacon	Of Wisdom for a Man's Self		

VENGEANCE AND GUILT

Montaigne	Of Conscience	Du Maurier	Rebecca
Poe	The Cask of Amontillado	Wallace	Ben Hur
Bacon	Of Revenge	Wharton	Ethan Frome
Hawthorne	Ethan Brand		
Blake	A Poison Tree		
Hawthorne	The Scarlet Letter		

are likewise merely suggestive, in this case all related thematically to the works being studied in class. Finally, it should be noted that some attempt to relate one group to that immediately following has been attempted here in order to provide a feeling of continuity that is not always evident in thematically organized units. Reference to the lists in the Appendix will show that many additional works could be fitted into the themes used here.

Chapter 5

What form of introduction?

The preceding chapters have dealt only with preliminaries: before works are actually taught, they have to be selected, placed, and arranged in some kind of order.

But with Introduction we cease to deal with preliminaries and move into the classroom. We have selected, placed, and arranged works according to the best judgment we had. Today we have a poem—"Lycidas," let us suppose—and there sits the class in front of us. What do we do now?

We may, of course, skip Introduction entirely. We may simply instruct the class to open their books, clear our throats, and start reading the poem aloud while the class follow in their texts. Omitting Introduction (the business of the present chapter), we have begun the Presentation. Possibly this is the best way to proceed with "Lycidas"; possibly it is not.

Perhaps we should have prepared students' minds in some way or other before we began reading. What might we have done?

"Lycidas" is an elegy. We might have had students read about elegies in reference books, might have lectured on elegies for half an hour, tracing the form from Bion to Milton, or might have assigned a committee, well in advance, to investigate and report. We might also have read another elegy or two, by way of illustration, before tackling the complex "Lycidas."

"Lycidas" is a poem by Milton. We might have had students read about Milton in reference books, or lectured on him, or assigned students to report. We might also have read, or had students read, simpler poems by Milton before tackling "Lycidas."

"Lycidas" is an English poem written in 1637. We could have lectured on or had students read about "The Puritan Period." We might easily have spent a week in combined research, report, and lecture so as to get as much historical context into students' minds as possible before attempting the poem itself.

Should we have done any or all or none of these things before we began to read the poem? Deeper than the question "Should we or not?" is the question *How do we decide whether we should or not?*

Should we decide on the grounds that these are college prep students who "ought to know about such matters," and accordingly go into detail about genre, author, and period? Or, if our arrangement is chronological, should we decide to go into these matters on the grounds that we must leave no gaps in literary history? Or, if our arrangement is typological, should we decide not to lecture on Milton and period but to deal fully with the evolution of the elegy as a sub-genre? Or should we decide to have students do a week's research on Milton, age, and genre on the grounds that they should have experience in library work and in writing an "investigative report"? Are any of these reasonable grounds on which to decide, one way or the other?

If we are faithful to our principle, we must determine the introduction to "Lycidas" on only one basis: whether or not the introduction we make will enhance the likelihood that the poem will reach students with full force. This question is never easy to answer; but it is the question we should always try to answer. There is no other rational basis for decision.

For the moment let us leave the example of "Lycidas" and turn to *Julius Caesar*. What *might* we do before we start the actual reading of this play?

Julius Caesar is a product of the Elizabethan Period. We might spend a week introducing students to Shakespeare's age, Renaissance political and other ideas, the theater, blank verse, the author's life and works.

Julius Caesar is a tragedy. We might lecture on the genre, starting with Aristotle and the Greek drama, defining and illustrating "tragedy," moving up through Shakespeare's immediate predecessors, and ending with modern theory.

Julius Caesar is set in Rome, before and after the assassination of Caesar in 44 B.C. We might lecture on the place of Rome and Caesar in world history, on Caesar's campaigns, on Roman customs, political structure, social classes, costumes. If some of our students are also students of World History, we might plan with the history teacher to conduct a joint study of Roman life in Caesar's time. We might have reports on Roman banquets, baths, and togas; we might have bulletin-board exhibits of drawings made by students or taken from magazine and newspaper advertisements. We might even have students from the sewing class make some sample garments. If some students are also students of Latin, we might have them teach the rest of the class a vocabulary of key words relating to government, public buildings, citizens.

We might show a film-strip on Shakespeare's London, Stratford, the Elizabethan stage. We might even show the filmed play.

We might read some Shakespearean sonnets, to get students acquainted with Shakespeare's language and verse before they tackle the major work.

We could easily do much more by way of introducing *Julius Caesar* than we could possibly think of doing in introducing "Lycidas." Both the Age of Elizabeth and the time of Caesar provide almost unlimited opportunity.

We could; but the question is whether we should. Before we decide on doing anything, we ought to ask whether doing it will really help the work reach students with its force as an artistic work.

Having illustrated the problem, we now urge the need of the teacher to question similarly the introduction to every work in the program, whether it be a Shakespearean play that will consume five weeks of study or a sonnet that will take only half an hour. If we are to find it anywhere, we will find our cue for the nature of the introduction *in the work itself.* If we make a habit of always asking the same question of each work, "What can be done before the students read it that will enhance the likelihood of its getting to them with full force?" and then try to answer the question honestly, we will soon find the absurdity of using any single, ready-made form of introduction for all works. We will find that for certain works one kind of introduction needs to be made, that others require a very different one, and that still others will have a better chance of reaching students unimpaired if they have none at all.

If we manage to be wholly honest, we may be surprised by our main conclusion: *that many more works fit into the third classification than into the other two*. We may even find ourselves deciding that certain works that we would have thought *surely* needed extensive "background" treatment before students read them really need none and will do better with none. Let us imagine that we are to teach Poe's "The Fall of the House of Usher" in the ninth grade and that the class has never read a story by Poe or even heard of him. They do not know whether he was American or Greek, whether he wrote in the nineteenth century or the third. They know nothing at all about "The Short Story" as a literary genre—nothing of its origins, evolution, or techniques. And of course they never have heard of Poe's theories of composition—the single tone, the single impression. They have never heard of mood, tone, suspense as critical terms, and know nothing of how writers create and use these.

In these circumstances, the temptation to take whatever time is needed in order to inform the class on all these matters—historical, biographical, technical—is likely to be overpowering. If we are using a standard anthology, we may assign close reading, under threat of a test, of all the background material. If we are using a paperback that contains no historical and technical paraphernalia, we may prepare several lectures. There is more than enough available "background" information to use up a week before students read the opening sentence of "Usher."

But if we take this week to inform them, are we *really* doing so because we think the force of the story will strike them with greater impact because of the information? Or— let us be quite honest—is it that we somehow believe they "ought to know about" Poe and his theories? Is it really the experience of Poe's story that we want students to have —or is it knowledge of backgrounds?

If Poe did actually succeed, by applying his theories, in building a powerful single impression into his story, will not that impression communicate itself to students who read "Usher" with care, or with whom it is read aloud with care? And if it *does* reach them, have they not then gained the best thing that the story has to give? Have they not then had the experience that is our *sine qua non*?

If it were necessary for students to know about Poe and his theories in order to gain this experience, then obviously the teacher's introduction should include the relevant information. If they could not experience Poe's "single impression" unless they were first told about it, then obviously the introduction should tell them. If knowing where "The Fall of the House of Usher" stands in the history of the American short story were necessary before students could experience the force of the story, then the introduction should inform them. But we should be careful not to mistake "knowing about" Poe, his theories, and the evolution of the short story in America for an end in itself; it is at best only a means to the experience of the work—and in this case an extremely dubious means. If Poe's artistic devices do really work, then students will presumably feel their effects even though they do not know the author's name. And if they do *not* feel these effects, telling them about the author, his theories, and the evolution of "The Short Story" is not likely to cause them to do so. "Knowing about" an effect is not at all the same thing as experiencing it, and it is the experience, not the knowledge, that we want.

Or take Robinson's brief shocker, "Richard Cory." Because Robinson is more recent, and not, like Poe, identified with a famous theory of composition, we are less likely to be tempted to introduce the poem with a lecture on the poet, his life, and conditions of poetry in the early twentieth century. But it is likely that before we have students read the poem we will at least tell them the poet's name, his dates, his nationality, and some bits of information about him and his contemporaries—or, more likely, we will make them study what the editor of our anthology has provided. Do we do so because we really believe that doing so will better enable them to experience the poem? Or do we do so because we cannot quite escape from the notion that students "ought to know about" such matters?

But in fact will not "Richard Cory," dittoed on a sheet with no identification except the title, come through to students with just as much effect as when it is read following a three-page introduction or a half-hour lecture? Indeed, will not its chances of coming through be *improved* if students' minds have not been dulled, in the interests of "preparation," by factual information? Confronted with the dittoed sheet, bare but for the poem, students can see that the *poem* is the sole thing that matters. But the poem preceded by three pages of informational matter has a competitor: students conditioned by years of recitation and testing will see at once what it is that the teacher *really* wants them to "learn about."

If we are honest, we may conclude that the only works for which factual information is necessary in advance are those that refer to a special occasion or event that if unknown will leave the work meaningless. It would seem faulty to have students read Whitman's "O Captain! My Captain!" without first mentioning who the "Captain" is and the occasion of the poem. It would seem a little less faulty to have them read "Lycidas" without first telling them of Edward King's death, since the poem is not "about" this loss in the way in which Whitman's poem is "about" the loss of Lincoln; but it would be better to speak half a minute about King. Emerson's "Concord Hymn" requires half a minute's preliminary statement. Tennyson's "In Memoriam," Shelley's "Adonais," Arnold's "Thyrsis," Browning's "The Lost Leader," Milton's "On the Late Massacre in Piedmont," Dryden's "MacFlecknoe" all are examples of works with an obvious need for preliminary comments. But even some "occasional" works may not need an introduction. Take, for example, Milton's sonnet on his blindness. Will the force of this poem come through better if students are told in advance about Milton's life and religious faith? Or will it strike harder if they discover from the poem itself the fact of the blindness and the earnest soul-searching it caused the poet?

We have argued, in general, for the omission of matters of fact about author, age, and genre in the introduction. Do we mean, then, that we intend to leave students forever ignorant of such matters? Do we intend to teach works not in a context but in a vacuum? Will students read "The Fall of the House of Usher" and learn nothing about its author and his famous theories? In doubting the validity of any introduction that stresses "background information," are we conspiring to keep students ignorant of authors, literary periods, genres, as if it were wicked to know of them?

We intend no conspiracy. There are three possible times at which information can be introduced in connection with a work: before it is read, while it is being read, and after it has been read. We have argued that, in general, "before" is not the time to introduce it. We believe that the place to begin the study of *Julius Caesar* is not with Shakespeare's life, or the Age of Elizabeth, or the idea of tragedy, or the physical theater, or the time of Caesar, but with the opening lines that Shakespeare wrote:

> Hence! home, you idle creatures, get you home:
> Is this a holiday?

Later, when we have read into a work a little, we may want to say something specific about Shakespeare, Milton, or Poe; about the Age of Elizabeth, the Puritans, or American romanticism; about tragedy, elegy, or "The Short Story." And after a work has been read through, we may want to say much more about these matters. How much we should then say, and what, and why are discussed in the chapters that follow.

We are, however, not yet finished with Introduction. So far, we have considered only one general sort of material that might or might not be covered before a work is read. But typical introductions used by teachers involve two main classes of material in about equal amounts: informational and motivational. Of course these two classes are not always discrete. Informational matter may sometimes be used only to provide information, but it may also be used to provide motivation. If, for example, we excite students' imaginations and whet their eagerness for *Julius Caesar* by first telling about Shakespeare, we both inform and motivate. We similarly incorporate two purposes in one when, before reading "The Fall of the House of Usher," we recount the desperate life of Poe, his griefs, his poverty, his losing bouts with illness and morphine. If we are lucky, we may so involve students in Poe's life that they will be eager to give his story a hearing.

With a few flourishes, we can make a Horatio Alger story out of Shakespeare's success: a country lad whose father's business had fallen off, he went to the big town, won fame and fortune, and came home after ten years to buy the biggest house for miles around. Such a recital can capture the imaginations of ninth graders, as can some of the other biographical items of fact or legend: the poaching episode on the lands of Sir Thomas Lucy, the famous will that leaves the dramatist's second-best bed to his widow, the first proof of his success in London when a bitter rival playwright castigated him as an "upstart crow, beautified with our feathers" who supposes himself "the only Shake-scene in a country." Anecdotes like these, often used by teachers at all levels, no doubt do help to put students on the author's side and predispose them to give his work a hearing. Used for motivation, they are no doubt more effective than when they serve only for information. Probably "background" introduced merely so that students will "learn about" authors, periods, genres is never justifiable as introduction; information that opens the work to immediate understanding is more nearly justifiable—though, as we shall note hereafter, even this is more useful if it is introduced *while* the work is being read or directly *after*.

Having now warmly complimented the "motivational style" of introduction, we can proceed with a clearer conscience to speak unkindly of its overuse and abuse. We should first name some popular forms of motivation that are peculiarly objectionable.

Certainly the most common of these is the use of excessive praise, in advance, of the author and the work. More students have been turned against Shakespeare by teachers' motivational effusions than by any other single means. That Shakespeare is great beyond our powers of expression, everyone knows who is literate; it would therefore seem impossible to overpraise him. But what purpose is served by lauding him over and over, just before one of his plays is read? A good story teller with a joke in mind that he knows to be hilarious never brags about its hilariousness before telling it. He just tells it, and the joke does all the rest. So let it be with *Julius Caesar*. To praise an author extravagantly in advance is to leave a suspicion that we do not really trust him as the storyteller with a great joke trusts it. It is as if we feared that students will fail to be impressed unless we tell them, and tell them, and tell them —all before we allow them to look at the opening lines. It is the task of Presentation, as we shall shortly see, to expose the greatness of a great work, or, rather, to show the work and let its greatness become apparent. But this is not the task of Introduction. It is appropriate here to restate the basic principle expressed in the chapter on Selection: the program should consist only of first-rate works. If we have made no mistakes, if they are all truly first-rate, their greatness will be manifest in the Presentation. If we have made mistakes, and included a phony or two, excessive praise will not help. On the other hand, excessive praise in advance can make even Shakespeare seem phony.

Akin to excessive praise, and even more repellent, is excessive stress on the "timeliness" of works, especially older ones. This is a large matter; we have touched on it in the chapter on Selection, but must now elaborate.

This form of "motivation" is vicious primarily because it motivates toward the wrong end—social experience rather than experience of the work as a work of art. Anthologists are perhaps guiltier than teachers in seeking to "sell" students on a particular classic "because of its special relevance to problems of today." The implication of this gross "pitch" is that the work's relation to today's problems is the justification for reading it. The trumpeting usually given on behalf of *Julius Caesar* is a prime example, and we cannot clarify the whole unsavory issue better than by quoting from the pages of a much-used anthology:

> Two thousand years have passed since Mark Antony stirred the Roman mob to revolt, and more than three hundred years have passed since William Shakespeare dramatized the episode in writing his play. Yet the problems of liberty and freedom posed in *Julius Caesar* are still important to people in this last half of the twentieth century.
>
> Today, we are still faced with the question of how men should govern themselves, how they can avoid giving over their rights to ruthless leaders. Today, we are threatened, as free men have been for centuries, by dictators' lust for power. When you read *Julius Caesar*, its timeliness will come almost as a shock. You will recognize the characteristics of modern dictators in Caesar's exalted opinion of himself. You will remember scenes in the newsreels showing how demagogues can win over the people with rabble-rousing speeches like Mark Antony's "Friends, Romans, countrymen." And you may shudder as you watch the cheering mobs idolize the very leaders who can enslave them. All such scenes are too familiar in the modern world. The problems of liberty and freedom that Shakespeare dramatized are still alive, still important, today.*

These claims are meant to put the play's best foot forward; but "timeliness" is not its best foot. To recommend one of the world's great tragedies on these grounds is to diminish it and to mislead students about the nature of the experience that is to be gained from tragedy. This is not to suggest that in the course of reading the teacher should strive to keep the class blind to the "timely" aspects of *Julius Caesar*; these will become apparent in close reading and discussion. But to make timeliness the basis

---

* From *Adventures in Appreciation*, Mercury Edition, edited by Luella B. Cook, Walter Loban, Susanna Baxter, copyright, 1952, by Harcourt, Brace & World, Inc. and reprinted with their permission.

of recommendation is to give Shakespeare "help" that he does not need.

It is unlikely that any anthologist or teacher can invent a better introduction to one of Shakespeare's plays than the dramatist himself provides. *Julius Caesar* opens on an exciting moment; it is presumptuous to suppose that the first scene stands in need of our tricks of salesmanship. In all the plays, the first scene sets forth the situation, introduces major characters, and sets the course of what is to follow. During the reading and discussion of the first scene, it is useful to clarify certain words and lines and to interpret crucial passages. But this is the job of Presentation, not Introduction. The teacher's function during Presentation is to help students see what the dramatist has created; if he succeeds, he can trust the dramatist to furnish the excitement. No great author, least of all Shakespeare, stands in need of motivational crutches.

In the category of superfluous crutches we should be remiss if we failed to mention introductory films, film strips, and similar audio-visual aids that are often used before students read the first pages of major works. Use of these devices only betrays the teacher's lack of real trust in the author himself. Again, this is not to doubt the occasional usefulness of such aids at later times in the study of a work or a group of works, and this question will be treated in a later chapter. But as Introduction they tend to deny the primacy of the work itself. In extreme cases, teachers actually show the filmed version of a novel or Shakespearean play before their students read it. This practice robs students of the privilege and the obligation to form their own images, from what the author tells them, of characters, setting, and action. When one has seen Orson Welles as Rochester in *Jane Eyre* before reading the novel, he continues to see Orson Welles throughout the reading. It may be quite true that Orson Welles is the perfect Rochester, but that is beside the point. An invaluable part of the total experience of reading a great book is the experience of building one's own images from the words supplied by the author. To equip students in advance with a ready-made set of images representing characters and setting is to deny them this creative experience. Seeing a novel or a play on film is an activity that should follow, not precede, reading.

Novelists like Hardy, Hawthorne, Dickens, and the Brontë sisters stand in no need of advance depiction through film strips representing Wessex, Puritan New England, London and Paris at the time of the Revolution, the moors and heaths of England. Meant to ease students into these strange and remote places, the films destroy more than they build, for they rob students of the right and need to create their own images; with that privilege removed, there is less reason to read great works at all. The great novelists always establish their own settings with sufficient clarity for the reader's imagination to take hold and build on. To provide the "help" of filmed detail in advance is to insult author, students, and work alike. How gross it is to show a film in order to "help out" Hardy's depiction of the scene that opens *The Return of the Native*:

A Saturday afternoon in November was approaching the time of twilight, and the vast tract of unenclosed wild known as Egdon Heath embrowned itself moment by moment. Overhead the hollow stretch of whitish cloud shutting out the sky was as a tent which had the whole heath for its floor.

The heaven being spread with this pallid screen and the earth with the darkest vegetation, their meeting-line at the horizon was clearly marked. In such contrast the heath wore the appearance of an instalment of night which had taken up its place before its astronomical hour was come: darkness had to a great extent arrived hereon, while day stood distinct in the sky. Looking upwards, a furzecutter would have been inclined to continue work; looking down, he would have decided to finish his faggot and go home. The distant rims of the world and of the firmament seemed to be a division in time no less than a division in matter. The face of the heath by its mere complexion added half an hour to evening; it could in like manner retard the dawn, sadden noon, anticipate the frowning of storms scarcely generated, and intensify the opacity of a moonless midnight to a cause of shaking and dread.

What reasonable teacher of literature can really suppose that Hardy needs the help of a film strip in easing students into the confines of Egdon Heath? And this is only the beginning; after a page or two, we are given this:

> Here at least were intelligible facts regarding landscape—far-reaching proofs productive of genuine satisfaction. The untameable, Ishmaeltish thing that Egdon now was it always had been. Civilization was its enemy; and ever since the beginning of vegetation its soil had worn the same antique brown dress, the natural and invariable garment of the particular formation. In its venerable one coat lay a certain vein of satire on human vanity in clothes. A person on a heath in raiment of modern cut and colours has more or less an anomalous look. We seem to want the oldest and simplest human clothing where the clothing of the earth is so primitive.

Throughout the first chapter, Hardy continues his description of Egdon Heath and the narrow road that traverses it, and after this initial account, which fixes its centrality and its brooding nature, the Heath is ever-present to the mind of the reader, silently and inexorably exerting its force on the lives of all who venture upon it.

It is conceivable that when students have finished reading the book they would gain some trifling value from seeing "The Hardy Country" on film; but they should not be shown it first and thus be robbed of the privilege of conceiving an Egdon Heath in their own mind's eye from the printed page. If we rob them of this privilege, we destroy one of the best values of reading.

Hardy is not unique among great authors in his habit of providing his own Introduction. The great ones always vividly establish their created worlds, and the notion that they need to be helped by audio-visual devices is presumptuous. We are mistaken in our supposition that because we are teaching twentieth-century American students who are directly familiar with present-day localities and persons they can make no beginning in a nineteenth-century tale of the Russian steppes or the Parisian *haut monde* unless we show them pictures in advance. Tolstoy, Dostoevsky, Flaubert, Hugo, Cervantes, Dickens, Austen create their worlds complete, *and establish the terms on which we are to perceive them.* That is a significant part of their business as novelists—it is, in large part, what their novels are —and the experience of reading their works as works of art is not enhanced but deformed by any Introduction designed· to "help out." Reading a great novel or play is an experience of re-creating for our own mind's eye what the author has suggested by words; we should aim to let students enjoy this experience, not occasionally but always.

Thus far we have raised, discussed, and ended by rejecting a variety of Introductions, and at one point, using *Julius Caesar* as an example, have suggested that the best one is to begin just where the author begins, with the opening scene. That is to say, we have suggested that the best Introduction is often no Introduction. In general, we shall stand by this conclusion, and will go further, extending it from the Shakespearean play to all other literary genres. It is tempting, before reading a pair of sonnets with a ninth grade class—perhaps the first that they have read—to lecture on sonnet form and history; for the sonnet is an exceptionally easy subject to lecture on and to appear learned about. But to lecture on "The Sonnet" and then to read two or three sonnets has the effect of placing these small gems in the position of examples or specimens, illustrating the lecture; and knowledge of the sonnet form and its history, the subject of our lecture, becomes primary at the expense of the experience of the poems. It is a temptation, therefore, that we should steel ourselves to resist. To lecture on Emerson and Transcendentalism before reading "The Oversoul" is similarly tempting—for who, given two hours with a good history of American literature, cannot talk at length on the subject? But, again, if we do so, this fine essay is reduced to the role of specimen. To show a film, or a series of slides representing modern scenes in Calaveras County during the annual jumping frog contest before reading "The Celebrated Jumping Frog" is also tempting; but why not trust Mark Twain *to set his own stage and tell the story with no advance help from us?* If we cannot so trust an author, we should not use him; we should find another whom we can trust. We have suggested that with works like "Lycidas," where a specific occasion prompted the work and should be known at once, there is reason for a few introductory words—the fewer the better. But otherwise, for poems, stories, essays, as with plays and novels, the best Introduction is no Introduction.

Nevertheless, before concluding, we shall illustrate one variant that can be used effectively on occasion. Let us suppose that a class is to read Poe's "The Cask of Amontillado." We say nothing about Poe or the "single impression" or "The American Short Story." We do not even announce that we are going to read "Amontillado." Instead, briskly, we touch off a discussion on the general topic of revenge. One way to start is for the teacher to tell about a case of revenge in everyday life—the story, for example, of neighbors, one of whom sawed off the other's overhanging limb at the property line; the other, after awaiting his opportunity for months, finding that his neighbor has left a wheelbarrow so that the handles extend across the property line, promptly saws them off. A free discussion ensues, during which students volunteer other incidents, perhaps even confess to personal acts of revenge, or at least to thoughts of it. If all goes well, the teacher can eventually shift the emphasis of discussion from the narration of incidents to an ethical problem: Is revenge ever justifiable? Does taking revenge reflect credit or discredit on the revenger? Is it a sign of strength, or of weakness? In the long run, is the admonition to "turn the other cheek" good advice or impractical idealism? At some point, the teacher may want to inject Bacon's famous definition: "Revenge is a kind of wild justice." Thereafter, the class can turn directly to "The Cask of Amontillado."

Or, instead, he may wish to extend his Introduction somewhat further to make it serve a double purpose. Having discussed revenge freely for fifteen minutes, he can put Bacon's sentence on the board and ask the class to write paragraphs using this sentence as the topic sentence. At the start of the next meeting he can read several of the paragraphs aloud—and then read Bacon's essay aloud, preferably with students following the same text, on dittoed sheets if necessary. And then he can turn to Poe's story. He will have accomplished much already. He will have introduced the theme of the story, induced students to read a great essay, and squeezed a substantial paragraph out of them.

The Introduction here illustrated is applicable to any work of literature in any genre. Like any other single method, it would prove intolerable if it were used invariably, but there is no reason it should not be used occasionally, especially when it can be made to serve multiply as in the illustration. The principle is clear enough: *it involves getting students' minds engaged with the theme, or subject, of a work just before that work is read.* The expectation is that, in this way, students will be receptive to the work from the outset, or in any event more receptive than had they turned to it "cold," while their minds were still on whatever aspects of their daily affairs were most pressing. When students enter the English classroom, their minds are rarely on English. They may be still engrossed in the subject of the preceding class, or with the conversation they had while walking down the hall, or with home and family problems. They may need a "warm-up." If a brief discussion can turn their minds to the subject of the work at hand, they can be ready from the first sentence on. In the chapter on Composition, we shall deal more fully with the possibilities of writing in connection with this form of Introduction.

But of course the method is also subject to abuse. To overuse it, we have implied, would be to establish a pattern of expectation that in time would become boring or laughable. To make the method too elaborate, to extend the period of discussion unduly would be to do more harm than good; any such discussion exists mainly in order to get at the literary work, which is the main thing always, and should not be prolonged as if it were an end in itself. Finally, overemphasis on the discussion of, for example, revenge, before the actual reading starts can make the entire enterprise seem to be a "lesson" on revenge, with the story merely serving as illustration. The method is thus subject to just such ills as we discussed in connection with thematic arrangement, where teachers find themselves teaching themes primarily and works secondarily. But as an occasional deviation from the Introduction we have recommended most strongly—no Introduction at all—this way is more to the point than any other that we have described.

Chapter 6

What method of presentation?

We mean by "Presentation" the actual reading of works. Obviously, no matter how much care teachers have taken with Selection, Arrangement, and Introduction, if they bungle the job of Presentation all will have gone for nothing.

But immediately a question arises with our definition of Presentation as "actual reading." Are there not other ways of making works known to students? Films, live performances, recordings are among the ways other than reading. Then, too, the teacher can tell the story of "The Cask of Amontillado" or summarize the message of "Self-Reliance." All these are in fact forms of Presentation, according to some definitions, but not ours. The basic work of the English teacher with literature, developing students' reading powers, will hardly be accomplished unless students read. We therefore regard films, recordings, narrative summaries, and the like not as Presentation but as Related Activities and will consider them in the next chapter. Here, then, Presentation means direct use of a written text.

Possible forms of Presentation include the following:

1. Independent readings by students at home
2. Silent supervised reading in class
3. Reading aloud by students in class
4. Reading aloud by the teacher while students follow
5. Playing a recording while students follow in their texts
6. A combination of these

With the exception of the fifth, which is limited to the particular works of which recordings have been made, the range of choice is open for every work.

We can also, with any work, break up the class into groups of five or six students and have them put their heads together and later report what they have agreed on.

Are all these possibilities equally good?

Or is there some one way that is simply best and should therefore always be used with every work in every genre?

Given the full range of possibilities, and assuming that not all are equally appropriate, we must consider what it is that we are trying to do. As with Arrangement and Introduction, we aim to give each work its best chance to reach students as a work of art. Of course we want it to do other things too—enlarge their vocabularies, acquaint them with other times, places, peoples, give them material and ideas for speaking and writing—but in choosing a method of Presentation we want to give each work its best chance to do what it can *best* do. It is in the Presentation, if ever, that the potential in literature for affecting students as human beings will be made actual. The problem of Presentation is thus the most crucial because the moment is crucial.

One fact is clear: there is no ready formula. But the starting point, always, is the work itself. We must take our cue from that, on the one side, and from the character of the class, on the other.

Clearly, some works included in a reading program will require a drastic form of Presentation if they are to be understood sufficiently for their potential force to reach students, while others can be understood fairly readily by students reading wholly or largely on their own. For example, *Johnny Tremaine*, a novel much used during the past quarter of a century, is a work that most members of an average ninth or tenth grade class can manage on their own. On the other hand, *Huckleberry Finn*—though one of the "easiest" of the world's supreme novels—contains depths, subtleties, ironies, insights into human character and behavior that the ninth or tenth grader on his own will simply miss. He may read along pleasantly enough, without much difficulty, and when he has finished, he may pronounce *Huckleberry Finn* "a good book." But if he has missed the qualities that make the novel great, he may as well have been reading *Johhny Tremaine*. There is much in *Huckleberry Finn* that needs the joint attention of teacher and student.

If we ask which of these novels ought to be read in the ninth grade, the answer is probably "both." But let us put the question somewhat differently: which kind of work, the *Huckleberry Finn* kind or the *Johnny Tremaine* kind, ought to be included in the *in-class program*?

Let us take another type of example. Teachers can, if they wish, use in the ninth grade an adapted *Julius Caesar* that begins like this:

FLAVIUS: On your way, there! Go home, you loafers! This is no holiday. Don't you know that workmen must wear their work clothes and carry their tools on a weekday. What's your trade?

FIRST WORKMAN: I'm a carpenter.

In the same version, Antony's oration begins thus:

> Friends, Romans, countrymen, listen to me. I have come to speak at Caesar's burial, not to praise him. The evil that men do lives after them; the good is often buried with their bones. Let it be so with Caesar. Brutus has told you Caesar was ambitious. If it is true, it was a serious fault, and Caesar has answered for it. Brutus is an honorable man. They are all honorable men. With their permission I speak to you.*

This version is replete with editorial comments and questions such as "Flavius speaks angrily to some of the excited common people" and "Why does Marullus scorn the common people? Do you think mobs of people are at times thoughtless and changeable?"—all of which students may imagine were written by Shakespeare himself.

Or teachers can use a standard text of Shakespeare's play—but to understand and enjoy what makes the trag-

* From *Julius Caesar in Modern English* by Elsie M. Katterjohn. Copyright © 1957 by Scott, Foresman and Company, Glenview, Illinois.

edy great they will need five weeks of close reading, wise direction, and steady discussion. Which version should be used?

Teachers' answers to these questions will determine the character of the whole English program.

For more than thirty years preceding the past four or five, the prevailing philosophy of English programs in the schools called for the use of reading materials that could be managed by students mainly on their own. If other criteria were also involved in selection, none took precedence over the criterion of "readability"—and a "readable" book was one that could be read by students independently. With independent reading, both at home and at school, as the principal—in many cases the sole—method of Presentation, it was necessary to bring into the curriculum an enormous number of selections that bear no resemblance to those listed in the Appendix. The selections thus introduced are of three general types: (1) good, but essentially easy short stories, novels, humorous pieces, and (in very short supply) poems; (2) "reading materials" that make no pretense of being literature—first-person accounts of climbing mountains, deep-sea diving, dangerous moments in daily life, explanations of why an airplane flies, biographical sketches of athletes, space fiction, "teen tales," and so on; and (3) adapted classics. The fullest evidence for these statements is contained in the major anthologies published between, roughly, 1940 and 1960, and in the nearly incredible number of adapted classics that appeared during that period: rewritten versions of Dickens, the Brontés, Hugo, Melville, Defoe, Twain, Homer, Shakespeare, and many others.

That independent reading is an indispensable experience for high school students goes without question. It must be provided for steadily during the four years. But that independent reading is an appropriate primary form of Presentation in the classroom is disproved by the very nature of the reading materials that this method has made it necessary to bring into the reading program. Teachers conditioned to the assumption that, if students cannot read *A Midsummer Night's Dream* on their own, it must be removed from the program *did* remove it. Chaucer, Spenser, Milton vanished entirely from the programs of many schools during this period. Such Homer as was read was mainly read in adapted versions that told the bare narrative in elementary-school prose. The supreme novels of the Western world were rarely attempted except in re-written versions. College-bound students typically read two of Shakespeare's plays in four years, but masses of students graduated without reading any Shakespearean play except in versions the character of which has been delineated by our quotation from *Julius Caesar*. Essayists like Bacon and Emerson—indeed, essayists in general— were replaced in the anthologies by articles like "We Took the Nautilus Under the Ice" and "With Plug and Casting Rod." For many students across the United States during this period, the most sophisticated literary experi-ence in four years was *Kon Tiki*.

During this long and regrettable period the standard reply of teachers and program planners to the question often asked by college professors, "Why do you not give them literature?" was invariably the same: "They can't read it!" What was meant was that they could not read it *independently*.

With the essential truth of this statement we have no quarrel. Aside from the rare exceptions, ninth graders sent home with instructions to read the first act of *A Mid-summer Night's Dream* for discussion next day most as-suredly cannot read the assignment adequately. They will either hate what they have been assigned to read or merely be indifferent to it. After two or three weeks they will "finish" the play, but they will not like it as well as *Little Britches*. Tenth graders, sent home with *Romeo and Juliet* (having read *A Midsummer Night's Dream* on their own the year before), will have the same frustrating experience with it and will dislike the whole undertaking, though they may enjoy *Johnny Tremaine*. Eleventh grad-ers sent home with *Twelfth Night* will fare no better, nor will twelfth graders with *Hamlet*.

After a year of frustration, teachers who still cling to the false premise that students should be given only what they can read adequately on their own literally have no choice but the obvious: to eliminate *A Midsummer Night's Dream, Romeo and Juliet, Twelfth Night,* and *Hamlet,* together with other works that make comparable demands, and to replace them with readings that students have proved they can manage on their own. The teachers who have "given up" on great works are teachers who tried to put students "on their own" with them.

We have already conceded that students on their own cannot read Shakespeare—or a great novel, poem, or essay —adequately. Indeed, we do more than concede: we insist that they cannot. Our basic disagreement with the past thirty years of professional English philosophy is over the action that should follow from this observation. Our conclusion is not that Shakespeare and the others should be removed from the program, but that a drastically different form of Presentation is needed in order to keep them in it.

We believe that the reading program should be dominated, not by works that students *can* read on their own, but by works that they *cannot* adequately read on their own. That students cannot read Shakespeare on their own is not a reason for removing him, but a reason for keeping him. That they cannot read Chaucer on their own is not a reason for removing him, but for reinstating him. And so also with other discarded writers of first-rate works from Homer to Eliot.

But now let us see what this means for Presentation. It means that classroom hours will be given over to the collective efforts of teacher and students, with much reading aloud and steady discussion. It means that teacher and students will make their way *together* through *A Midsummer Night's Dream* in the initial reading, as they will do also with "The Pardoner's Tale" and "Of Truth" and "Lycidas" and "The Bishop Orders His Tomb" and "Prufrock."

But we acknowledged earlier that independent reading by students is also an indispensable part of their high school experience and should be continued throughout the four years. How can they have this experience if they are to read and discuss everything as a joint enterprise of class and teacher?

The solution requires, in effect, two programs rather than one, each distinct yet related to the other. The first, the *inside* program, should include a select list of works that students cannot read adequately without the close cooperative effort of teacher and class. These are works that need to be *taught*; most in-class time will be given to them. The object in using these works is twofold: first, to gain from them the best experience they have to offer as works of art; second, to learn through the study of them how to go at other works independently. The second program, the *outside* program, should include a more extensive list of works that students can read independently with growing power as the continuing in-class demonstration carries over. The outside list should include works that the least capable readers can manage, but it should also include works that will challenge the powers of the most able.

But let us disregard the outside program for the moment and concentrate on the subject of Presentation with respect to the inside one.

Works included in it should both need and deserve the most drastic form of Presentation—close study in class, with continuing discussion. To use this method with works that students could handle alone would be not only wasteful of time and effort but also deadly for all but the least able students. Detailed in-class study of works that do not need it puts teachers themselves at a disadvantage. It is when the work read is such that students can cope with it adequately on their own that the teacher's help is least appreciated, and it is then that the teacher is most likely to be vexed with disciplinary problems. Whatever his own maturity and wealth of background, the teacher proceeding laboriously with *Little Britches* will find little to point out that students cannot see just as well for themselves. Students often respect an algebra teacher, even if they hate algebra, because he can show them how to work a problem with which they would be quite helpless alone. What comparable usefulness can an English teacher demonstrate in dealing with *Little Britches?*

Moving through *King Lear* line by line, opening meanings fathoms deep to the view of students is hard work; but it is surely easier, in another sense, than similarly moving through *Our Town* and wracking one's brains for something to add to what students can see for themselves. For this reason alone, if there were no other, the best of teachers are sometimes heard to say that they would rather teach *Moby Dick* than *The Yearling*, Katharine Mansfield than O. Henry, and "Of Truth" than "Little Mo—Queen at Sixteen." Respect for both teacher and the subject of English is easier to gain and hold with Chaucer than with "The Cremation of Sam McGee."

Of course if there were no better reason for teaching a Shakespearean sonnet than that it affords the English teacher opportunity to shine almost as brightly as the math teacher, we should hardly be justified in preferring it to "Get Along Little Dogies." But the point is one to consider: the generally low regard of most students for the English teacher and the subject of English has unquestionably grown from the use of insignificant reading materials and activities that make the teacher seem useless.

The great argument for using a drastic form of Presentation is that it makes possible the reading of great works. Further, not only do students, in this way, have the invaluable experience of first-rate works of art, but they thus develop their own powers to read and enjoy. Let us put it this way, as a rough approximation: after four years of the kind of in-class study that we have suggested, supplemented by an outside program of independent reading, many students will be capable of reading *King Lear* on their own; but after four years of reading, on their own, the only kinds of things that they *can* read on their own, most students will have developed only enough to read, let us say, *Our Town*, *To Kill a Mockingbird*, and *Annapurna*—and will be as helpless as ever with *King Lear*, having had no experience with works of its stature.

If we believe that it is just as good for students to read *Little Britches* as to read *Crime and Punishment*, if we believe that the works they can read adequately on their own are just as "good" for them as the works of great novelists, poets, and dramatists whom they cannot read adequately on their own, then by all means the former are what they should read, and they should read them independently. But if we truly believe that there is compelling reason for them to read the latter, we have no alternative but to adopt as drastic a form of Presentation as these authors require.

Poetry

Because many poems are short and represent highly concentrated expression, they lend themselves especially well to close reading and discussion in class; and because they are concentrated, they especially need the intensive study that they get only in this way. Further, as every writer on the teaching of literature has insisted, poetry demands to be heard, not merely seen, and it is only in the classroom that we can be positive it will be heard. To miss the sound of most poems is to miss much of the beauty that is a great part of the total experience. Of course beauty of sound is not limited to sweet and mellifluous notes, as in the most musical of Shakespeare's sonnets or Tennyson's lyrics or Conrad Aiken's minor melodies; it extends also to the shocking, the deliberately harsh, as in some of Browning and in Wilfred Owen's "Dulce et Decorum Est." But whether mellifluous or grating, the sound of poetry must be heard.

The best of teachers manage to have a short poem read three or four times in the course of an hour—the first time by themselves, while students follow in the text, the subsequent times usually by students, when questions of interpretation invite rereadings. At best, these subsequent readings are prompted by differences of opinion, with one student after another reading aloud in order to argue his point about tone, emphasis, or meaning. Finally, after all the problems of the poem have been discussed and, hopefully, solved, teachers often end by reading through once more, so that the poem is heard with all its meanings "in."

If there were any such thing as an inflexible pattern for

the Presentation of poems, the steps might be these: (1) with no preliminary ado whatsoever, the teacher reads the poem through aloud, clearly but without ostentation and without stopping, while students follow the text; (2) discussion begins, concentrating on the whole meaning and moving back to the details of thought, structure, imagery; (3) students offer additional readings of the whole or parts, as discussion occasions; (4) the teacher gives a final, clear reading without stopping.

This treatment may be heavier than some poems require; further, the length of some poems may make it impossible to read the whole more than twice. If it is objected that a good many poems—light, humorous, open ones—need no such elaborate form of Presentation and may even be ruined by it, the best answer is that these should be left for students to read on their own in the outside program—which is likely to be short on poems. We hold to our earlier statement that works chosen for the inside program should be those that do need and deserve drastic treatment. The general pattern, therefore, should be appropriate for any that are chosen.

But it is in the detail of discussion that we cannot expect to make a single pattern fit any two poems. What is to be discussed about a poem? The cues must always come from the poem itself. As examples, let us take three well-known works: "Richard Cory," "Dover Beach," and "Lycidas." The first is very short and comparatively easy; the second is longer and somewhat more complex; and the third is longer still and infinitely complex. Among them, they represent a wide range for purposes of illustration.

Of "Richard Cory" we should first ask whether anything is needed by way of introduction. Need we tell who Robinson was, when he wrote, what the period was like, or what poetic form the work uses? Surely not: the place to begin "Richard Cory" is with the first line—and many teachers prefer to provide students with a dittoed sheet that carries the bare poem, so that the anthology's gratuitous information about author, post-World War I America, and the rest will not stifle the experience of the poem.

Omitting Introduction, then, the teacher reads the poem through, not as a demonstration of voice control and diction, but so unpretentiously that not a single student looks up from his page during the reading.

And then what? It is unlikely that any student in the class has failed to get the "point," for the impact of the last line is abrupt and resounding, like a thwack. And if students have *felt* the impact of the poem, what more is there for analysis and discussion to do?

The question is not an idle one, nor is it relevant only to "Richard Cory." It pertains to the case of any work of literature the main force of which is released by an initial, able reading. But perhaps the basic issue is uniquely vivid in the case of "Richard Cory": here is a fine short poem about which we can assume that students felt its force from a single, clear reading. We have insisted from the outset that this is the finest thing to be had from a work of art—the force of it as a work of art. Why not simply stop there?

If we go back over the details, our purpose is presumably to explain *how* the poem managed to produce the effect that it has just had on the class. We aim to show what the poet *did* artistically in order to get the poem to produce this effect. But *because* the poet did what he did —whatever it may have been—the poem has already *had* its effect on students before we attempt any explanations. So why explain? Do we, after all, want students to have "knowledge of" even more than we want them to have "experience of"? Or do we perhaps believe that understanding the artistic means by which the poet caused the poem to have its effect will enhance the effect, or that this understanding is necessary for the poem to have its *full* effect? Let us see what explanations can accomplish.

We begin discussion by centering on elementary matters of form—the stanzaic divisions, the meter, the rhyme. There is nothing unusual or striking about any of them; it might be hard to find in English a poem that moves along a more ordinary course. Was this, perhaps, deliberate? Does the very ordinariness, running through fifteen lines, accentuate the sudden jolt of the sixteenth? We turn next to observe words: "crown," "imperially," "arrayed," "glittered," "king," "grace." What have these in common? Why are they "right"? Very unobtrusively, they contribute to our sense of a kingly man. We finally center on the name—Richard Cory. Why not Richard Adams, or John Cory? If we are lucky, some imaginative student will hit upon a great idea: Richard, Coeur . . .

Of course Robinson was not writing about a king, and certainly not about Coeur de Lion; but the more splendor he could suggest for Richard Cory, the greater the impact of that stunning last line. Students, we can be sure, had no conscious recognition, when the poem was first read aloud, of the means by which the poet created the force that struck them—they were only struck. Our question remains: now that they have been led to see how it was done, is the force greater? Will a work of art do more for them as an aesthetic experience if they comprehend its artistry than if they do not?

The impulse of most teachers is to assert an emphatic "Of course!" Most of us are eager enough to justify our labor spent in getting students to recognize similes, metaphors, devices like alliteration and assonance, and a dozen other elements of poetic technique. But perhaps we should not answer the question too easily or too positively. Teachers have traditionally been accused of concerning themselves and their classes so much with the *mechanics* of art that the *force* of art never reaches students; the only "experience" they have is acquisition of terminology, skill in identifying devices and techniques. If we cannot be sure that experience of a poem is richer when students are aware of the artistic means than when they are not, we can at least be sure that awareness of the artistic means *instead* of experience of the work is not what we want.

The answer of this book to the basic question is therefore not an emphatic "Of course!" but a guarded "Yes." We believe that understanding the means of art is an aspect of the total experience of art. We believe that students who are aware of the means gain a fuller experience than those who merely respond without awareness. By reading a poem through carefully first, without explanation, we can give it a chance to get through as an experience—and, once had, this experience certainly cannot be snatched back again, by any amount of subsequent probing into the poet's mechanics. Then, after examination and discussion of technical aspects, we can read the poem through a second (or third or fourth) time. We cannot be positive that the final reading, with all the understanding of technique now supporting it, will strike with any more force than it did the first time. But there is a good chance that it will.

We should now turn to the second of our three poems. "Dover Beach" is longer than Robinson's poem, but we can still count on getting it read through two or three times in the course of an hour. Following our pattern, then, we should first read it through without preliminary explanations and without stopping to explain anything while we read. We should read carefully and clearly, of course, with the intention of giving the poem its chance to do as much as it can unaided. But what next?

With "Richard Cory" we debated whether any kind of explanations could really add to the initial effect. With "Dover Beach" the question needs no debate: there is much both without and within the poem that, made clear, will make the final reading more potent than the first. Certain details both from the life of Arnold and from the Victorian Period are indispensable to an understanding of "Dover Beach," and if these are made known between the initial and final readings, they will enrich the students' experience of the poem.

The spirit of scientific inquiry had delivered smashing blows to comfortable Christian faith. The work of Darwin had been going on since the 1830s, though the *Origin of Species* was not actually published until 1859. Lyell's work on geology and the antiquity of the human race, which completely revolutionized ideas of the age of the earth and of man, had also become known since the 1830s. The life of Jesus and the Bible were coming under the stern gaze of science, and Arnold himself would soon be drawn into the controversy over science and religion. Thus a momentous revolution lies behind the central metaphor of the poem:

The Sea of Faith
Was once, too, at the full, and round earth's shore
Lay like the folds of a bright girdle furled.
But now I only hear
Its melancholy, long, withdrawing roar . . .

And surely it is just at this point in the discussion of the poem—not in the introduction—that the facts should be made known to students.

What, concerning Arnold himself, will enhance the force of his poem? Mention, perhaps, of his classical learning is relevant, for the tone of melancholy that pervades "Dover Beach," as it does the mass of Arnold's poetry and prose, is illuminated by this background. Arnold's is never a shrieking lament, a romantic agony, but is a quiet, dignified melancholy, disciplined by classical restraint. In connection with the opening lines, when the poet stands looking across the Channel to where, on the French coast, the light "Gleams and is gone," reference to the romantic story of Arnold's love for Marguerite, whom he met long before in Switzerland, will add a special resonance. The memory of that youthful love gives a special poignancy to the "eternal note of sadness" that he hears in the sound of the sea. Possibly, too, we should find a metaphorical significance in the light that "Gleams and is gone." During discussion, reference to and readings from certain other poems by Arnold may enrich the meanings of the opening stanzas. Two or three of the Marguerite poems express the same sense of loneliness that dominates "Dover Beach." The sense of isolation, of being divided by the sea, is a feature of these poems, and the fact adds poignancy to the scene described here. One of these poems, "Isolation," begins with the line "With echoing straits between us thrown," and ends thus:

A God, a God their severance ruled!
And bade betwixt their shores to be
The unplumbed, salt, estranging sea.

Selected information on the life of Arnold notably enriches the experience of "Dover Beach."

So much for what might be introduced from outside the poem. Now, what can be said of what is even more important, the art within it? We must again raise the question posed in connection with "Richard Cory": if, after the initial reading, students feel the effect of the poet's art, what is to be gained by explaining how the poet achieved the effect?

One point about the opening stanza can be made easily and quickly. It concerns the contrast in the sounds of the first and second halves of this stanza. The first six lines build an impression of quiet serenity by using words like "calm," "full," "moon," "fair," "gleams," "glimmering," "tranquil," "sweet." In these lines nothing disturbs the beautiful scene. All is serene, unruffled: this is how the world seems. Then comes the seventh line, which is like a grating hinge, and the remaining lines bring in a new sound, first harsh and disagreeable, then melancholy. "Meets," "blanched," "grating," "draw back" (one version of the poem, used by Lionel Trilling, has "suck back") —these are harsher sounds that disturb the earlier serenity: this is how the world is. Then the final lines of the stanza, describing the coming and going of the waves on the shore, turn to onomatopoeia:

> Begin, and cease, and then again begin
> With tremulous cadence slow, and bring
> The eternal note of sadness in.

In the final stanza the pattern of the opening stanza is repeated, the first lines creating the illusion of serenity with words like "love," "one another," "seems," "land of dreams," and the closing lines reasserting the harsh reality with "confused alarms," "struggle and flight," "ignorant armies," "clash."

Arnold's North Sea of the first stanza is linked to Sophocles' Aegean Sea in the second by "a thought." What is this thought? That is the substance of the third stanza. The first two stanzas prepare the dominant metaphor of the poem: the sea, and the Sea of Faith. The first stanzas are barren of metaphor, and no doubt deliberately, so that the great metaphor, when it comes, looms up in isolation. The entire third stanza is given to it. Thus the first stanza is linked to the second, the second to the third, and the poem could stop there, its "point" being the metaphor of the third stanza. It may enhance the force of the poem for students if they learn that Arnold originally wrote the final stanza to stand alone, and then, years later, wrote the first three stanzas, which now stand together as the preparation for the eventual point of the entire poem:

> *Ah, love, let us be true*
> *To one another! for the world—*

"cannot be counted on," as we may paraphrase the thought. Ultimately, thus, "Dover Beach" is not "about" the sea, or the decline of faith; the decline of faith is the background for the plea made at the opening of the final stanza. And here, too, a reminder of Marguerite may add a dimension.

It would be a sad waste to explain these matters, about the age, Arnold's life, and the structure and vocabulary of the poem during the greater part of an hour after the initial reading—and then not to read the whole through once more, so that students can hear it with a new awareness.

We turn finally to "Lycidas," thinking of it as exemplifying the opposite pole to "Richard Cory." With the latter, we questioned whether anything that might be said about author, period, genre, or artistic qualities is really needed or useful. With "Dover Beach," a middle ground between the poles, we have no question but that illumination of the poem both without and within will greatly enhance its power. But with "Lycidas," the question is whether enough can be said about author, age, and genre to release its great potential unless the readers already possess more maturity and literary sophistication than is usual in high school students.

Our uncertainty is not whether, with sufficient instruction, students can be brought to understand the poem. The text of "Lycidas" has been so elaborately annotated by scholars that a good teacher in possession of any standard edition can clarify the details of the poem. But understanding a work is not synonymous with experiencing it; understanding is only a foundation for experiencing. After all elements have been explained, is there a likelihood that students will get an experience at all, or will they have gained only knowledge of pastoral conventions and a mass of allusions, classical, Christian, and other?

"Lycidas" is one of the most difficult poems in English —not, indeed, merely to "understand" but to experience as a work of art. If students are likely to gain knowledge only, and not experience, should the poem be taught at all? Teachers and anthologists generally have evidently decided that it should not be taught. The finest of recent high school anthologies of English literature include "L'Allegro," "Il Penseroso," a few sonnets, and a sample of Paradise Lost, but no "Lycidas."

But no twelfth grade teacher should give up "Lycidas" without having an honest try at it in three or four classes. If it then seems beyond reach, it should no doubt be abandoned. It should be taken as the greatest poetic challenge of the year, for both teacher and students. Teachers who have taught it for years would not think of not teaching it. It is not likely that they would stand by the poem with such persistence if they had found their labor wasted. "Lycidas" is hard work but the rewards are high, for there is no finer poem in English.

To teach the poem adequately is likely to take three or four class meetings. Once again, the first step is to read the whole aloud without stopping. What will students get from this first reading? With "Richard Cory," we said, they will get everything, or nearly so. But from "Lycidas," so far as detailed meaning is concerned, they are likely to get nothing. If they have been told in advance that the poem is an elegy for Milton's classmate, they will have that straw to grasp throughout the reading and occasionally will be cued by it to catch a passing reference. But most of the poem will remain a profound mystery. On the other hand, if the teacher has read faithfully, they will have gained something else that may, in this case, be as precious as meaning: the sound of the music, the noble notes of what has been called "the high water mark of English poetry." Before the reading has ended, some will have been caught up in its subtle rhythms, its intricate phrases, and may have surrendered to the magic of the cadence. For a little while afterwards ordinary speech will seem gross. Who is to say that they have had the least of what the poem has to give if this happens to them? Fra Lippo Lippi comes to mind:

> *If you get simple beauty and naught else,*
> *You get about the best thing God invents.*

"Lycidas," of course, is a rare case: really to *hear* its music is to have an experience of art.

Even so, to be borne along on the wings of majestic sound with little or no understanding is not enough. To get that understanding, teacher and students, equipped with a scholarly text, must go through line by line, often pondering single words. We cannot possibly make that explication here, nor is it necessary now to do more than suggest what it entails. First of all, it entails changing the figurative to the literal. Consider the first seven lines. Taken literally—which is exactly how students will at first take them—they say that the speaker is setting out to pluck the berries and crush the leaves of laurel and myrtle before they are mature. Most students will be astonished to learn what these lines really signify: that the young poet (Milton was twenty-nine when King was drowned) has no choice but to undertake a high poetic task before he is ready for it. This beginning exemplifies the basic fiction of pastoral allegory that runs throughout the poem. But besides interpreting this basic fiction, teacher and class will need to spend much time in merely identifying the nearly incredible number of allusions that compose the fabric of the text. "Lycidas" is the most allusive great poem in English—and since the allusions are the very brick and mortar of the basic fiction, or allegory, they must be not only identified literally but also interpreted, their significance for both the allegory and the literal statement made clear.

Still, the explication *can* be made, and the whole poem

worked out, even by students who never before encountered Muses, Nymphs, Furies, Druids, Mona, Deva, Or-
pheus, Hebrus, Naera, Arethuse, Mincius, Camus, and so
on and on. With effort, all can be duly identified and
related to the two levels of the poem. But the real question is whether, after "understanding" has been gained,
"Lycidas" can reach students as artistic experience.

It is in the most rarefied literary atmosphere that the
poem moves and in which the reader must come to move
who genuinely experiences "Lycidas." To feel the poem as
experience, the reader must accept its basic convention,
its use of elaborate trappings of classical pastoral. The
elevated tone of the poem can be heard through a good
reading, and the details of the text can be understood
through patient explication; but to relish the very basis
on which the art of "Lycidas" rests takes a degree of
literary sophistication that is possibly more than we can
reasonably expect of high school students. The problem
is somewhat like that of getting immature readers to appreciate Henry James at his most Jamesian, as in, say,
The Golden Bowl. Students who have grown up to Dickens, Homer, Shakespeare, Dostoevsky falter with James,
not because he is harder to "understand" than the others
(though certainly he is often hard enough) but because
of the nature of the things that *concern* him and his
characters and about which he writes whole chapters.
Shakespeare is filled with murders, ghosts, battles, gross
jests, love affairs, betrayals, jealousies, fierce arguments
about tangible matters; it is easy to be concerned with
the matters that concern Macbeth, Hamlet, Falstaff, Viola,
and even Andrew Aguecheek. But to be concerned with
the subtle issues that occupy the minds of main figures
in a James novel is to move on a level of civilization not
only far above that on which high school students and
most other people actually move but far beyond the reach
of their sympathies. "Lycidas" is artistically esoteric as
The Spoils of Poynton is socially and psychologically
esoteric.

But "Lycidas" and *The Spoils of Poynton* should stand
as ultimates toward which we should keep students stead-

ily pointed. To be able to respond sympathetically to such works, to be able to live imaginatively for even a little while at their level, is to have attained, for the moment, to a rare height of being.

Students will not reach this height on the first reading of "Lycidas," though they may be moved by the sounds of its music; nor will they reach it during the patient explication, when relevant facts of Milton's life and period are introduced and the details of word and line clarified. If they reach it at all—and there is no assurance that they will—they will do so during the final oral reading, when they catch both sound and meaning. Perhaps at some point in the discussion, before the final reading, Milton's way of sublimating his feelings by clothing them in the fiction of classical pastoral should be contrasted with the more direct expression of grief by other poets—Poe lying down by the side of his Annabel Lee, Tennyson lamenting to the "cold gray stones," Whitman fairly shouting his grief for his fallen Captain. Whitman's poem may help to make the transition, since it employs a fiction, as "Lycidas" does. But the very palpableness of Whitman's fiction, like the loudness of his poetic voice, will contrast strongly with the sophisticated art of "Lycidas," and to hear the lofty strains of Milton's poem immediately after Whitman's outburst may prove a welcome experience.

Short stories

Most poems selected for reading in high school will necessarily go to the inside program, where they can be read and discussed by teacher and class together. With short stories, the case is reversed: most stories should go to the outside list and comparatively few to the inside one; and of these few, fewer still should need a drastic method of Presentation such as we have urged for poems. Probably none at all should be read aloud, discussed, and then again read aloud; some should be read aloud, discussed, and then quickly read again by students independently. Though many short story writers make much of tone (Poe, for example) and therefore of sound, few short stories need to be heard, whereas all good poems do.

Typical high school anthologies of literature give approximately one-third of their space to short stories—more than to any other genre. The number of selections included in a series volume for any one year runs between fifteen and twenty-five. Further, teachers usually supplement the anthologized stories with those in current issues of magazines and with short story collections. The many attractive paperback editions now on the market make hundreds of deserving stories readily accessible. A fair estimate is that most high school students read at least twenty short stories each year for their English classes. This is surely a minimal number; they could easily be expected to read fifty or more.

But most of these should be read outside, with a minimum of direct help. In insisting on this point, we do not discriminate against stories or question their appropriateness for school programs. Our point is that it is a disservice to students and stories alike to use a more drastic form of Presentation than is needed. Most first-rate stories are highly readable, and to inflict on them unneeded analysis, to lecture on techniques, to belabor matters like "evolution of the short story" and "characteristics of the short story" will surely decrease rather than increase the potential enjoyment. Mainly, good stories need to be allowed to be just what they are—good stories. If, as we repeatedly insist, what we really want is the enjoyment of works of art as works of art, and not knowledge of techniques, types, historical contexts, we can best serve the purpose by steering students toward first-rate stories and leaving them alone together.

Unfortunately, we do not now seem to be going in the direction of leaving students and stories alone together. Colleges and universities now have specialists in the short story on their faculties; seminars in "The Short Story" are not unknown. These trends suggest that we may be in for even more academic analysis of stories than in the past. Teachers often justify elaborate analysis of stories and deliberate contrasting of famous stories with run-of-the-mill ones on the grounds that these are means of fixing students' standards of taste. Students are asked to bring in stories from their favorite periodicals and to compare these with the "classics," the teacher's aim being to demonstrate through analyses of plot, character, style, and technique the superiority of the classics. But the very nature of the undertaking—comparative studies of good and poor stories in order to show the differences—reduces the likelihood that students will truly experience any of the stories thus studied, for they will be reading not to experience but to compare and contrast techniques. The entire enterprise assumes the character of an exercise. The primary object of reading first-rate works of literature is not to learn how to distinguish these from mediocre ones—though one may hope that the ability to distinguish will develop as a matter of course—but to gain the experience they offer.

Despite our contention that the best thing to do with most stories is to leave students alone with good ones, we stand by our more basic argument that the best possible use of the in-class time of teacher and students is made by close cooperative study of selected texts, and we do not exclude short stories from this principle. But if twenty-five stories are to be read in a given year, we believe that not more than four or five should be examined in this way. Which ones should they be? The choice is probably harder than for any other genre. According to our principle, they should be works that both *need* and *deserve* this drastic form of Presentation. We assume that *all* the stories to be read are first-rate, but most can be left to outside reading simply because they have less need for close study and may even be spoiled by it.

Take, for example, Mark Twain's story of the jumping frog. Though there is no such critical consensus about supremely great short stories as there is about supremely great novels, the chances are that able critics would include the jumping frog among the world's best dozen. If the list were restricted to "the ten best humorous stories," it would probably stand at the top. But should Twain's frog story be included among the few stories selected to be given drastic treatment in class? Surely not. Students can read it on their own, with a few minutes for laughter in class the next day. To make it the subject of close study would almost certainly result in its being used to illustrate local color, dialect, exaggeration; the teacher would feel obliged to point out the many devices of humor that are characteristic of Mark Twain at his best. To subject the story to such analysis would be as faulty, we believe, as to send students home to wrestle with "Lycidas" on their own.

Much the same may be said of O. Henry's stories. A ninth grader who can read much of anything by himself can manage "The Ransom of Red Chief" and "The Gift of the Magi," and he stands in no need of lecturing on the surprise twist, the O. Henry technique of characterization, the jaunty style, or anything else. It is doubtful that a single O. Henry story needs analysis in class. The little story of "The Last Leaf," sentimental as it is, provides the young reader with a sudden, potent experience. Studied as if it were "Lycidas," it cloys. As a work for serious in-class study, it is absurd; but as one story among many fine ones that can be read independently, it is superb.

Most major writers of short stories frequently read in high school belong with Twain and O. Henry—on the outside list. We do not slight them by placing them there; we give them their best chance to do what they can. Harte, to add another, is spoiled by being made to serve as the example of local color. Sentimental as it is, "The Outcasts of Poker Flat" deserves better than to be studied as an "example" of something. Poe will do better when he is left to students on their own than as the example of "single impression." Left alone, Poe can be exciting; analyzed to illustrate a theory of composition, his stories are among the great bores of literature. De Maupassant, the most popular of French short story writers, writes with such clarity, plots so deliberately, and characterizes so pointedly that analysis is superfluous. "Saki," whimsical and odd, is harder to read than these, but good readers succumb to his charm better alone than aided. The same is true of Lord Dunsany. Jack London's "To

Build a Fire" is strong, suspenseful, once-over-quickly reading; but, studied in an anthology, buttressed with "aids" and questions, it is a nuisance.

Stories by Henry James are a different matter. Any of a dozen James stories need and deserve the scrutiny of an able teacher and a twelfth grade class. Kafka belongs here, as does Katharine Mansfield, with "The Garden Party," "Miss Brill," and "Bliss"—stories that only *seem* easy to the uninitiated. Conrad, Hardy, Conrad Aiken ("Silent Snow, Secret Snow"), Faulkner, Katherine Anne Porter, Thomas Mann, two or three stories by Chekhov, Tolstoy's "The Death of Ivan Ilyich," two or three by Balzac, Crane's "The Open Boat"—all will be helped rather than hindered by in-class study and discussion. The long, less concentrated ones, like Tolstoy's "Ivan Ilyich," need only some good discussion in class after independent reading; at the other extreme, James and Mansfield need reading aloud and immediate discussion.

A somewhat uncertain case is Hawthorne. "The Great Stone Face" is among the best-known, most often anthologized stories in English. It is sometimes read by ninth graders as an outside assignment, then discussed; but because of the heavy allegorizing in this story, it is better read aloud and discussed in the same hour. The fact is that though students who read it independently may "like" it, they will surely have missed what makes it a masterpiece. "The Minister's Black Veil," "Dr. Heidegger's Experiment," and, most of all, "Rappaccini's Daughter" need similar treatment: allegory is not, like the humor of Twain's frog story, spoiled by explanation.

With these stories, the necessity for close study is not so much to analyze and tabulate techniques, identify devices, reveal subtleties of style, and classify according to sub-genres; it is mainly for getting meanings clear. Sometimes, as with Kafka's symbols and Hawthorne's allegory, it is necessary to go into sophisticated devices *in order* to unlock meanings; but teachers should not use Kafka and Hawthorne in order "to introduce students to symbolism and allegory." Such terms should come into the discussion only as they implement the primary purpose of Presentation, which, always, is to release the force of the work as a work of art.

Essays

Most non-fiction prose included in the major anthologies used in high schools consists of nearly every type of non-fiction prose *except* essays. Included in quantity are biographical sketches, short excerpts from full-length biographies and autobiographies, account of personal adventure, items from popular science periodicals, newspaper and magazine articles, bits and pieces from journals and diaries, letters and excerpts from letters, excerpts from political speeches and famous orations, sections of historical documents, and so on. Much of the material is hardly classifiable except under a broad heading like "miscellaneous non-fiction prose." The best of the pieces are valuable as historical documents or as sources of scientific, sociological, biographical, or other information; the worst are merely "timely." Few, perhaps none, appear to have been chosen for literary value. Nothing in the anthologies so ill becomes them or the English program as does the bulk of this prose. The essay, however, is a work of a different order from these.

Though essays often present information, often are entertaining, and sometimes are timely, they are distinguishable from the merely informative, entertaining, and timely by their devotion to *ideas* and their care for form. Back of every proper essay can be sensed a mind intent on shaping, ordering, composing—sometimes to make an idea clear, sometimes to express an attitude, sometimes to tease the reader into an excitement of thought and emotion. The good essayist is conscious of unity and style; he may be graceful, light, airy, witty, or he may be deliberate, ponderous, coldly intellectual. But he is always *something*, and makes his presence felt. He may write "On Liberty," or he may write "On Chasing One's Hat"; he may write "On a Piece of Chalk" or "On the Knocking at the Gate in *Macbeth*"; the nature of the subject does not matter at all, but there always *is* a subject of some kind, and never merely a topic.

A legitimate essay is a work of literature no less than a poem or a short story is, and like the poem and the short story, it deserves whatever form of Presentation is needed to open its values for students.

Essays are not easy to teach. Few people read essays for pleasure as they do stories, novels, even plays and poems. Most teachers will probably acknowledge that they do a poorer job of teaching essays than any other form—if they teach them at all. These, surely, are among the reasons for what has happened to the essay in anthologies and school programs: while poetry, drama, and fiction have held their place, the legitimate essay has all but vanished and been replaced by miscellaneous non-fiction prose.

If the essay is to be restored, as it deserves to be, it must be well taught. Stories, novels, and plays have plot, characters, action, physical setting. As we read them, our minds are busy with images of scenes and people; the mind's eye watches these physical objects as though they were flashed on a screen. Poetry has its own lures: rhyme, rhythm, music, color, imagery, striking lines. But essays deal with *ideas*, and ideas are bodiless. As we read *Moby Dick*, we visualize Ahab and Queequeg as though they were flashed on a screen. But what is there to flash on the screen as we read "Self-Reliance" or "Of Truth"? True, the essayist may inject persons and scenes in order to illustrate an idea, and the mind's eye may briefly busy itself with these; but the idea itself remains invisible and impalpable. The essay-reader's mind is on its own, grappling with what cannot be seen or touched, and with no such inducements to continue as plot gives to stories and rhyme to poems.

Because it is harder to excite the mind with ideas than with people, actions, and things, essays are hard to read and hard to teach. But this is also why studying first-rate essays is an indispensable experience for high school readers. For most of them, the essay will provide their first introduction to the world of ideas. The very idea of "idea" is new and strange to ninth graders. Their worlds are only people, events, and things. And, indeed, many students arrive at college with no notion of ideas and no experience in extracting ideas—as opposed to information—from a printed page. Since the central concern of a liberal education is with ideas, they are at a serious disadvantage; and as for those who do not go to college, most will never enter the wonderful world of ideas at all. They are the truly deprived ones.

The main objects, then, of using essays in the reading program are these: to introduce students to the world of ideas, to give them experience in getting and understanding ideas from the printed page, and to excite them about ideas. (The important relation of essay study to composition we shall discuss in the chapter on Composition.)

What form of Presentation will best serve these purposes? Students can much more reasonably be left on their own with narrative forms than with essays. With essays, as with most poems, teacher and students must work together, reading aloud and immediately discussing. In fact, this form of Presentation is even more essential for essays than for poems. With poems up to the length of "Lycidas," we insisted that there be no stopping for discussion until the whole has been read through; the reason is obvious. But with essays, where the whole concern is to gain clear understanding of ideas as they are developed, there is sometimes need to stop for discussion after each sentence. It is more precise to say, then, that with essays discussion should not immediately follow reading but should be simultaneous with it. To intrude on the harmony of sound that is "Lycidas" is to break its spell and risk losing the impact of the whole; but "Self-Reliance" demands discussion as and when each gem of thought is encountered. In many essays the paragraph units tend to identify appropriate stop-to-discuss points.

With poems, the questions that should arise are of all kinds: they concern not only meaning but the great variety of poetic devices. With essays the necessity is to follow the emerging thought. This is not to imply that there need be no discussion of style and structure, of transitions, use of illustrations and examples, and so on;

but the central concern is with meaning. For this reason, especially, there is great advantage in conducting the discussion simultaneously with the reading. If students mull over an essay independently and then attempt to discuss it the next day, the task of generating excitement proves almost impossible. Ideas encountered and only half understood yesterday have a warmed-over taste when brought up for discussion today. But when teacher and students together encounter ideas as they read, the game is fresh. Few students will ever have guessed before that there is beauty in an unfolding idea; when teacher and class go at an essay together, there is at least the possibility of generating true intellectual excitement.

Left on their own, ninth graders can manage the expository prose of an article about scuba diving; they can read popular accounts of the polar ice caps, why birds go south, climbing Annapurna, Helen Keller's struggle to master communication, Willie Mays' rise to fame, an astronaut's day, a submarine voyage under the ice, ant and bee civilizations, the perfection of a new vaccine. There is nothing at all wrong with any of these; people who have grown up to be avid readers are almost invariably those who have always read everything they could get their hands on. So students should read all these—*on their own*. But in the close company of a teacher, ninth graders can take on Bacon's "Of Ambition"—Latin quotations, classical allusions, and all—and take a step into the most exciting of all worlds, the world of ideas.

Essays are things to weigh and consider. If their ideas are to be found exciting, it will be in class, not at home. What looks cold and uninteresting on the printed page and is likely to continue to look so when immature readers read in solitude can become hot enough in classroom debate. Bacon, Emerson, Thoreau, Lord Chesterfield, Chesterton, Bertrand Russell, George Orwell can always be counted on to start an argument if they are given a chance; and when students read and discuss together, they get a chance. Even Addison and Steele—traditionally deadly assignments for students on their own—will come alive when they are discussed simultaneously with reading. Essays are solitary affairs for essay writers, but they need readers sitting in a circle. Not even poems have such compelling need to be treated in this fashion.

When students have been awakened to the possibilities latent in ideas, they can be put on their own with some essayists. Lamb, Leacock, Tomlinson, Morley, Shaw, Goldsmith, and of course Thurber and Benchley can be read with enjoyment even in solitude. But Chesterton and Shaw are good cases in point: even though able juniors and seniors can read them independently, their real excitement is missed in that way; they will do better in class. As for Bacon, Emerson, and Thoreau, their ideas ought always to be aired where there is opportunity for instant discussion. Bacon, in particular, so grates on the built-in attitudes of modern American students brought up in a vastly different political and social environment that he is good for an argument in every paragraph and often in every sentence. Every teacher in grades 9, 10, 11, and 12 should want to use him again and again—never for home reading but for the excitement his ideas engender in the classroom.

Both Bacon and Emerson are specific antidotes for the sickness of "presentism" that sometimes turns English classes into social studies classes concerned mainly with current issues. There is a world of difference between getting students excited about current and local affairs and getting them excited about the ideas that underlie the special issues of any time—and, better still, about ideas *per se*. Bacon and Emerson invite excitement *in the idea itself*, and can breed respect for the very *idea* of ideas.

Novels

Experienced teachers know very well what is the biggest problem with the novel: getting through it without taking the whole semester. Regrettably, during the past generation or two this merely practical difficulty has too often been solved in one of three ways: (1) by using slight "best sellers" that students can whip through on their own; (2) by using very short, though good, novels, leaving the full-length masterpieces unattempted; (3) by using drastic abridgements of the great novels. There are better solutions.

Here we are first concerned with the inside program, works that both need and deserve joint attention of teacher and class. The greater number of novels can go to the outside program, to which they will no doubt contribute more reading than any other form. On their own, students can read six to eight novels in a year; but for the classroom we shall be thinking of only one or two each year.

But how can a major novel be dealt with adequately in that time? If we study it line by line, like a poem or essay, a novel of eight hundred or a thousand pages will take all year. On the other hand, if we leave the whole novel to outside reading, reserving class time for discussion only, we will be forced to use novels that, though good, lack the high distinction that should characterize all works that make up the inside program. *The Good Earth* is a good novel and was a great best seller; *The Yearling* is in roughly the same class; *Johnny Tremaine*, widely used for many years, often even after the ninth grade, stands a little lower than these; *Giants in the Earth* fits the general category also; so does *Northwest Passage*; and so, more recently, does *To Kill a Mockingbird*. These, and many like them, are good novels and some are even excellent. They should all be included—on the outside list.

But for the inside list we want novels comparable to the distinguished poems, plays, essays, and stories included there; we want the most distinguished works in the genre: *Pride and Prejudice, Moby Dick, The Scarlet Letter, Anna Karenina, Huckleberry Finn, Madame Bovary, Crime and Punishment, Jane Eyre, David Copperfield, Les Misérables, Père Goriot, Vanity Fair.*

On the plane barely below these are *Wuthering Heights, A Tale of Two Cities, Great Expectations, The Return of the Native, Tess of the D'Urbervilles, The Mayor of Casterbridge, Lord Jim, Victory, Sense and Sensibility, Emma, The Portrait of a Lady, The Wings of the Dove,*

The Ambassadors, The Portrait of the Artist as a *Young Man,* and *Of Human Bondage.* We might list a dozen more on this plane, any of which is appropriate for the in-class program. And after all these, we should drop a level or two before we came to novels that we thought appropriate only for the outside program.

We should note here that high distinction among novels (and other works) is not necessarily to be equated with difficulty in reading. Several novels on our second plane are much harder than some on the first plane. Probably the hardest on the first plane are *Moby Dick* and *Crime and Punishment;* next, because of their irony, are *Vanity Fair* and *Pride and Prejudice.* Least difficult of the first group are *Huckleberry Finn, David Copperfield,* and *Jane Eyre. Les Misérables,* the longest of the group, is easy except for its size and the necessity to remember the details of several lines of action; much the same is true of *Anna Karenina. Madame Bovary* and *Père Goriot* confront students with a social milieu that is strange and perplexing, but their narratives move along with classic simplicity.

Harder than the hardest novel on the highest plane are the three James novels named on the second plane, and nearly as hard as these are the two by Conrad, where the technique of narration puts barriers in the way of the uninitiated. Dickens' *A Tale of Two Cities,* long a widely used novel in the tenth grade, is much harder than *David Copperfield. Wuthering Heights,* again primarily because of its narrative device, is harder than any novels on the first plane except those of Melville and Dostoevsky. Probably the least difficult of the second-plane novels are Hardy's—but even these are harder than *David Copperfield* and *Jane Eyre.* The moral that emerges from this brief table of approximate difficulties is this: that teachers who shy away from novels in the very highest rank because they are "too difficult" and tackle those on the second plane under the impression that they are easier are wrong more often than right. The twelve hundred pages of *Les Misérables* offer some of the easiest reading in all the world's distinguished prose fiction; the relatively brief *Wings of the Dove* includes some of the hardest.

Still, the least difficult of the supremely great novels need as close attention as teachers and classes together can find time to give them. In the era of leaving students on their own with novels, *Johnny Tremaine* was as good a novel as most tenth graders could manage. Worse, they read an adapted *Tale of Two Cities* or *Great Expectations*. But together teacher and ninth grade class can begin with *Jane Eyre*, *Huckleberry Finn*, or *David Copperfield*, any one of which is infinitely superior to *Johnny Tremaine* or any adapted classic. Twelfth graders who, on their own, might have reached no higher than *Mutiny on the Bounty* can, with the teacher, take on *Moby Dick* or *Crime and Punishment*. With novels, the difference between what students can be expected to read on their own and what they can be expected to read under the close direction of a teacher is so very wide that we shall suffer a great loss unless we find a satisfactory means of "getting through" a big novel in class. Since lack of time prevents reading and discussion of a whole novel in class and since the inability of students to manage the supreme novels independently prevents assigning all the reading for homework, our only choice is to combine in-class and out-of-class reading.

Some teachers assign all the reading for outside, but first identify key or peculiarly different sections to be reread aloud in class. Other teachers also assign most of the novel for outside reading but reserve predetermined parts to be read first in class. Yet others assign the whole for outside but do much rereading in connection with classroom discussion; this is probably the most widely used method.

The three variations have a common disadvantage: the greater part of class time is spent discussing what students have already read on their own—sometimes only the night before but sometimes a whole week before. Especially with long novels, class discussion often lags far behind reading. Such discussion is rarely other than dreary. The situation is worsened when, instead of assigning a set number of pages for next day's reading, the teacher has instructed the class to "go ahead and finish the book as soon as you can." After a week or two, students are strung out over hundreds of pages; some have finished and are ready for the next book, while others are barely up to the point to which discussion has progressed. Under these conditions, discussion is confused, wasteful, and boring. It is after such frustrating experiences that teachers turn to novels that students can manage on their own. Instead, they should change their method of presentation.

When discussion today concerns what was read yesterday or a week ago, the good students pretend to be interested, the mediocre ones are indifferent, inattentive, uncooperative, though not directly rude, and the remaining ones get out of hand. Each period is made unpleasant for everyone because the teacher must repeatedly admonish students: "John, pay attention!" "Bill, I asked you a question!" Nor can students be held wholly to blame; yesterday's or last week's reading, warmed over and hashed over, is not appetizing. When a student has floated down the river on Huck's raft, he cannot easily be stirred to real excitement about events that took place far upstream and that he remembers vaguely. His mind is mainly, and quite properly, occupied with where Huck is right now.

There is a second serious objection to warmed-over discussion: it has about it the disagreeable aroma of a recitation or oral quizzing. From the point of view of students, the only purpose seems to be to test whether they can recall details, and there is much waving of hands and snapping of fingers when some lucky fellow happens to remember one. Students are not genuinely involved; they are trying to survive the hour. Whatever good is accomplished during such an hour has little to do with "experiencing the work as a work of art." What is worse, the dread of tomorrow's discussion stands perpetually in the way of enjoying tonight's reading. To read the best of novels knowing that tomorrow or a week hence one will be called on to regurgitate the details of a particular chapter is to read it in desperate circumstances.

But there is one happy solution to the problem of combining in-class and out-of-class study of novels, and some teachers have discovered it. Let us say that the novel is *Huckleberry Finn*.

The teacher begins the novel by reading aloud while students follow in their copies. Words, difficult sentences are dealt with summarily in passing. Occasionally, when something of key importance comes up, there is a brief discussion to make sure that all students are abreast of developments.

The combined reading-discussion continues until ten minutes before the end of the period. If the teacher can manage to reach a point of particular interest, so much the better. The teacher then asks students to read on to a definite point, perhaps fifteen pages ahead, for tomorrow. He then drops them, with directions to read on silently until the end of the period, and at home. Teachers who have never tried the method will be gratified to see how students who have now become involved in the story will go straight on reading without raising their heads until the bell rings.

On the next day, teacher and students take ten minutes to summarize and discuss the pages read by students independently. This brief discussion need have no odor of oral quizzing about it; the necessity for discussion is obvious to students, and the time is brief. The object is to get ready to read on.

As soon as the gap has been bridged, the teacher resumes the reading, conducting discussion as he goes. And again, just before the hour ends, he drops students with a new advance assignment.

Thus class and teacher move through the novel, with the teacher doing much "playing by ear"—increasing or decreasing the length of advance assignments, lengthening or shortening the discussion time as seems right. Teachers who have used this way of presenting any one of the very great novels have found it not merely effective but dramatically so. The principal advantages are these: (1) It combines the virtues of close in-class study with those of independent responsibility. (2) Using both in-class and out-of-class time, it enables the class to complete the novel in good time. (3) It avoids the rehash, question-answer kind of discussion that is both useless and demoralizing. (4) It holds the class together, so that in discussion all minds are intent on what is being read or has just been read. (5) Most important of all, it comes nearer than any other method to guaranteeing that the *whole* class will understand and enjoy a great work.

One point, hinted at earlier, should be made explicit here. It is often argued that students should not all be held to the same place in reading a long work, that the assignment to "read to the end of Chapter 5 for tomorrow" blocks the incentive of capable readers who may want to read on and on. The method outlined does indeed fix the points to which students are expected to read in advance assignments, and must do so, since the teacher's in-class reading will resume at these points. But no student is prevented from reading a book to the end on the first weekend if he wishes to do so. The advance assignment should make it clear that students are expected to have the next few pages ready for quick discussion; if they have read farther, they need merely go back to these pages to refresh their memories. Such students will, in effect, have the advantage of reading much of the book through twice.

A final virtue of this method is its flexibility. It can be precisely adapted to class and novel. *David Copperfield* is a long, open narrative, much of which can take fast reading and little discussion. The teacher who knows the book well will know when to increase the outside assignments from fifteen to thirty pages and when to decrease them to ten. The same applies to *Les Misérables*, hundreds of pages of which read as easily and excitingly as any thriller. Even *Moby Dick*, a very difficult novel, has long open spaces where thirty pages for an overnight assignment will not be excessive; it also has some spots where ten pages will be too much. Students should not be given advance assignments that will take more than a few minutes to discuss. If a great part of the hour is needed for discussing what was read independently, one unique feature of the system—its avoidance of hour-long rehash sessions—will be lost.

Plays

With drama as with the novel, we are here concerned with the works that both need and deserve a drastic form of presentation in class. More specifically, that means we shall deal mainly with Shakespeare. Other dramatists— Sophocles, Ibsen, Shaw, Rostand, Goldsmith, Sheridan, Wilde, Chekhov, O'Neill, Miller, Anderson, Wilder, Williams—appear in many school programs also, as they should, but with much less frequency than Shakespeare. Some of these require in-class reading and some are better off without it. Sophocles requires as intensive treatment as Shakespeare. Most of the others are better trusted to able readers, especially those who are drawn to drama by choice, for reading outside. Here is not the moment to debate the question whether it is better for students to read *King Lear* than *The Glass Menagerie*, *Macbeth* than *Death of a Salesman*, *Twelfth Night* than *Our Town*, *As You Like It* than *Ah, Wilderness*, *Romeo and Juliet* than *Cyrano de Bergerac*. Our point is that Shakespeare most needs and deserves intensive classroom study. That students should read a wide range of plays other than Shakespeare's we have no doubt; but the place for most of these is in the outside program.

We have acknowledged that Sophocles needs intensive treatment. We do not mean that none of the others needs or is worthy of it. Ibsen, Shaw, Goldsmith, Sheridan, Wilde can profitably be read and discussed in class. But to give a good stage play like *Our Town* a line-by-line examination in class as if it were *King Lear* is needless and does the play disservice. Next to Shakespeare and Sophocles, probably Ibsen and Shaw can best bear intensive treatment. But with both, ways should be found to get along rapidly. *Hedda Gabler*, *A Doll's House*, or *The Master Builder* should be finished within a week. So should *Man and Superman*. So should *She Stoops to Conquer*, *The School for Scandal*, *The Importance of Being Earnest*. By using both in-class and out-of-class reading, as was recommended for the novel, teachers can move through these plays rapidly to better effect than if they took five weeks. More harm than good is done to the experience of *Death of a Salesman* by scrutinizing the play as if it were *Lear*.

But the experience of *King Lear* is not damaged by five to six weeks of line-by-line reading and discussion; and, conversely, only the most superficial experience of it can be gained by high school students in a one-week reading. If only a week is to be given to a play, the play should not be Shakespeare's, not even an "open" one like *As You Like It*. We may sum up the situation thus: to give only one week to a Shakespearean play is as faulty as to give five weeks to *Our Town*.

How should the five weeks on a Shakespearean play be spent? We can begin our answer by noting three widely used ways of dealing with the text: (1) independent reading, with subsequent discussion in class; (2) reading aloud in class with students alternating in parts; (3) reading the text silently while a recording is played, with intervals of discussion. Before adding a fourth way, let us briefly consider these in turn.

Independent reading • Probably more teachers have given up Shakespeare entirely or turned to adapted versions because this method failed than for any other cause. Ninth graders, sent home to prepare the first act of *A Midsummer Night's Dream* for discussion, do not read it well enough to justify reading it at all. The truly conscientious and the plain-scared ones plod faithfully through, looking up words and striving to make sense of obscure passages. The middle range of students read through the act in half an hour and get only a rough notion of what is happening. The lower ranges either make no attempt at all or meet frustration. Next day's discussion is utter waste. The very conscientious make energetic efforts to prove to the teacher that they looked up all the classical allusions— with which the first act of *A Midsummer Night's Dream* is packed—and they venture wild opinions about Theseus, Hippolyta, Demetrius, Egeus. The middle ranges volun-

teer vague information at the level of "what happened."
The lower ranges slouch down in their seats, trying to
look as if they were absent. Whatever scraps of information the class may gain from reading and discussing in
this fashion, they certainly do not gain any kind of pleasure, least of all the kind that a work of art is designed to
give. And the teacher—though he may have contrived to
look pleased with the discussion, happy to settle for any
kind of comment—thinks in his heart that ninth graders
truly cannot read Shakespeare, as indeed they cannot, and
resolves to use *Sorry, Wrong Number* or *Juliet in Pigtails*
next year. For this year, however, he has been so foolish
as to select the play and must get through it somehow.
Thereafter the class hours are punctuated by his glowing
comments meant to stimulate interest—how great Shakespeare is, how great his poetry is, how great his characters
are, how much good it does students to read Shakespeare.
But the cause is lost. The polite students nod and try to
look as if they agreed, the middle group try to look as if
they were listening, and the others roll up their eyes.

Reading aloud by students • Unlike the teacher above,
who has "had it" long before the hour is over, the teacher
who merrily begins by assigning Johnny to read Theseus,
Jane to read Hippolyta, Mary to read Helena, Agnes to
read Hermia, Joe to read Lysander, Arthur to read Demetrius, and Ernest to read Egeus is convinced, at the end
of the hour, that he has had a great day and is *really*
teaching Shakespeare. What is more, students leave the
class in high spirits, chatting, laughing, mimicking one
another, slapping one another on the back. They have had
a good time. They have giggled when Agnes mispro-
nounced a word ludicrously, guffawed when Joe read the
wrong line, reached across the aisle and poked Ernest
when he missed his cue, whistled when Mary (who
blushed in confusion) got a little too much feeling into
a line, snickered when Arthur finished his passage and
went right on reading a stage direction. Each waited
breathlessly to be called on to take over a role. They were
amazed to see their teacher all smiles throughout the hour

and incredulous when the bell rang so early.

Surely this is the only way to teach Shakespeare! Students have enjoyed themselves hugely, go away happy, and will be eager to return tomorrow. They have felt themselves drawn together by participating in a mutual undertaking. The rapport of teacher and class is wonderful; morale is higher than it has ever been. Above all, half the class has already had the experience of reading magnificent verse aloud, and the other half will have it tomorrow. All in all, the experience has been invaluable and is one that students and teachers should enjoy often.

It may seem churlish to assert at this point that however valuable was their experience, it was not an experience of A Midsummer Night's Dream as a work of art. But assert it we must.

We do not dispute the possibility that the experience was as good as or even better than the experience of a work of art. But an experience of a work of art it was not. It was different in kind, and in fact did not even remotely resemble the experience of a work of art. And since the primary object of Presentation is to allow an artistic work its best chance to get through to students with its unique force, this method, whatever its other virtues, misses the mark and will not do for the initial Presentation. The time for students to read and to act out parts in A Midsummer Night's Dream is not now, but later, after the initial Presentation has been completed. We shall return to this and similar issues in the chapter on Related Activities.

Recordings • The fault of student reading as a form of initial Presentation, namely, that students cannot read well enough and hence draw attention to themselves rather than to the text, is avoided by the use of a professional recording, which students follow in their books. Fine recordings of all Shakespeare's major plays are now available, and that students should hear the appropriate one before the study of any play is considered complete we have no doubt. But the use of a recording as initial Presentation is not satisfactory.

The root of the trouble is that no mechanical device, whether record player or tape recorder, is sufficiently flexible for the purpose. Shakespeare's dramatic verse is of a high specific density. Even if it were not written in Elizabethan English but in American English, it would still place a greater demand on the understanding of students previously unacquainted with the text than can be accommodated at the speed with which it is spoken by actors. This is not to say that students cannot get a general sense of "what is going on," nor that they cannot gain real enjoyment from the recording. But if they are previously unfamiliar with the text, they will miss all but the obvious effects. They will miss, that is to say, what makes Shakespeare Shakespeare—and if they miss this, there seems no valid reason why they should be reading Shakespeare in particular.

However admirably professional actors may read—and they will read not only better than students but better than teachers—the speed is too rapid for the mind to assimilate meanings, despite the great help that right intonations and sharp characterizations give. Any Shakespearean text is laden with meaning. Passages teem with ideas. Images are piled on images; there are images within images. Though Shakespeare worked with the hearer in mind, he could not wholly succeed in raising the full wealth of his thought to the surface so that it could be instantly apprehended. There is simply too much. Take a passage almost anywhere:

DUNCAN: The love that follows us sometime is our trouble,
Which still we thank as love. Herein I teach you
How you shall bid God 'ild us for your pains,
And thank us for your trouble.

LADY M: All our service
In every point twice done and then done double
Were poor and single business to contend
Against those honours deep and broad wherewith
Your majesty loads our house: for those of old,
And the late dignities heaped up to them,
We rest your hermits.

This is no deep soliloquy in which a Lear or a Hamlet probes the mysteries of the universe or his own soul; it is only an exchange of greetings between guest and hostess in the doorway. Hearing, students will understand—from the actors' tones if not from the words themselves—that Duncan greets his hostess warmly and that she thanks him for having always been so kind to her and her husband. But if this is to be the depth of students' understanding here and elsewhere in the play, there is no compelling reason they should read *Macbeth*.

Really to apprehend what is here, even in this doorway exchange, it is necessary to stop, reread, consider, discuss, give time for the mind to take in what has been said. With any kind of recording device, the best-intentioned attempts to provide the necessary time are frustrating. Teachers sometimes play a recording of a Shakespearean play completely through in three or four successive meetings without stopping for comments and discussion, the object being to hear it first as a whole. Or they sometimes play through a scene or an act and then stop to discuss, going back over what has been heard. The second way is preferable, from at least one point of view, but even it is unsatisfactory. To wait until the play has been heard through before returning to examine the early acts is to wait too long; the process of line-by-line study is then unappetizing. The time to understand the meanings of lines is right then and there, *when they are heard in context*. To wait until the end of the scene or act before going back is better, but there is no substitute for getting meanings *precisely at the moment of need*.

Reading aloud by the teacher • We have rejected the method of independent reading because students miss too much and have a painful time both in reading and later in discussing. We have rejected the method of oral reading by students in class because, though the experience may be enjoyable, the enjoyment derives not from the work but from students themselves. We have rejected the method of the professional recording because it either postpones necessary discussion until it is too late to be effective or introduces jarring discord by interruptions. Further, we have rejected these not partially or inconclusively, but categorically. We have only one major possibility left—reading aloud by the teacher while students follow in their texts, with comments and discussion carried on at the moments of need.

Why is not this just as bad as using the recording and interrupting it? In fact, why is not this even worse? The teacher will certainly not read all parts with a skill to match that of professional actors; hence the teacher's reading will lose the principal advantage that the recording has.

The difference is that the teacher is not, like the recording, engaged in a performance. Teacher and students are engaged in a joint enterprise of discovery. If the teacher reads appropriately, there is no sense of performance; the object is to get words, lines, passages open for discussion. When really accomplished teachers proceed in this way, students actually forget that they are hearing a reading. Following the text intently, not looking up, they seem *themselves* to be reading. When teacher and class pause to discuss, they pause as a unit; they do not change from one operation to another, but in effect continue with another aspect of the single operation they are engaged in—that of discovering "what is there." But when the recording is used, discussion intrudes on performance. The recorded performance is like a stranger in the room, a party alien to the enterprise of teacher and students. When the teacher pauses in reading in order to comment or ask a question, he does so with the same voice with which he was reading. But when the teacher stops the recording to comment, he shuts off the performing voice and the class hears his own. It is not a single process of study that is going on, but two—performance and study—with a jarring division between.

No recording device has sufficient flexibility to serve the needs of initial Presentation. The recording is an intruder that cannot become part of the intimate relationship that exists when teachers and students join wits to study a text. It demands students' awareness of its presence, diverting attention that should go to the printed text. But the teacher's voice can move in and out of the text without jarring because it is the same voice, sometimes reading, sometimes commenting. Since there is no performance, no performance is interrupted by discussion.

Of course, if the teacher has confused reading with performing and sometimes reads in such a way that students look up to admire his diction and feeling, he will have the same disadvantage that the recording has. We do not imply that the teacher should read Shakespeare badly—feebly, flatly, monotonously. He should read faithfully for meaning, but as inconspicuously as possible. If a student looks up, the teacher should realize that he has stopped reading and slipped into performing; the tones of reading and performing are markedly different. But neither do we say that a teacher who is an able performer should never perform. If he can read Macbeth's dagger speech as an actor does it on the stage, then he should by all means demonstrate. But his demonstration should not serve as his initial reading of the passage for meaning. It is often useful for the teacher to show how the actor would speak a passage, and to do so with gusto. During the usual reading, students will watch the text; during the demonstration, they will watch the teacher. When the demonstration is finished, teacher and students should return to their regular business of perusing the text.

We should now turn to two or three questions that always arise when teachers discuss this way of working with a Shakespearean text. Heading all other questions are these: How often and how long should reading be interrupted for discussion? What sorts of things should be discussed? How deep should the teacher try to go in critical analysis?

The questions are rarely asked by teachers experienced in using this method of presentation; they are asked by inexperienced teachers and by others who have tried other methods but not this one. For after brief experience the questions tend to answer themselves—and the answers that come rather automatically with "teaching by ear" are much more satisfactory than those that can be given arbitrarily here.

Certainly no arbitrary answers to the question "How often and how long should the teacher stop for discussion?" should be given here. These answers depend on the particular text and the particular class. The main object is to keep the students' understanding abreast of the reading. Sometimes, without pausing, the teacher drops in an explanatory word. Sometimes he stops to clarify at the end of two lines. Most teachers find that extended passages of ten to thirty lines, such as soliloquies, are best read through without stopping—as we have said poems should be. Further, there is advantage in keeping certain scenes whole in the reading: the two balcony scenes from *Romeo and Juliet*, for example, need to be heard intact; but this does not mean that the teacher dare not supply a clarifying word in the same breath with reading. A very long scene, such as the great court scene from *The Merchant of Venice*, which runs to more than 450 lines, should probably be read through without discussion, but there is frequent need for abrupt clarifying comment. The trick for the teacher to master—and it is an astonishingly easy one—is that of commenting without causing students to look up. If they do not look up, it has been mastered.

Much the same must be said about the nature and depth of discussion: all depends on the play and the class. It is possible to generalize to this extent, that discussion usually involves both little things and big ones. On the one hand, it is obviously necessary to keep the running details of word and line clear, and abreast of the reading. But on the other hand, the reading of any extended work also involves looking before and after, and not only at the present instant. The mind of any able reader is packed with awarenesses that set the particular moment of action in a context of what has preceded and what may be expected to follow. When, for example, Romeo kills Tybalt, it would be a poor reader whose whole consciousness was devoted to the act itself; here the mind must flash back to Act I and the Prince's ominous edict:

> *If ever you disturb our streets again,*
> *Your lives shall pay the forfeit of the peace.*

Now Romeo has disturbed the peace—and what must be the consequence? Awareness should include remembrance of Juliet, also—only two hours a bride, and impatiently awaiting night and Romeo: what implications has Romeo's act for her? Thus, at any given moment in a great action, the able reader's mind is busied with complex awarenesses. In large measure, the teacher's task during the combined reading-discussion process is to demonstrate how the able reader moves through a work, his mind actively relating the present instant to past and future. For the experienced reader much of this activity is involuntary. But the immature reader is engaged in practice to become an experienced reader—and no way is better for the purpose than this of combined reading and immediate discussion.

It is in discussion, too, that much of the material which we said should not be included as Introduction becomes relevant and can be introduced effectively. Rather than lecture on the Elizabethan stage before reading the play, the teacher can await a propitious moment in the text when it will mean something to students to learn that there was no front curtain, that there were several playing areas and levels, and that there were no stage furnishings in the modern sense. In Romeo and Juliet, the first urgent place to introduce information on Elizabethan staging comes very early indeed: the initial Chorus speaks of the "two hours' traffic of our stage." In Macbeth, after twelve lines, when the scene shifts from "a desert place" to Duncan's camp, remarks on the absence of elaborate settings become relevant. When at the end of a scene orders are given to carry off a dead body, there is point in telling students about the lack of a front curtain. Rather than lecture on the nature of Shakespearean tragedy before a line of Julius Caesar is read, the ablest teachers wait until Brutus, in the second scene, bares the central fact of his character:

> If it be aught toward the general good,
> Set honor in one eye and death i' the other,
> And I will look on both indifferently.

> *For let the gods so speed me as I love*
> *The name of honor more than I fear death.*

Here is the time to speak on Bradley's "character as Fate" in Shakespearean tragedy; thereafter, when Cassius announces precisely how he will work on Brutus' sense of honor in tempting him to join the conspiracy, and, again, when Brutus commits a succession of tactical errors because, being a man of honor, he cannot choose otherwise, the basic ideas of what tragedy was to Shakespeare can be shown. If, finally, a definition of Shakespearean tragedy seems appropriate, it can be attempted after the death of Brutus, when the full evidence of one play has been observed. Arrived at inductively, the definition will have meaning.

Analysis of such technical matters as characterization, plotting, irony, soliloquies, asides, imagery, climax, denouement, like discussion of historical and biographical matters and characteristics of the genre, best arises from the details of text and should normally await the propitious moment; then, when the teacher points out a dramatic device and invites class discussion of it, the relevance is apparent. Students who go through a Shakespearean play in this fashion will end by knowing more about the dramatist, his age, his theater, his language and verse, the theory of comedy or tragedy than if these topics are lectured on in advance. But more than that, the timely introduction of precisely relevant information will help them to experience the play as a work of art.

Chapter 7

What related activities?

We have ended a long era during which the term "Activities," after a spectacular heyday, slowly but surely acquired
unfortunate connotations and eventually became disrepu-
table. It is today a bad word that loosely sums up the
abuses and mis-emphases of the past thirty-five years.
Significantly, recent writers of textbooks and designers of
English programs, who formerly wove everything around
the concept of Activities, now shun it. From the 1930s
through the 1950s, editors of anthology series were less
concerned with the quality of literary selections than with
the range of Activities to which the reading selections conveniently lent themselves. The literary work was not the
thing of first importance, but a device for stimulating
Activities. One reason for the decline in the quality of
literary selections in the anthologies of this period is unmistakable: first-rate poems, essays, plays, stories, novels
are less effective for stimulating Activities than ephemeral
pieces from newspapers and current magazines. The variety of Activities that can conveniently be sparked by
"Self-Reliance" and "Lycidas" is less impressive than that
which can grow from a magazine article on "Space Pioneers" or "Why an Airplane Flies." When Activities
were an end and literature only a means, poems by Milton
and essays by Emerson were obviously poor choices and
were dropped.

Anthologists and curriculum specialists vied in invent-
ing activities to accompany reading, including all sorts of
"doing" that could somehow be related. Students might
read "The Celebrated Jumping Frog" in groups of five or
six around a table and then put on a fifteen-minute radio

or television program during which Smiley was interviewed about his frog; other groups, each having read different stories, would think up similar activities, the performance of which would consume all in-class time for two weeks. This illustration is not extravagant and is certainly more than fair; in that it refers to activities growing out of a first-rate work of literature, it is superior to the plethora of mere doings that were prompted by non-literary pieces.

Still, the variety of activities that was undertaken in connection with reading was as nothing in comparison to that which, during the same years, grew from the "other half" of the English program. The enormous textbook series that supposedly centered on grammar and composition were steadily expanded to include telephoning, interviewing, introducing persons, ordering meals in restaurants, social and business communications of all kinds, panel discussions on any and all topics, conducting meetings, planning and presenting radio and television programs, giving directions, getting along with people, asking for a date, improving the personality, and applying for a job.*

Indeed such activities have brought the terms "English Activities" and "Language Arts Activities" into such disrepute that we hesitate to use "Activities" in the title of the present chapter. Whether the term can ever be restored to respectability is uncertain. But the fact is that *certain* activities are both respectable and indispensable concomitants to the study of literature, and it is with these alone that we shall be concerned.

The two foremost activities, however, we shall not discuss in this chapter. The first, Discussion, we have considered in the chapter on Presentation, characterizing it as an integral part of Presentation. The second, Composition, deserves a chapter of its own. Just now we shall be concerned with Outside Reading and with several lesser but important activities: Vocabulary Study, Reading Aloud and Acting Out, Memorizing, Using Recordings and Films.

* For a full account, see *High School English Textbooks: A Critical Examination.*

Outside reading • Earlier, we distinguished between two programs that together make up the full reading program: the in-class program, works that both need and deserve a drastic form of Presentation; and the outside program, works to be read independently, or largely so. It is with this latter program that we are now concerned. What sorts of works are appropriate for the outside list that would be inappropriate for intensive study in class? What should be the relation of the outside list to the in-class selections? How guide the outside program, yet keep it independent? How arrange for students to report on their reading?

Though works in every genre can be included, the outside program uses fewer poems and essays, more stories, novels, and plays, and, in addition, autobiographies, biographies, journals, travel books, and other sorts of nonfiction prose not included in the in-class program.

Let us now illustrate. We are reading *Huckleberry Finn* closely in a ninth grade class during a period of four weeks. On their own, students can be expected to read two or three novels from an extensive list accommodating a wide range of reading abilities. The best readers should be able to manage *David Copperfield* or *Jane Eyre*—works that might, instead, have been chosen for in-class study. *The Yearling* would suit many, boys and girls alike. The less able should manage a novel or two by Stevenson, *The Three Musketeers*, *The Human Comedy*, *The Red Pony*, *The Pearl*, *The Light in the Forest*. Twain's *Life on the Mississippi* and *A Connecticut Yankee* are obvious choices. The ninth grade is not too early for best sellers like *To Kill a Mockingbird*; neither is it too immature for *Catcher in the Rye* and *Lord of the Flies*. Indeed, the list of available novels to accommodate all abilities at this level is unlimited; nor need it be confined to novels: here is a place for the Halliburton books, for biographies of statesmen and scientists. Though we would object violently to the use of a week for intensive in-class study of *Annapurna*, *Hiroshima*, or *Kon Tiki*, we object not at all to these for the outside program: a prime advantage of confining the in-class program to first-rate works that require joint study by teacher and students is that students can be left the freer in their outside choices. Ninth grade choices can range from *Little Britches* upward to *David Copperfield*, from *The Count of Monte Cristo* to *The Red Badge of Courage*, from *The Old Man and the Sea* to *Ivanhoe*.

Let us next suppose that in class teacher and ninth graders are studying some highly select short stories: one or two by Hawthorne, others by de Maupassant, Gogol, Bierce, Chekhov, Tolstoy. Including reading, discussion, writing, the stories will take about three weeks. Independently during this period students can be reading short stories very nearly wherever they find them. The present availability of paperback collections offers an unlimited range. There are volumes of Modern Short Stories, American Short Stories, English Short Stories, Russian, French, German, Spanish, Irish Short Stories; there are selected volumes by de Maupassant, Chekhov, Mansfield, Poe, O. Henry. There are Best Short Stories, Great Short Stories, Stories of Suspense, Favorite Short Stories, Great Ghost Stories. Indeed, any volume of an anthology series includes fifteen to twenty stories that are eminently satisfactory for independent reading though not, with some exceptions, for close class study. While half a dozen masterpieces are being read and discussed in class, each student should manage ten to twenty stories on his own. Those who like O. Henry can read a volume of O. Henry; others, a volume of de Maupassant; those who prefer variety can read a national collection or a world collection. Nor need we exclude stories in modern periodicals: a student whose family has back issues of *Harper's* or the *Atlantic* can find more than enough excellent stories.

Or suppose that teacher and ninth graders are studying *Julius Caesar* closely for five weeks. Unlike short stories and novels, dramas appropriate for the ninth grade outside program are limited in number. In the eleventh and twelfth grades, students can read widely in American and English plays on their own, including some Shakespearean plays, but ninth graders will generally be wiser to read in other genres. However, the ablest can attempt *The Mer-*

chant of Venice; others can read a collection of one-act plays. The radio and television scripts that clutter major anthology series are pieces to see performed, not to read, even in the outside program. It is better to let students continue to read short stories, novels, or biographies than to offer them radio plays like "The Rock," "Out of Control," "The Hitch-hiker," "The Snow Goose," and "One Special for Doc," typical of the anthologies. However exciting some of these may have been on radio or television, they are flat and unprofitable reading. Possibly the in-class program for the ninth grade should include one or two fine one-act plays, to be read aloud and discussed, perhaps just before *Julius Caesar.* Plays like Chekhov's *The Boor,* Dunsany's *A Night at an Inn,* Synge's *Riders to the Sea,* often placed in the twelfth grade anthology but more appropriate for the ninth, Glaspell's *Trifles,* and Lady Gregory's *The Rising of the Moon, Spreading the News,* and *The Workhouse Ward* may stimulate students to try a collection of good one-act plays independently.

After the ninth grade the outside choices in most genres increase yearly, and during the twelfth grade they are unlimited. If sophomores study *Romeo and Juliet* in class, they should manage *As You Like It* on their own. If juniors read *Macbeth* in class, they should manage O'Neill, Wilder, Anderson, Miller, Williams, Goldsmith, Sheridan outside. If seniors read *Hamlet* or *King Lear* in class, they should be able to manage any play from Sophocles to Ionesco. If sophomores read *The Scarlet Letter* in class, they should be able to read the Brontés, Scott, Eliot, Dickens, Austen outside. If juniors read *Moby Dick* and seniors *Crime and Punishment* in class, they should be capable of Hardy, Conrad, Faulkner, Thackeray, Flaubert, Balzac outside. The ablest and most ambitious can take on *War and Peace;* all should be able to handle *Anna Karenina.*

In discussing the ninth grade outside program, we deliberately avoided mentioning poetry and essays; perhaps even few sophomores should read in these genres outside of class. But poems, essays, and books of ideas should be included on the outside list for juniors and seniors. If juniors study a few poems by Dickinson, some may be moved to read her complete works; the same is true for Robinson, Frost, Wordsworth, Tennyson, Whitman. If seniors read Book I of *Paradise Lost,* the ablest should try the whole poem outside; others may follow up with Shelley, Keats, Browning. If the Prologue and two stories from the *Canterbury Tales* are read in the original in class, some seniors should read the whole collection in a modern version. If two or three essays by Emerson and Thoreau are read in class, some students should undertake the whole of *Walden.* Bacon's essays, some of which should be read in class in each high school year, might be read as a collection by juniors and seniors. Essayists like Tomlinson, Orwell, Chesterton, Mencken, Leacock should do admirably as whole-volume undertakings in the upper years. Juniors and seniors should read outside a substantial number of critical essays, usually in connection with works being read in class. Wordsworth and Arnold on poetry, Hazlitt, Coleridge, Shaw on Shakespeare, Sainte-Beuve on classics, Virginia Woolf on "How to Read a Book," Pater on style, contemporary critical studies of individual novels will help to illuminate a particular subject of study in class.

The separation of inside and outside programs not only permits concentration in class on absolutely first-rate works that need the joint attention of teacher and class but also allows for much freer range in outside choices. The outside list should include works that otherwise would not be read at all or only in fragments. Franklin's *Autobiography* is regularly represented by only three or four pages in the anthologies, and these sample pages are presumably to be *taught.* But in fact books like the *Autobiography* should not be taught at all; they should be read, not in samples, but in complete form by students on their own. There is no literary point in introducing students to three pages of Franklin; there is at most only historical point. But there is literary point in reading the whole *Autobiography.* In recent anthologies *The Diary of Anne Frank* is sometimes similarly represented by a few entries. But, again, the book needs no teaching; it should be read outside, as a whole. The outside program is also the place for Dana's *Two Years before the Mast* and Parkman's *The Oregon Trail*, both often represented by mere scraps in the anthologies. These are not books to teach; they are books to be read more freely. Ambitious seniors can take on Cellini's incomparable *Autobiography*. They can read modern lives of people like Michelangelo, Leonardo, Rembrandt, Renoir, lives of poets, statesmen, scientists. They can read *whole* books instead of the snippets to which the anthologies limit them.

Though we have illustrated it only briefly, the outside program as we intend it is of far greater scope than that associated with the traditional book-report system. Our outside program rests on the assumption that the in-class program will be precisely that: in-class works will be read and discussed in class, with few home assignments except in the case of long novels. Freed from the task of preparing in-class works for discussion next day, students can be expected to read more extensively outside.

In the past, "book-report reading" has rarely had any connection with the "regular" reading that was carried on both in class and out. While *Julius Caesar* was being read, one student might be reading *Little Britches* for a book-report, another *Up from Slavery*, another *Annapurna*, another *Kim*, with thirty students reading as many different books, none related to *Julius Caesar* by time, genre, topic, theme, or otherwise. In contrast, what we intend is that some kind of relationship be maintained between the inside and outside programs so that they will reinforce each other. The relationship can be flexible in order to permit wide range of choice. While a novel is being read in class, students might choose to read independently any other novel, another novel by the same author, another novel from the same period, a life of the author, short stories by the same author, any works having a thematic or even topical affinity. While *Romeo and Juliet* is being read, students could choose another play by Shakespeare; another play from any period; a life of Shakespeare; a novel like *Kenilworth*, with an Elizabethan setting; a novel like *Wuthering Heights*, with a tragic love story; the complete collection of Shakespeare's sonnets. If *Moby Dick* is being read, students might choose other novels and stories by Melville, like *Billy Budd*, *Redburn*, *Typee*, *Omoo*, *White Jacket*; *Two Years before the Mast*; a volume about famous voyages—Drake, Magellan, etc.; a critical volume like *Call Me Ishmael*; Melville's poems; a book on whaling; stories, poems, essays of approximately mid-nineteenth century America. In practice, the relationship of inside and outside reading can be even looser than these few examples suggest; but some degree of connection is certainly desirable and will benefit both programs.

We have, finally, to consider possible ways for students to report on their outside reading. First of all, the teacher must be aware at all times of what each student is reading. Students who are reading books that bear on the text being read in class can often contribute to discussion when their outside reading illuminates points at issue. Occasionally, when someone has read a work that relates significantly to the in-class text, he should be given five minutes to discuss it. For more formal reporting, many teachers use a card file in which students briefly record their outside reading. But a more interesting and substantial way of accounting is to have each student keep a private log of his outside reading, which is periodically checked by the teacher. Many mature readers keep such a log, in which they jot down not only the gist of a book just finished but personal notes that will best bring details back to mind. The habit, if students will but form it in their high school years, will prove invaluable all their lives. The log serves also as an adequate reporting device.

But the most effective single way of reporting outside reading is through the writing program; this is discussed in the next chapter.

Reading aloud, acting out • In discussing Presentation, we have insisted that not students but the teacher should do the initial oral reading of the text. But, especially with poetry and drama, reading aloud by students is an indispensable activity *after* the initial presentation. Let us look first at poetry.

Short poems up to the length of "Lycidas" should be read twice by the teacher, first without comment, and finally after discussion has been completed. But between these readings discussion creates need for the rereading of parts or in the case of short poems such as sonnets, of the whole. In the course of asking a question or making a point, students often reread lines aloud without being asked expressly to do so. A student whose interpretation differs from that implied by the teacher's inflection in reading certain lines can make his point by rereading them aloud. Probably few moments are more satisfying to teachers than those in which many members of a class insist on reading passages aloud in just the way *they* think they should be read; their insistence means that they have become involved. Often the teacher can help create these productive moments by deliberately raising a question on certain lines. Take, for example, the opening line of Browning's monologue:

> *That's my last Duchess painted on the wall* . . .

Remembering the occasion of the poem—the Duke's meeting with the Count's representative to make final arrangements for acquiring a *new* Duchess—how should the line be read? Indeed, which word in the title should bear the stress? Or take the first line and a half of Arnold's final stanza in "Dover Beach":

> *Ah, love, let us be true*
> *To one another!*

The problem is to hit the precise inflection for "us" and "true"; if one remembers that Arnold goes on to say, in effect, "for the world—isn't," the emphasis comes clear, and the whole poem is unified in an instant. All fine poems, whether great resounding ones like Milton's or minor-key ones like Emily Dickinson's, contain such lines, and part of the problem of understanding is to find the precise inflection. Student discussion of poems can be exciting when there is repeated rereading of parts to unlock meaning; reading aloud in order to make a point about meaning is far more satisfying to students than reading aloud at the teacher's command, merely for the practice of reading aloud.

Reading aloud from stories, essays, and novels, too, is most satisfactory when it is done in the normal pursuit of meaning or making a point about the text. When, for example, students discuss the characters in a novel, one way to have them support their contentions is to ask them to read the relevant passages; this method affords them practice not only in reading aloud but also in using evidence.

But it is drama that affords the best opportunity for large-scale experience in reading aloud. We insisted earlier that the teacher do the first reading of a play with students following in their texts. We should now complete the argument: the study of a Shakespearean play should not be considered finished until *every student in the class* has read several hundred lines aloud.

One way is a rapid rereading of the entire play with students taking turns in the roles. If there is not time to read the whole play, students can read through major scenes, with narrative bridges supplied quickly by teacher or students. Besides giving substantial practice, this admirable method reassembles the play after the fragmentizing study that has taken several weeks. The method is subject to one notable abuse: teachers often choose the best readers for the big parts, leaving the scraps for the meek and insecure. It is true that hearing great passages read by feeble readers is a trying task; still, the meekest boys in class should have their turn with Antony and Shylock and the meekest girls with Rosalind and Juliet. In the initial reading, this method would destroy the likelihood that anyone would gain an aesthetic experience from the play; but the second reading serves a different purpose.

Another method is to have students stand in front of class for a token acting-out of selected scenes. Overnight preparation is necessary if students are to be reasonably effective. This method puts emphasis on the performing experience; it serves less well the other purposes of quick reading and rapid review.

A third way, more elaborate, allows students in groups to choose scenes they would like to present before the class. The groups themselves assign or choose parts and manage at least one rehearsal. Shakespeare's plays contain many scenes—the casket scenes of The Merchant of Venice, the husband-wife scenes of Julius Caesar, the death scene of Romeo and Juliet, the discovery of Duncan's murder in Macbeth—in which two to six people have strong parts, with action, business, and a sense of wholeness in a small unit. These productions take time, but they acquaint students with some elements of drama that they otherwise miss. Here again, an abuse of the method lies in limiting weaker students to weak roles while class leaders get the plums. Sometimes it is possible to place a student in two acting groups, with a minor role in one and a major in the other.

Memorizing • Though memorizing has long been out of fashion, many teachers always have students learn poems by heart.

That memorization should have been neglected during the past thirty-five years is understandable, for memorizing lines of poetry was incompatible with free reading in indiscriminate texts, incompatible also with other activities in an activity-centered program. In an atmosphere of panel discussions, parliamentary activities, dynamic group discussion of Johnny Tremaine, mass media activities, make-believe telephone conversations, and practice in "using the language of guest-host relationships," an assignment to commit "When in Disgrace" to memory could have meant only one thing to students: their teacher had gone mad. But with the in-class program of combined close reading and discussion of great texts that we have described, the activity of memorizing is in perfect harmony.

What should students memorize? When should they memorize? And above all, why should they memorize?

They should memorize many poems of sonnet length,

a few of the length of "Dover Beach," and passages from longer poems like "Lycidas," "Tintern Abbey," and "Prufrock." They should memorize fifty or more lines from each Shakespearean play they read. There is no such thing as a particular poem that they "must" memorize, though probably no one who memorized the opening of the Canterbury Prologue through "Whan that they were seke" ever honestly regretted doing so.

Short poems that are read, reread, and thoroughly discussed are already half-memorized. The great sonnets of Shakespeare, Milton, Wordsworth, Keats, Elizabeth Browning, the Rossettis are so well composed that one word brings on the next, one line the next, one movement the next; when one has firmly grasped the main idea, the precise language, with the prompting of rhymes, almost supplies itself. After thorough discussion, half an hour's concentration followed by overnight jelling and occasional checking will fix a sonnet in the mind forever. The great passages from Shakespeare's plays are among the easiest in the language to memorize, and students who prepare a scene for acting in front of the class can often take care of the memory assignment simultaneously.

"Checking up" on memorization is always a problem. To save time, teachers often have students write a poem from memory; but it is a waste and a chore to write out, rather than speak, a poem. At the opposite extreme, teachers give several class meetings over to individual recitation; but this painful ordeal can make a shambles of the whole program. A better way is to break the class into groups of five or six, with each student saying his poem for other members of his group; every student can be heard in twenty minutes with a minimum of strain for speakers and listeners alike. Some teachers improve this method by having each group choose one speaker to record his poem to be played back to the whole class. The system works as well with passages from plays as with poems.

Finally, why should there be any memorizing of poems and passages? We should remember that poetry is in large part "the way it is" because it was originally composed to aid the memory of the speaker; hence the experience of memorizing affords a special insight into the elemental nature of poetry. But if we are really to justify memorizing, we must relate this activity to the primary "why" of studying literature. We have upheld the power of art to affect the innermost being, and this principle governs all our decisions about Arrangement, Introduction, and Presentation. Memorization is the ultimate degree to which all our methods can be carried: it aims at literally incorporating certain works of art in the being. The closest reading and the fullest discussion are, in a sense, only approaches to this end; it is the final act, commitment to memory, that seals the artistic force inside and gives it there, over a long period of time, its best chance to work.

Library study, vocabulary study • Doubtless students need experience in finding books in libraries and experience in using wanted information from these books and periodicals. They also need steady stimulation for vocabulary growth. In the following chapter on Composition, we shall relate library experience to the study of literature. Just now we shall consider only "vocabulary work."

Typical "Grammar and Composition" texts include sections headed "Vocabulary Study," "Using the Dictionary," "Word Study." These sections usually claim twenty to thirty pages in each volume of a series, or about one hundred pages in a four-year series. In addition, many schools use a second series of vocabulary workbooks which include lists of words to be looked up and used in some sort of assigned exercise. And, finally, series workbooks for each grade, though they chiefly emphasize exercises in punctuation, sentence structure, and other mechanics, regularly include also a section of exercises for vocabulary development.

These three sorts of textbooks would seem to provide amply for direct action on vocabulary, quite apart from the study of literature. However, the effectiveness of "direct attack" on vocabulary through word lists is strongly suspect. Anyone who has learned a foreign language knows that the *massive growth* of vocabulary does not come through the memorization of words in lists, duly defined at the head of the lesson, but afterward, in the course of extensive reading. Granted that at first we need to learn *le crayon, la plume:* the best way to acquire a large French vocabulary is to read French copiously—unless, of course, one resides in a French-speaking community, where the ear will prove even better than the eye, at least up to a point. In using workbook exercises and word lists with students of English, we are proceeding as if these students were in the very first stage of learning their language, at the point of *le crayon* and *la plume.* But of course native English speakers of high school age are far beyond the point where word lists can bring significant growth. What will do that is steady reading in first-rate books.

What is here proposed, therefore, is total abandonment of "vocabulary work" in grammar and composition series, vocabulary booklets, and workbook series, the enormous time thus gained to be spent on reading.

Do we mean that no deliberate study of words, no deliberate effort at vocabulary development, should accompany the reading and discussion of texts? We certainly do not: attention to words is the first necessity in close reading and discussion. The first objective of reading and discussion is meaning, and meaning is founded first on words. It would be folly to discuss the images in a poem or the symbols in a story with students ignorant of the words that compose the images and symbols. Care for the meaning of words—which often involves considerations of etymology—is properly the initial step in discussion. Some teachers appoint a different student each day to manage "the big dictionary"; when the reading of a poem is finished and discussion begins, his job is to supply whatever authority is needed. Reading at home, students should be advised to keep a dictionary always at hand.

But now that we have categorically dismissed vocabulary workbooks and unrelated vocabulary exercises of every sort and have placed the great responsibility for vocabulary development upon the close reading and discussion of literary texts, we need to add a word of caution.

Among the many ways of ruining the experience of a work of art, one of the deadliest is to approach a poem, story, or other form as though the main object were a vocabulary lesson. Teachers have been known to pass out dittoed copies of Tennyson's "Ulysses" with words underlined "to be looked up and used in sentences"; they might as well have distributed the list of words without the poem—in which event they might as well have used a vocabulary booklet in the first place. They have been known to assign Galsworthy's story "Quality" for home reading, distributing a list of "study questions," the first of which is "What new words did you learn from this story? List them, and use each in an original sentence." They have been known to assign the first act of A Midsummer Night's Dream with a list of instructions beginning "Watch for any unfamiliar words. Look them up in the dictionary, and copy the definitions in your 'Notebook of New Words.'" Worse still, a common practice of teachers is to extract from each scene in a Shakespearean play every word that is likely to be unfamiliar and to have students look up and define these words before they read the scene. Even Shakespeare cannot survive this treatment.

The aesthetic experience of Tennyson's poem and Shakespeare's play cannot, indeed, survive any such brutal treatment. The experience of art is fragile, touchier than a seismograph, shyer than Wordsworth's violet. Any gross approach intimidates it, and these approaches are gross beyond measure.

Zeal for vocabulary development is commendable, but not at the expense of the experience of art.

Recordings, films, film-strips • We have insisted that the time to use recordings, films, and film-strips is after, not before or during, the initial presentation of a work. The "first round" with any work should involve teacher, students, and a written text, with the teacher, not a machine, controlling the text. This close-knit group resents the intrusion of any outsider into its intimate doings. But after class and teacher have done their utmost, professional recordings can enrich the experience of the work. With poems there is no problem; short poems can be heard in a few minutes, and longer ones easily within one class period. With a Shakespearean play, however, the problem of time is severe. One purpose in using a recording of a play is to hear the whole in as short a time as it would take for performance. Several weeks of line-by-line reading and discussion, necessary for understanding, rob a play of that major part of its force that depends on the speed with which it is experienced. In three hours *Macbeth* builds momentum that yields a mighty impact; in three weeks, the concentration of its power is dissipated. If it is true that any work of art represents a concentrated experience, the description seems peculiarly apt for the effect of tragedy: when we receive a lifetime of experience in three hours, we know we have had something done to us.

Unfortunately, it is impossible to play a three-hour recording in a forty- or fifty-minute class period. An uncut recording of *Hamlet* takes a week of class meetings; the "two hours traffic of our stage" of *Romeo and Juliet* takes four meetings. Though students are assured of hearing dramatic poetry well read, they miss the force of concentrated experience that is possible when the sweep of action is uninterrupted. If the first class period ends in the midst of the balcony scene of *Romeo and Juliet,* the spell is broken, and after twenty-four hours of thinking about other matters no class is ready to start the second day's meeting on the high pitch of emotion to which the play had lifted them the day before. Juliet's

> *Thou know'st the mask of night is on my face,*
> *Else would a maiden blush bepaint my cheek*
> *For that which thou hast heard me speak tonight* . . .

will fall on ears attuned to last hour's biology discussion and to five minutes' hallway bedlam—ears quite unprepared for the sudden onslaught of passion.

Teachers can avoid breaks in the middle of high dramatic moments, or, the next day, can replay a little to let the dramatist build to his peak again; but this way takes time, and the essence of the problem is to avoid extending the performance. Some teachers use recordings that hit only high spots in the great plays; it is possible to do *Hamlet* thus in two meetings. The trouble is that it is during the low spots of a Shakespearean play that the audience is prepared emotionally to encounter the high spots.

Teachers sometimes devise means of keeping a class together for three hours—a Saturday morning, an evening at someone's home, a special dispensation to use a whole Friday afternoon for the English class. Ways can be found, if the teacher's will is strong enough.

We also argue against the use of a filmed play or novel before the original is read. Not the least valuable part of the experience of reading a great work is that of creating one's own images from what the author supplies in the text. One's personally imagined Hamlet, faulty as it may be, is the product of a process that cannot take place when one is supplied on stage or film with a physical Hamlet in the shape of Olivier or Burton, complete to the last details of hair, eyes, ears, nose, and mouth. To prevent students from imagining their own Hamlet, Rochester, Heathcliff, Ahab, Micawber, Jean Valjean, Karenin, or Becky Sharp by confronting them first with the physical features of actors is to deny them creative experiences. To one who has seen Olivier as Heathcliff before reading *Wuthering Heights*, a personally imagined Heathcliff is forever impossible. Olivier is no doubt a finer Heathcliff than the reader is capable of imagining, but that is not the point.

But Olivier, Burton, and even Orson Welles do no harm to the imagination when they are seen *after* students have evolved their own images through reading and discussion.

The same is true of film-strips, available for nearly every major literary figure, work, age, or locale. The excuse for using these devices before reading is motivation: get them interested in the Shakespeare Country, the Elizabethan Stage, the Wessex country, Puritan New England, whaling ships, Dickens' London, Hugo's Paris, the Lake Country of the Romantic poets, the Brontë moors, the white cliffs of Dover, the Canterbury route, or Mississippi riverboats —and *then* take up the play, novel, or poem. But a work that needs a film-strip to arouse interest is a poor work, and the teacher who needs it is a poor teacher. The time to use film-strips is *after* reading a work, not before. Film-strips need the motivation of great artistic works more than great artistic works need the motivation of film-strips.

Testing • The best thing that students can get from litera-ture, enhancement of their own humanity, is unfortu-nately hardly testable, at least not with enough accuracy to suit the necessities of grading. The best that the teacher can do is test the understanding of works and trust that if understanding has been gained, the work has at least had a chance to affect the being. That the emphasis of testing should be on works themselves rather than on the factual peripheries—period, biography, characteristics of genre—goes without question here: all that we have said about Selection, Arrangement, Introduction, and Presenta-tion points toward this conclusion.

The main burden of testing, aside from daily discus-sion, is borne by the writing program. What students say about works in class and what they write about them in their compositions should together constitute the "testing program," and should give ample evidence for the de-cisions that teachers eventually have to express with stark symbols. The varieties of writing experiences we shall explore in the next chapter.

But we should not leave the immediate subject without one or two mild and possibly unexpected words in behalf of the much-maligned objective test. For years it has been heresy for an English teacher to confess to the use of true-false, fill-in, multiple-choice, and similar testing de-vices; other teachers might be suspected of using these, but the English teacher—never. Since the English teacher, if no one else, is expected to make students *write*, ordinary sense demands that he avoid tests in which they do not have to write. We have no wish to dispute the point.

Nevertheless, an informal five-minute objective quiz dictated by the teacher at the beginning of an hour, with answers jotted down quickly by the students can serve multiple purposes: (1) it can get students back on the track after a twenty-four-hour absence from the English class; (2) it can review yesterday's reading, in-class or out, and set the stage for continuing with the text; (3) it can help by re-emphasizing matters previously discussed, underscoring important textual details; (4) it can even serve as a morale builder if it is kept informal and un-burdensome. Many teachers have students exchange papers and mark them as teacher and class together supply answers. This method has the advantage of reviving yesterday's discussion and getting students reinvolved before reading and discussion resume.

What use the mass of quiz grades should serve in establishing the term's grade is for the teacher to decide. Quiz papers should certainly be collected and the marks recorded; if nothing else, they enable the teacher to keep close check on which students are "with it" in the daily reading-discussion and which are lost and need to be drawn more into discussion. Some teachers make a great point of having a show of hands by those who make a perfect score; not the least of the purposes served is that of en-couraging the whole class toward the day that everyone present will be able to raise his hand.

Perhaps even more useful and no more time-consuming is the one-sentence quiz on the reading assignment or discussion of the previous day. The question can be so framed that the response must be cast in the form of a comparatively sophisticated sentence. A general weakness of the writing of even the best students is flimsy sentence structure. These one-sentence responses oblige students to coordinate and subordinate more carefully than they do when they can sprawl their ideas over an entire para-graph. It is a comparatively easy matter to correct them, assign a numerical value from one to ten, total them at the end of two weeks, and assign a letter grade. If the teacher announces that the quiz may deal with absolutely any detail in the reading assignment but that students should feel free to ask questions about matters that are not clear, the number of probing questions and the ensuing discussion that will precede the quiz will be as valuable as the quiz itself.

Chapter 8

What about composition?

What should they write about?

What should students write about? This is not only the first but the last and the perennial question that confronts students, teachers, program planners, textbook authors. If the energy annually spent in "thinking up topics" could somehow be stored in a giant battery, the Atomic Energy Commission could disband.

Before we discuss the question, we should quickly survey typical writing assignments in typical widely used grammar and composition textbooks. Here are a few from a ninth grade volume:*

1. Write a newsy letter to a sick friend or classmate. Be sympathetic and cheerful.
2. On a bus or train, at a station, at a game, at a play, or somewhere else observe an interesting stranger. . . . Prepare an oral or written description that will give your classmates a vivid picture of this stranger.
3. Compare a typical summer day at home with a day you've spent at the beach or in the mountains.
4. Write a theme on one of the following: my hobby, scouting, lifesaving, raising a calf, building a model, making a dress, planting a home vegetable garden, jet propulsion.

Here, again at random, are writing assignments from the twelfth grade volume of the same series:

1. Write a theme on one of the following: bargain hunters, hi-fi as a hobby, new frontiers in science, college

* J. C. Tressler and H. I. Christ, *English in Action,* Course One and Course Four, D. C. Heath and Company, 1960.

scholarships, apartment living vs. home ownership, what makes a happy marriage, places of interest in our community.

2. To a friend or a relative—boy, girl, or adult—write a lively letter.

3. Write an informal essay on one of the following: cats, snakes, bells, the weaker sex, do-it-yourself, family chores, sports cars, family life on television, going steady, beach picnics.

We might continue with hundreds—indeed, thousands —of such examples.* Writing assignments in the tenth and eleventh grade volumes of the series are identical to these in kind, and writing assignments in all other widely used series are similar. What we have seen, therefore, is an incomplete but accurate representation of the high school writing program as it has stood for many years. But there has been a violent reaction against such "theme topics." Many teachers today flatly deny that they use, or could be induced to use, these or others like them. They ignore the textbook topics and devise their own.

The justification given for the use of such topics is similarly uniform throughout the grammar and composition textbooks: students should write about what they know and are interested in. Since students have favorite uncles, pets, hobbies, friends, since they have had experiences in camping, hiking, playing games, baking cakes, flying kites, living in town or country, apartment or house, since they have ambitions, girl-boy and parent-child problems, personal likes and dislikes—all these should furnish the subject matter for exercises in writing.

But this is the underlying fault of all such topics: they can serve only as "exercises in writing." The universal loathing of students for "themes," whether laboriously worked out word by painful word or hastily scribbled off in desperation, is clearly traceable to the writers' own sense that these are only "exercises in writing." All English teachers should follow the example of those who have already eliminated this approach to writing.

* For a detailed account, see *High School English Textbooks: A Critical Examination.*

Let us clarify the issue by exemplifying two basically different kinds of writing assignments. The first is from a twelfth grade textbook chapter called "A Clinic for Paragraphs":*

> In using comparison or contrast, set all the points on one side against all the points on the other; or compare or contrast them one point at a time. . . . Write a paragraph of comparison and one of contrast, using two of the topic sentences below. Proofread your paragraphs. (1) Books offer greater enjoyment than television; (2) A brown winter coat is more practical than a pink one; (3) The plots of all the stories in this magazine are alike; (4) I am like my father in many ways.

The second, of our own devising, may be described thus:

> A twelfth grade class has just finished reading *Hamlet*, IV, 5, where Laertes, armed and furious, breaks down the doors and confronts Claudius with a demand for satisfaction on the score of Polonius' murder. Discussion accompanying the reading has come to a focus on the striking contrast between Laertes and Hamlet as avengers. Some students think that Laertes' fiery entrance and argument with Claudius glaringly show up Hamlet's shortcomings as avenger; others maintain otherwise. As the hour ends, the teacher instructs students to write single paragraphs on the question at issue and announces that reading of two or three of these will open the hour tomorrow. The teacher may present a topic: Hamlet and Laertes as avengers; or pose a question: Does the evidence of the play so far suggest that Hamlet or Laertes is better qualified for the role of avenger? or dictate a topic sentence which allows for choice: Their conduct through Act IV, Scene 5, suggests that Laertes (or Hamlet) is better qualified than

---

* Matilda Bailey, Marcillene Barnes, and Edna M. Horrocks, *Our English Language, Fourth Course*, American Book Company, Second Edition, copyright 1963.

Hamlet (or Laertes) to solve a complex problem of revenge.

Let us consider these assignments in turn. The first is an assignment made in connection with a chapter on the paragraph as a unit of composition. In the section "How Paragraphs Are Developed," students have learned that paragraphs can be developed (1) by details, (2) by reasons, (3) by examples, (4) by comparison or contrast, and (5) by definition or explanation. This information is standard enough, and is, besides, well illustrated by numerous short paragraphs showing development in these ways. But though the world's prose abounds with paragraphs developed in these ways, probably not one was written for the purpose of developing a paragraph by details, examples, reasons, comparison, contrast, definition, or explanation. All were written by authors intent on saying something about something and saying it as clearly and forcefully as they could. If they used details, they did so because details served their purpose. If they used comparison or contrast, they did so because the subject lent itself to development by comparison or contrast. But their purpose was not "to use details" or "to use comparison or contrast."

A paragraph written to illustrate a method of paragraph development is false because its purpose is false. What is worse, it plants in students a false notion of what writing is and why people write. The same objection holds for all types of assignments that approach writing as an exercise in using special devices and techniques: "Write a paragraph in which you use at least three figures of speech," "Write a paragraph in which you use only periodic sentences," "Write a paragraph in which you use vivid verbs." Teachers have been known to dictate ten "spelling words," with the instruction to "Use these words in a theme of 500 words." About what?

To approach writing not by specifying devices to be used but by listing topics like "My Favorite Uncle," "My Hobby," "Our Camping Trip" is only slightly less objectionable. It is from writing on such topics that students acquire their well-known aversion to "theme writing" and to the subject of English. Not only can they think of little to say—they have no reason to say it. Knowing that the assignment is only an exercise, they obediently set down 500 words, and the teacher duly corrects their mechanics and urges them to "get more life" into their compositions next time. But the next set of themes will be just as bad.

After a few years of this, students come to suppose that writing is always an exercise: a "theme" is something written only for an English class. If they ever do learn to write well and with the pleasure that honest purpose makes possible, it will be because they somehow managed to free themselves from the false notion of writing as "exercise."

Now let us examine the second assignment, which asks students to assess the relative qualifications of Laertes and Hamlet for the task of revenge. This assignment grows directly from the continuing classwork; it asks students to continue with a subject they have been discussing, but to do so in writing. The advantage is obvious: the assignment does not, like the other, set writing apart as a special exercise; it emphasizes the close affinity of writing and discussion. It makes the point that people write on the same sorts of subjects they discuss, and they write about them for essentially the same purpose that they discuss them—to have their say about them. Few English classes, one may hope, spend time discussing "How to Train a Dog" or "I Am Like My Father." When, however, they are assigned to write on such topics, they cannot fail to assume that we discuss some topics but write on quite different ones, that we discuss to prove a point but write to have an exercise.

Of course, oral discussion and writing are not identical in their demands. The writer must marshal his material and shape it so that it will be effective without benefit of gesture, facial expression, and voice. But as discussant and as writer the student is pursuing the same goal: he wants to say something about something. Given this sense of writing, students are at least off to the right start.

Yet this is only one reason why teachers should make

literature the basis for composition. Literature is the natural material, at hand, available, abundant—so obviously the natural choice that college teachers are often incredulous when they learn that high school students, though they read and discuss books, write about anything and everything but books. As supplier of substance, idea, and inspiration for composition, literature is inexhaustible. Steadily read and discussed, it steadily feeds the mind; its potential is only half realized if students do not follow up discussion by writing. Literature teems with ideas. It demands that attitudes on important issues be taken, judgments arrived at, views expressed. Was Brutus right in setting the good of Rome above personal inclination? Was Shylock justified in seeking revenge on one Christian for the whole history of wrongs done Jews by Christians? Was Huck Finn's revolt from the attitudes of his society an act for all boys to emulate? Was Milton's decision right: *is* it better to buckle down to duty than to "sport with Amaryllis in the shade"? It is impossible to read great books without confronting fundamental human issues, for these are what poets, novelists, dramatists would have us concern ourselves with. Grappling with these issues is a function of classroom discussion, and writing about them is only a more formal way of grappling with them. Students can write about them with more honesty and conviction than about favorite uncles, taking care of goldfish, or setting up tents.

These issues make composition a more significant experience because they keep students' minds working on the plane of *ideas* rather than on that of physical facts and acts. We shall suggest hereafter "idea" subjects with which the very young and unsophisticated can work: but indeed even these students can debate in writing, at their own level, within their own limits, ethical and moral propositions. If a ninth grader cannot write as profoundly as a scholar about Huck's switch to Jim's side or Brutus' decision to kill Caesar, yet the experience of writing about it is at least as good for the ninth grader as for the scholar. It is impossible to write about such matters without thinking about them, and if one thinks fairly steadily about them, they leave their imprint. A composition program based on literature cannot fail to consolidate some of the effects that the reading and discussion of literature introduce into students' minds.

When should they write?

We must deal with "when" in two senses: first, in relation to time of year; second, in relation to particular works.

For many years, throughout the United States, it was standard practice to separate "English" into halves: one semester for writing and mechanics (spelling, grammar, punctuation, etc.), the other for reading. This arbitrary division is still reflected in the existence and continued use of two entirely discrete sets of textbooks—literary anthologies and grammar and composition volumes. During one semester students read and discuss literature; during the other they write, do sentence exercises, and busy themselves with a wide variety of "language arts" activities. With literature confined to one semester and writing to another, a reading-discussion-composition program conceived and managed as a single program is of course impossible.

Many teachers, even while the semester-semester division was standard, adopted shorter periods of reading and writing. They would read for one quarter, write for one quarter, read again, and write again. Others would read for two weeks, write or do mechanics for two weeks, and so on. In extreme cases, students would read on Mondays, spell on Tuesdays, do grammar exercises on Wednesdays, write on Thursdays, and do "vocabulary work" on Fridays.

But whether it is semester by semester, week by week, or day by day, separation is separation and means that "English" is conceived not as a single program but as several unrelated activities. So long as students read "The Celebrated Jumping Frog" and then write a theme about their favorite uncle, the programs are discrete even if they do both in the same hour. But if they read and discuss the story one day and the next day write a comparison of Mark Twain's humor with Salinger's, then literature and composition are one program. In the next chapter we shall be concerned with making Mechanics a partner in the same program.

In this program, reading-discussion-writing continues throughout the year. Though at times reading and discussion must be briefly suspended in order to get compositions completed, they remain vital because students write about what they have read. In this program, further, there is no occasion to fear that writing will be scanted. The Conant report and other reports have urged the need for greater attention to writing than has been usual in the past, and recently some influential administrative groups have charged that "English teachers just want to teach literature; they don't want to bother with teaching students to write decently"—as though there were no connection. But in our program writing is involved in the teaching of literature, just as literature is involved in the practice of composition. A work is not considered "taught" until it has served both discussion and writing. The whole program flows steadily; no part of it is ever blocked. It calls for steadier attention to composition, throughout four years, than has yet been the case.

We should now turn to our second sense of "when": at what point or points in relation to the reading of a work are students to write? With a short work, or a group of short works, the obvious time to write is after the reading has been completed and discussion has brought issues into focus. But with longer works—novels and plays—it is possible to have students write *before* they read, at many points *during* the reading, and *after* the reading has been completed. Teachers who have converted to this system from the barren program of "themes" on random topics painfully devised and accepted by students with groans have found themselves suddenly overwhelmed with abundance.

FORMS AND MODES OF WRITING
IN CONNECTION WITH READING

Before • In discussing Introduction, we made the point that some teachers, before starting a major work, initiate conversation on a theme or subject prominent in the work. Without mentioning the work itself, they get students to express ideas on this subject orally, and when minds have been sufficiently stimulated, propose a specific subject, or several choices, for writing. A tenth grade class, let us say, is about to start *Romeo and Juliet*. The possibilities are many: a discussion on misunderstandings between parents and children; on the existence or non-existence of "fate"; on feuds between rival students in school, between neighbors, within families, between neighboring towns; on apparent evil bringing about ultimate good. It is impossible to predict what developable subject for writing may grow from discussion of these general topics. The last-named, for example, might evolve into a statement like "Often what first appears to be misfortune turns out to have been a blessing in disguise," which can be offered as topic sentence for a paragraph, the substance of which students will draw out of real or imagined experience. When they have finished, they will no doubt have written a paragraph developed "by examples"—but they will not have set out to develop a paragraph "by examples"; they will have set out to argue their point.

All large works offer similar possibilities of initial discussion, and from the topics that stimulate most interest the teacher should select subjects for writing. A discussion topic need not center on the primary theme of the work to be read, but it should relate significantly enough to the work that discussion and writing will prepare students for the reading that follows.

Short works, too, can be introduced through discussion and writing that, in turn, will stimulate reading. Some teachers appropriate the "point" of a poem before students read the poem, make it the subject of discussion, and end by framing a topic sentence to be developed out of students' own experience. When, having thus tried their hands at the subject, students see how the poet developed it, they may gain a sudden new respect for poets. Again, some teachers pluck a line from a poem—"A thing of beauty is a joy forever"—and offer it as the topic sentence for a paragraph after discussion. The same device works with essays. Bacon's initial sentence, "Revenge is a kind of wild justice," can be used as topic sentence for a paragraph (it will probably turn out to be a paragraph developed "by definition") after discussion and just before reading the essay. Bacon and Emerson are peculiarly rich in such developable idea-sentences.

The possibilities of writing before reading are only hinted by these examples. We should not leave the subject before mentioning a much more frequently used kind of preliminary writing: library assignments in looking up and writing a brief account of an author, an aspect of his period, or the genre represented by the next work to be read. When a tenth grade class is about to read a group of Shakespearean sonnets, some members might prepare a 500-word paper on the history and form of the sonnet. Others might read an account of Shakespeare's life—not a full biography, but such an account as is to be found in an encyclopedia, the *Dictionary of National Biography*, or a volume of the complete works—and write a résumé of their reading. Or a ninth grade class ready for *Julius Caesar* might investigate and write about Shakespeare's life, the idea of tragedy, the Elizabethan theater, or the Caesar-Pompey situation just preceding the assassination.

But we mention this sort of preliminary writing only because teachers often use it. We do not recommend it. It affords an inferior *kind* of writing experience because it involves mere compilation of information rather than development of idea, which involves creativity. Students cannot conceivably learn enough about such topics as these to have anything to say "on their own"; they can only summarize, paraphrase, or directly copy. Further, this kind of assignment constitutes the least desirable form of Introduction to a literary work because it emphasizes backgrounds rather than the work itself. The time for writing of this kind, if there is to be any of it, is not Before, but After.

During • Here we can eliminate short works at the outset: no teacher is likely to interrupt the reading of a sonnet to have students write on a subject that has emerged from discussion of the opening lines. We are concerned here with the kinds of writing that can be undertaken in the course of reading a novel or a play.

Some teachers manage to get a dozen or more pieces of writing from students during the reading of a major work like *Hamlet*. Though each piece is short, the total wordage is considerable. The writing represents serious thought and includes experience with various compositional problems. A special virtue of writing assignments made during the period of reading-discussion is that they are related closely to the continuing oral discussion and thus serve to remind students that writing and discussion do not essentially differ. These assignments avoid the unfortunate "theme" connotation, the mistaken supposition that writing is a special, artificial exercise.

Since *Hamlet* has been mentioned, we can conveniently use it for illustration of possible writing assignments. It is unrealistic to suppose that the specific subjects here named will turn out to be the subjects that teachers and students will arrive at; we have asserted that writing subjects should *grow out of discussion*—and the subject that is brought to a head by discussion in one class will not necessarily be the one that emerges in another. The teacher can so direct discussion as to *make* it come to a predetermined point, but the main feature of the system is sacrificed if he decides in advance that students are to write on certain subjects and no others and accordingly forces discussion toward those subjects. Discussion, if it is to be faithful to the text, must go where it will, and writing should follow its lead.

The very first scene of *Hamlet* provides subjects for a paragraph because it *is* the opening scene, fraught with significance for what follows. One possibility is to phrase a question that will require a succinct digest of the information provided. This suggestion is applicable to all other Shakespearean plays as well. The opening scene is always crucial in what it tells of situation and character, in the mood it creates, and in its preparation of subsequent action. With ninth graders starting *Julius Caesar*, we might ask for no more than an efficient retelling of the action. But with seniors starting *Hamlet* we should use a more sophisticated approach to get at the same kind of review. We can do so by phrasing a topic sentence to be developed into a single paragraph from the evidence of the text: "Past, present, and the immediate future are all represented in the first scene of *Hamlet*." Or we can shift the emphasis to technique and still get a review by phrasing such a topic sentence as this: "In introducing us quickly and fully to the complex opening situation, Shakespeare uses Horatio as a dramatic device." If this topic sentence looks like a stopper, it should be remembered that teacher and class will already have read and discussed the scene, and discussion will certainly have revealed Horatio's usefulness to the dramatist: Horatio, like the audience, is brought into a situation of which he knows nothing, and, like the audience, he is a disbeliever in ghosts; he and the audience see the ghost for the first time together, so that the experience of each is also the experience of the other; then, in the center of the scene, between the first and second appearances of the ghost, Shakespeare has Horatio tell of the past event—the wager in which the elder Hamlet slew Fortinbras—which underlies the whole of *Hamlet*; and, finally, Horatio announces his intention to carry news of the ghost to Hamlet and thus links the opening to what follows. But though classroom discussion should have covered these and other aspects of Horatio's service as a dramatic device, it will have covered them disconnectedly, in passing, so that students still have a compositional problem in bringing them together to form a well-ordered paragraph.

This type of initial writing assignment is neither very exciting nor very demanding. But it serves two purposes: it gets the program of writing underway, and it focuses students' attention on situations from which will flow the action of the play. A more demanding assignment might concern the specific devices by which the dramatist, beginning with the first two lines (when the wrong man, the relief rather than the sentry on duty, demands "Who's there?"), creates the extraordinary atmosphere of tension, mystery, and suspense that envelops the scene. And yet another would attempt the subtlest task of all: it would probe the secrets of the dramatic magic by which Shakespeare, in less than 200 lines, tears us from our familiar world and makes the business of remote medieval Denmark engross our minds. The dramatic craftsmanship of every opening scene in the major plays is expert, but the skill of this one is dazzling. Any writing assignment that focuses attention on dramatic technique is therefore peculiarly appropriate here.

The twenty-two scenes of *Hamlet* can all yield at least one good subject for writing, and many can yield an indefinite number. Obviously students should not be asked to write on every scene, or they will come to think that scenes are read only to motivate writing—a misconception to be avoided at any cost, since the primary object is always the experience of the play as a work of art. The best way to avoid this misconception is to let subjects for composition emerge from discussion. Once reading is well underway, most writing assignments, though they have their point of departure in a particular scene, will require reconsideration of much that has preceded—a distinct advantage because students are thus steadily reviewing.

Especially with *Hamlet*, many writing assignments will turn on character and the interpretation of action in the light of character. Writing assignments developed from discussion tend to center on the perennial question of Hamlet: his delay. A series of writing assignments will inevitably bring this question into focus repeatedly. "Why does Hamlet delay?" is implied in the question "Why does Hamlet decide to put on an 'antic disposition'?" "Why does he devise the 'Murder of Gonzago' scene?" gets at the same underlying question. "Why, just after he has elatedly fixed on the 'mousetrap' device, do we find him debating the question of suicide?" raises it again.

"Why can he not bring himself to kill the king in the prayer scene, although, a few moments later, he can strike a vengeful rapier through the curtain into what he thinks is the king's body?" again questions the cause of the delay by probing the character of the man who does the delaying. A series of such questions leads straight to the final scene: "Why, knowing that the king is bent on killing him, does Hamlet accept the challenge of the fencing match?" "Why, at last, can he kill the king when he never could do so before?"

But the play is not *all* Hamlet: Claudius, Gertrude, Ophelia, Polonius, Laertes, Horatio, and Fortinbras, although they function mainly in relation to the story of Hamlet, also offer subjects for writing. The easiest, least satisfactory, and most frequent type of assignment instructs students to "write a character sketch of Ophelia" —or Polonius, Gertrude, Horatio, Laertes. This kind of assignment gives no focus for composition and invites "mere writing" rather than composition, whereas, to repeat an example cited earlier, "Laertes is better qualified than Hamlet to carry out a task of revenge" *directs the writer to assemble the evidence needed to demonstrate the assertion.* His final answer may be quite wrong, in another writer's judgment—but his composition will have unity and coherence because he has aimed to make the point in which *he* believes. "Polonius gets exactly what he deserves"—if that is what some students want to argue after discussion of Act III, Scene 4—will produce pointed and coherent writing about Polonius; so will "Polonius is the unfortunate victim of circumstances beyond his control." But "Write a character sketch of Polonius" will produce a dull and rambling piece of "mere writing," and the writer will learn nothing about composition.

Such assignments are most appropriate for long works. Preferably they call for single paragraphs rather than "themes" consisting of a dozen or more alleged paragraphs that often contain only two or three sentences each. They should ordinarily run to nearly a page. They can be written at the end of a class period, or they can be started near the end of a period and completed at home; the next day's meeting can begin with reading of two or three by students before they are handed in. So used, they unite the study of literature and the practice of composition. They should be a staple of the English program from the ninth grade through the twelfth.

We should not leave this particular form of writing, however, without stating what is possibly its greatest virtue. These experiences should do much toward building in students a sense of responsibility for *honest* writing, writing that supports and advocates what is true, or what the writer believes to be true. Here again we assert the necessity of preceding writing with discussion: discussion should explore possibilities of wide variety, but it should lead at last to thesis statements that students honestly believe they can support with evidence because they believe them to be true: "Polonius gets exactly what he deserves" should *not* stand as the topic sentence for a student who does not believe it to be true; such a student should adjust the statement until it expresses what *he* believes is true.

If it did nothing else, this approach to writing would nurture integrity. The usual "writing exercises" never imply that students should associate writing with truth: an exercise is an exercise, and "truth" is involved only in reporting honestly how many words the student managed to write. If students can be brought to understand writing as existing to express and support truth, they will have mastered something more than mechanics.

After • With writing done after a work has been read through, we shall be concerned with all genres, the short as well as the long; and, in addition, we shall be mindful of out-of-class as well as in-class reading. Let us begin, however, with long works, once more using *Hamlet* to illustrate.

Reading and discussion are finished. A round dozen of substantial paragraphs have already been written. What more is appropriate? Many teachers like to conclude the study of a major work with an essay that involves the structure of the entire work. Such an essay serves as a method of serious review in the course of which students perceive much that was missed in day-by-day reading; in this way, they consolidate their experience of a whole work of art. In addition, they may find new interest and even pride in writing.

Obviously, if writing a single essay is to accomplish any of these near-miracles, the subject must be well-chosen. Above all, it must be one that the student—with suggestive direction from the teacher—has claimed for himself. One way *not* to handle the situation is for the teacher, on the last day of reading *Hamlet*, to hand out a list of a dozen topics with the instruction, "Choose one and write an essay of 2,000 words due next Friday."

A better way is to advise the class early in the reading to be alert for problems of personal interest. Daily discussion uncovers all sorts of possibilities. By the end of Act I a student may have taken a fancy to imagery. As he reads along with everyone else, noting and discussing all aspects of the text, he also conducts his special study of this particular element. He begins marking lines, passages, jotting down notes, keeping a close, private record. He becomes aware of recurrent patterns, perceives that certain speakers tend toward favorite images, finds that images tend to cluster, at certain points, around prominent ideas. By the end of Act V, he will have, at the least, a collection of factual data; but if he has been both thoughtful and lucky, he will have much more than this: a tentative theory about the imagery of *Hamlet*. He may be able to state a demonstrable thesis: "In *Hamlet*, Shakespeare's choice of imagery helps to define the character of the individual speaker." If his observation has been accurate, his thesis should be true; and if its truth holds up under further examination, he should be able to assemble the evidence that demonstrates it. If, thereafter, he goes to the library and consults Spurgeon and Clemen on Shakespeare's imagery, he will be able to do more than merely read and copy out the data provided by these scholars. He will go to them knowing what he is looking for—further illumination of a subject about which he already has some definite ideas. He is in position to use secondary sources properly and honestly, as tests of and supplements to his own observations. He may find that Spurgeon and Clemen offer genuine aid and comfort for his own theory. He may find that their evidence forces him to modify his thesis. He may even find it possible to modify *their* conclusions. But whatever he finds, he will do more than summarize and paraphrase.

This approach to "the long paper" differs fundamentally from that of passively accepting the bald, thesis-less topic "Imagery in *Hamlet*," with instructions to "go into the library and look up all you can find about it."

But it differs more drastically still from the type of "long paper" assignment that is regrettably in even more common use. All major grammar and composition textbooks include chapters variously headed "Writing the Research Paper," "The Investigative Report," "The Term Paper," "Preparing the Long Paper." Section headings of such chapters commonly include "Choosing the Topic," "Narrowing the Topic," "Gathering Material and Listing Sources," "Taking Notes," "Organizing the Material," "Writing the Paper," "Preparing the Final Copy." That high school students, at least as early as the eleventh grade, should get experience in finding and using secondary materials and in writing a "long paper," complete with footnotes and other scholarly paraphernalia, goes without argument; the experience is, even, an indispensable element of the English program, a "must" for college preparatory students and valuable for others as well.

But the experience should not be approached as an exercise in "Writing the Long Paper." Like all other activities of the English program, it should grow from a center. Too often, a senior class that has finished reading *Hamlet* finds that the next item in the course outline is "Writing a Research Paper." Accordingly, the teacher instructs the class to lay aside *Hamlet* and take up the grammar and composition textbook. There, in Chapter 12, they find the headings listed above. One page lists thirty possible topics, among them these: Auto Design, Cancer Research, Guided Missiles, Educational Television, High School Athletics, The Olympic Games, New Discoveries in Medicine, Opera, Plastics, Skin Diving, South America, Texas. Each student selects a topic; then, during the next two weeks, he follows the steps of the outlined instructions, from "Narrowing the Topic" to "Preparing the Final Copy." He has then "had" his experience with the Research Paper and goes back to literature or on to grammar. The research paper is thus an unrelated episode.

Many of the "long papers" thus prepared may prove mechanically superior to that in which our student attempts to explain his own theory of Shakespeare's use of imagery in *Hamlet*, for they are limited to concern with the mechanics of collecting and organizing information, whereas the latter involves the development of idea. It is not impossible that in the process of compiling information on "Plastics" some student will formulate a theory of his own about "Plastics" and that he will then be directed, in the presentation of his research, by this thesis. In that event, he may at last even have something of his own to say about the subject. But his chances of doing so are negligible. Nothing about the topic or the manner of his undertaking it suggests that having something of one's own to say is relevant to the purpose.

The long paper is also useful in connection with the outside reading program. In the past, reports on outside reading have been typically brief and mechanical. The traditional book report outline—author, title, setting, principal characters, summary of plot (or other content), and evaluation—is designed to allow students to report quickly and teachers to check quickly. Some such mechanical device is probably indispensable if all outside reading is to be duly reported. The objections to the form are two: it is merely mechanical and it invites plagiarism. The long paper used in connection with the outside reading program goes much beyond this form and should be manageable at least twice in a year. Let us see how it works.

While students and teacher are reading *Hamlet*, students on their own are reading various works, all of which have some connection with *Hamlet*. Mainly, perhaps, they are reading other plays—Miller, Shaw, Sheridan, Ibsen, Williams, Anderson, Wilder, Wilde, Goldsmith, O'Neill.

The teacher has suggested that they watch, as they read the outside play, for a subject that relates it to *Hamlet*. The subject may concern techniques of characterization, creation of atmosphere, use of irony, moral and ethical attitudes, themes, big ideas. For the student who has read *Hamlet* and a nineteenth-century comedy like *The Importance of Being Earnest*, significant points of comparison are less evident than, say, between *Hamlet* and *Macbeth* or even *Hamlet* and *Death of a Salesman*. But *Hamlet* and *The Importance of Being Earnest* are both dramatic in form, are staged, have characters, action, settings—and in each case the hero has a problem. Further, *Hamlet*, though a tragedy, contains abundant comic elements in language, situation, and character—as many, in fact, as are to be found in most comedies, not excepting Wilde's. The chances of identifying a fruitful subject for an essay linking even these two dramatic opposites are therefore real enough.

The same holds for linking outside reading, through essay assignments, with other in-class genres. When teacher and class are studying *Pride and Prejudice*, probably the outside reading will be dominated by novels, including others by Jane Austen. Some novels on the list may be related to *Pride and Prejudice* through their use of irony, some through their characteristics as novels of manners, yet others through period. A profitable essay might be written on the "worlds" of a widely divergent pair: *Pride and Prejudice*, with its tightly ordered social universe, *Wuthering Heights*, with its wild setting and wilder passions that defy order. Are these so discrete that a writer would end by having two separate essays on his hands rather than a unified one? One of the most exciting challenges that composition can offer is that of uniting matters that seem poles apart: does not the common femininity of Jane Austen and Emily Brontë, after all, impress itself on their violently contrasting novels? Class discussion will often turn on Jane's orderly, highly civilized milieu; but does nothing ever happen that betrays the existence, in this tight circle, of romantic impulses that will not be excluded? Students who think seriously about

these two violently contrasting works will eventually find
a thesis that they can support—and both the discovery
and the composition can prove an exciting, creative experience.

We now turn from plays and novels to short works—
poems, stories, essays.

A tenth grade class has just finished studying Shelley's
"Ode to the West Wind." Discussion has probed the
meanings of word, line, and stanza; tone has been considered; imagery has been discussed in relation to meaning; the various manifestations of Nature have been re-
marked: the wind itself, the leaves, clouds, waves. Some
students have likened Shelley to Wordsworth as a poet
of Nature; others, though admitting the ubiquitous presence of Nature in the poem, argue that this is not Words-
worthian, not a "Nature poem" at all. The dispute eventually becomes a central issue; finally, the teacher writes
two assertions on the board:

1. Since every stanza is packed with references to Nature,
   from "Wind" and "Autumn" in the first line to
   "Winter" and "Spring" in the last, "Ode to the West
   Wind" can best be described as a Nature poem.
2. Though stanzas are packed with references to Nature,
   "Ode to the West Wind" cannot properly be called a
   Nature poem, because it is not essentially *about* Na-
   ture.

Students choose the statement they prefer and are free to
reword the thesis statement to correspond with their idea of
what is true.

An assignment of this kind is possible when discussion
has centered on a debatable proposition. It would be absurd to suppose that discussion will always lead to an
exciting point of departure for composition: sometimes
the teacher will have no choice but to rely on "standard"
directions: "Write a paragraph in which you explain the
symbolism of the poem." "Write a paragraph in which
you explain the relation of the last two stanzas to the first
three." "Write a paragraph in which you explain 'O
Wind, If Winter comes, can Spring be far behind?' in

the light of the rest of the poem." "Write a paragraph in which you show how Shelley 'uses' Nature to make his true point." All these topics involve some of the same elements of the poem that the "assertion" assignments do, and certainly they are superior to assignments like "Read reference material on the life of Shelley and prepare a brief written report" or "Read reference material on 'The Ode' and write a brief report on its characteristics and history"—though even *these* are preferable to setting Shelley's poem aside and assigning a "theme" on favorite uncles or making ice cream. The "explain" topics, however, give students no *focus* for composition and no purpose except to "explain." The "assertion" assignments do give focus, and they give the most effective kind of purpose, that of inducing others to see and to believe what the writer sees and believes.

Let us turn to a second genre, the short story. A ninth grade class has just studied de Maupassant's "The Necklace." Even the unsophisticated ninth graders have felt the shock of Mme. Forestier's devastating final remark: "Oh, my poor Mathilde! My necklace was paste! It was worth at most five hundred francs!" They see that the story would end flatly but for this unexpected twist and are content to let this reason suffice. It is the teacher who must introduce an idea new to these readers: in a good story even a surprise twist is prepared for; if not, the end is merely cheap, like Mme. Forestier's beads. To demonstrate, the teacher leads them back to re-examine Mme. Loisel's character. An astute student may remark that she resembles Miniver Cheevy, dissatisfied with her lot. Bit by bit they piece the portrait together. They find that though at first they had noticed nothing special, de Maupassant in fact took pains to expose specific traits of character in this woman. Why did he do so? Why did he not instead make her just a normal, honest wife? By now, most students assume that the teacher will direct them to "Write a character sketch of Mme. Loisel." But the teacher has a little surprise of his own. After the discussion, he writes on the board: "It is through his precise characterization of Mme. Loisel that de Maupassant renders the final twist artistically appropriate." The assignment calls for a paragraph developing this topic sentence. It will certainly involve "character sketch," but it will be a character sketch with point. Students will not merely write; they will compose.

We turn finally to the essay—the genre often used as a basis for writing in connection with literature even by teachers who do not otherwise have students write in connection with literature at all. The essay treats ideas directly, in expository prose, as students themselves are expected to do when they write; the relation of essay reading to essay writing is therefore obvious. Typical college anthologies used in freshman composition courses include essays only (though recently some have added other forms), and high school anthologies that offer suggestions for writing do so more consistently for essays than for other forms. The basic assumption of our program, however, is that students will write in connection with all genres. Though appearances would lead us to the contrary conclusion, there is really little more reason to write an essay in connection with an essay than to write one in connection with a sonnet or a tragedy. The essay has one obvious advantage over other forms, namely, that it *is* the form that students themselves use, and it therefore serves automatically as a model. But the degree to which teachers should encourage students *deliberately* to use other writers' essays as models is debatable. Certainly students should analyze the process of idea development in the distinguished essays read in class—not only in order to understand what the author says but to learn what they can of method. The most convenient way to have them understand what it is that *they* are expected to produce is to confront them with great examples of the form. But to say that they should study the techniques of essayists is not to say that they should model their own composition on a particular essay. If they do so, they will only be engaging in an "exercise." To say "Write an essay, modeling your technique on that of Huxley in 'On a Piece of Chalk,'" or "Now that you have read Orwell's 'Politics and the English Language,' write an essay in which you develop your ideas in similar fashion" is to mislead students with that false purpose to which we have objected so often. Though more sophisticated, the instruction is basically as faulty as "Write a theme in which you use at least three compound-complex sentences." No writer actually sets out to use compound-complex sentences, though all mature writers use compound-complex sentences in the course of expressing their ideas.

There is also a second reason not to instruct students to "write like" the essayist they have just read: the essayist's manner may not be right for the student or for our time. A famous professor always advised his freshmen to study Bacon's thought and style minutely, but added, "If you write like him, I'll flunk you." Much the same can be said against writing like any other great essayist. Not only are writing styles personal; they change from period to period. Celebrated nineteenth-century essayists like Hazlitt, Pater, and Stevenson wrote well, but not as we would have students write. Hazlitt looks archaic, Pater excessively "fine," Stevenson too literary. Emerson's great "Self-Reliance" is a collection of provocative profundities, and any contemporary student who composed so loosely would deserve to fail.

These strictures apply less to first-rate essayists of our own time. Though these write in a wide range of personal styles, all are "right" for our time, and we could wish nothing better than that our students learn to write like them. Should we therefore have students read contemporary essays only, so that all can serve as models for writing? Certainly not. The usefulness of essays as models for composition is indisputable, but this is the least important reason for including them in a reading program. Ironically, the exclusive use of contemporary essays damages not only the reading program but the writing program itself, since it encourages the deliberate use of them as models for writing with the result that writing is approached as "exercise" rather than as development of ideas.

We should not leave the essay without an illustrative writing assignment that does not make an "exercise" of writing. A tenth grade class has just read and discussed

Bacon's "Of Wisdom for a Man's Self." Most members have been irritated by Bacon's contention that it is more acceptable ("tolerable") for a ruler ("sovereign prince") to act in self-interest than for a private citizen to do so. Brought up in a democratic society, they find this idea in conflict with our sense of the public official as the servant of the people. But further discussion of Bacon's idea (perhaps supplemented by the teacher's reading a speech from *Hamlet*, III, 3, "The single and peculiar life is bound . . . Never alone/ Did the king sigh, but with a general groan") opens the possibility that a sovereign prince might indeed act only in self-interest and yet prove himself a faithful servant of the people. The teacher provides a topic sentence that allows students to argue either way: "Bacon's contention that acting in self-interest is acceptable in a high public official is (is not) compatible with the democratic concept of the official as servant of the people."

WRITING IN CONNECTION WITH READING: A SUMMING-UP

Our quick tour of writing assignments before, during, and after reading, with only one or two specific illustrations for each genre, can hardly have done more than scratch the surface. We have not touched, for example, the possibilities of writing in connection with *groups* of works arranged thematically. But obviously a unit having an anti-war theme, and including a novel, a pair of short stories, an essay, and half a dozen poems, offers opportunities for comparative writing and synthesis. A unit having to do with love, including Bacon's irritating essay set amid seven or eight works in several genres all extolling the virtues of what Bacon calls "this weak passion" that "doth much mischief," should provide a variety of springboards from which students can develop their own ideas.

Further, our illustrations represent only two forms of composition, the paragraph and the essay. These choices have been deliberate, the intention being to emphasize the forms that should be the staple of a writing program.

The advantages of paragraph writing as the day-in, day-out staple cannot be exaggerated. First of all, because the composition is short, it can be written quickly by students and graded quickly by teachers; thus class and teacher can handle many paragraphs in a semester. Second, the paragraph is the ideal unit for grasping the meaning of *composing* as opposed to mere "writing." Students learn little about composing by writing rambling papers of a thousand words in which paragraphs are undeveloped and in which there is neither unity and coherence, nor emphasis. The teacher's best standing injunction to students is "Write less, and better," and the paragraph unit best implements this direction. Students gain a sense of the *whole*, without which there can be no composition, only writing. In reading first-rate essays, they should discover that an unfolding idea is an exciting experience; and through writing paragraphs they should eventually find that *making* an idea unfold is even more exciting.

A paragraph is a whole composed of sentences; an essay is a larger whole composed of paragraphs. In moving from paragraph to essay, students should be taught that the topic sentence stands in relation to the paragraph as the thesis statement, or thesis paragraph, stands to the essay. The elements within the paragraph and the elements within the essay cohere for the same reason: they relate to the whole that they develop. If the sense of the whole, the *idea* being developed through the parts, is clear to the writer, coherence will take care of itself; this is the main concept that can best be grasped through writing paragraphs from *given* ideas expressed as topic sentences: "Revenge is a kind of wild justice." This does not mean that students should spend the ninth and tenth grades writing paragraphs before attempting essays in the upper years. They should write both paragraphs and essays throughout four years; but the ratio should be twenty paragraphs to one essay.

Nor does this emphasis on the development of ideas through paragraphs and essays mean that students should write in no other forms. We should now consider "writing in connection with reading" in a different perspective.

"Writing in connection with reading" is not synonymous with "writing on or about reading." When we have students write a critical analysis of character or poetic techniques, for example, we are indeed having them write "on or about" the work, and it is this that students should do most often and that we have illustrated.

But what if we have them write a paraphrase of a passage in *Romeo and Juliet* or make a précis of "Self-Reliance," or write a narrative summary of the first scene of *Twelfth Night*, or prepare a dramatic adaptation of Galsworthy's story "Quality," or devise a parody of Poe's "The Raven"? Clearly, these are not ways of writing "about" a work, but are rather ways of "reproducing" an original; and though none ought to be a staple of the writing program, all have their uses and some should be frequent.

Paraphrasing enthusiasts (rarely students) argue that the paraphrase (close, literal rendition in the student's own prose) forces accurate reading of a text and requires economy and precision of expression. In proper paraphrase, the writer is faithful to the tone and spirit of the original, omits nothing, keeps the original emphasis, and avoids personal comment. Paraphrasing is thus an exacting discipline for both reading and writing. It works best with poems and short passages within poems and plays, especially Shakespeare's. There are various ways of using it, one of which follows. Students and teacher are reading *Henry IV*, Part I. Normally, after reading through an extended passage, students and teacher paraphrase orally, to make sure that everyone understands, before continuing. But occasionally the teacher may vary the pattern. He reads through Prince Hal's speech ("I know you all") at the end of I, 2, a passage indispensable to the understanding of Hal's conduct through what follows. Then he gives students fifteen minutes to paraphrase in writing. Students should be advised that they are not to begin "In this passage Prince Hal says that . . . ," but are to use first person. Individuals then read their efforts aloud, and difficulties are ironed out. The teacher should certainly collect the papers and check them as "in"; he should rarely grade them, but he will find them extremely useful in identifying students with serious troubles that might not become evident in oral discussion. A variant of this practice is also useful. Though usually teachers will not make advance reading assignments in Shakespeare, it is sometimes good to experiment by having students read through the next scene overnight to find how well they can manage. At the next meeting, the teacher may assign a key passage in the scene for paraphrasing. After several students have read their efforts and discussion has clarified the passage, these paraphrases should be collected and, unlike those in the former illustration, should be graded.

The limitations of paraphrase are as definite as its virtues. First, it is frankly an exercise, and we oppose assignments that encourage students to think of writing as exercise. Second, it is perverse in that it requires students to unmake the beauty that a poet has wrought by reducing it to literal and often inept statement. Third, it forbids creativity, for the student must add no thought, feeling, or attitude of his own. And fourth, it is hated by students because it is exacting labor that ends in something inferior to the original. These disadvantages would ordinarily be enough to condemn any writing device. But here some of the faults work in reverse, too. By rewriting an artistic passage in plain prose and comparing the result with the original, students may become suddenly appreciative of the beauty of the original. Further, by recognizing how far short of a total poem even the best literal statement falls, students may gain an insight into the mystery of the poet's comment that a poem "should not mean, but be." When these values are added to the disciplinary services rendered to both reading and writing, paraphrasing may be found worthy despite its limitations. But it should not be used too often.

Much the same holds for the précis, a first cousin of the paraphrase. It has the same limitations as the paraphrase and approximately the same virtues. It is entirely uncreative, for students are permitted to contribute nothing except wording. It differs from the paraphrase in that it attempts to distill the thought of the original, whereas the paraphrase records literally; accordingly, a paraphrase often runs longer than the original passage because it takes more words to reproduce what the poet wrote, whereas the précis shrinks the original and should rarely be more than one-fourth its length. The paraphrase is most often used with poetry and drama, but the précis works best with expository prose. A typical assignment is this: "Write a careful précis of 'Self-Reliance' in the space of a single page." Students who rejoice at the prospect of writing only one page will soon learn that it is much harder to reduce "Self-Reliance" to one page than to six.

Teachers sometimes use the précis for a more specific purpose. Students who have paraphrased Prince Hal's speech at the close of *Henry IV*, I, 2, are then immediately instructed to write a précis of the same speech. If this assignment seems like mere busy work to students, the need is apparent enough to experienced teachers who have observed that students can paraphrase a passage accurately, word for word, and yet have no sense of what the passage as a whole says. The précis serves as a corrective; it is impossible to write a satisfactory précis without understanding the original.

The remaining ways of "reproducing" an original need little comment. The narrative summary should rarely be used beyond the ninth grade. A typical assignment is this: "Retell in your own words the story of *A Midsummer Night's Dream* to the end of Act I." Adaptation (as from narrative to dramatic form) and parody not only allow but require a degree of creativity. Groups of students working together sometimes adapt a short story or a chapter in a novel to play form for performance before the class. Parody should rarely be assigned to a whole class; but a talented student can use the form to whet his sense of style or to express his sentiments about a work of dubious literary quality.

From writing "on or about" literature and "reproducing" originals, we turn finally to a third general class of writing in connection with reading that we may call writing "out of" literature.

Teacher and eleventh grade class have read and discussed Browning's "My Last Duchess." This superb dramatic monologue ends as the Duke and the Count's representative prepare to separate, having, presumably, settled details of the Duke's impending marriage to the Count's daughter. In the poem, the Count's man says nothing, is left uncharacterized, expresses no attitude. What manner of man is he? What will he report to his master, now that he has glimpsed some dark qualities of the Duke's character? His report can be made the subject of an original monologue. If students wish, they can write it in blank verse; but of course they should write in prose if verse intimidates them.

Any of Browning's dramatic monologues can be used similarly as a springboard for original composition: "Andrea del Sarto" can be the basis for a monologue with Andrea's wife speaking confidently to her "cousin" about her husband. "The Bishop Orders His Tomb" can spark a new monologue that begins directly after the Bishop's death, with the favorite son, Anselm, "child of my bowels," doing the talking.

These are illustrations of a kind that is widely adaptable. Writing "out of" literature offers a multitude of possibilities, usable with all genres. At one extreme, representing examples of writing done very "close" to the original, students might write their own essays on parents and children after reading Bacon's "Of Parents and Children." At the other extreme, they might take off from a mere suggestion given by half a line in a poem or play to write an essay. Between these extremes, the possibilities are endless. Students might write, in narrative or dramatic form, a "missing" scene from a Shakespearean play: what did Fleance do after he escaped Macbeth's murderers? What of Shylock's immediate reaction when he returns to discover Jessica's elopement? What of Horatio's promised accounting, to Fortinbras and the Danish court, of the events that led to the bloody ending of *Hamlet*? What of Malvolio's departing threat, "I'll be revenged on the whole pack of you"? The possibilities are as numerous as the situations that abound in literature.

These are rather "far out" ways of writing "out of" literature. They should not serve as a staple of the composition program, and no students should be required to undertake such flights, nor should any enthusiastic student be permitted to indulge in them to the exclusion of more prosaic experiences with the development of ideas. Chaucer, Spenser, Shakespeare, Milton wrote "out of" their predecessors' works throughout their careers, whether they were using a bawdy Italian tale or the Bible as the source. It would be harder to name a dozen authors who never wrote "out of" literature than to name a hundred who did. Raleigh's "Nymph's Reply to the Shepherd" was written "out of" Marlowe's "The Passionate Shepherd to His Love." One of the great sonnets of the language was written when Keats first looked into Chapman's Homer. We may even imagine that *Bleak House* was written "out of" just three words of Hamlet's soliloquy: "the law's delay."

We emphasize again the distinction between "writing in connection with literature" and "writing on or about literature." The charge is often made that using literature as the main basis for composition means confining students' experiences too narrowly. The validity of the charge would at least be arguable if our intention were to have classes write nothing but literary criticism, to have them write always "on or about" literature. Even so, the charge of narrowness would be essentially false, since literature itself is infinitely broad. But the charge is doubly false when we include writing "out of" literature, for then there are literally no limits. Here literature provides the impetus, but the student's own experience provides the material.

Chapter 9

. . . And mechanics?

The term "mechanics" is often used in a very narrow sense: under this term, one widely used textbook includes only four items—capitalization, abbreviations, writing numbers, and italics. More commonly, punctuation is included also; sometimes the term is stretched to embrace everything having to do with correct and effective sentences.

Here we shall stretch it even further to include all the *formal* aspects of composition, from those that pertain to the whole composition down to those that have to do with the single word.

Mechanics comes last in this book, not because it is least important, but because that is where it comes in the constantly revolving pattern of the English program: students first read and discuss a work of literature; they next write in connection with their reading; and finally they and the teacher discipline what they have written. Disciplining means the application of mechanics to the composition in all its aspects, the final act of the writer.

Though Shakespeare was said never to have blotted (corrected) a line (Jonson: " . . . would he had blotted a thousand") and some twentieth-century novelists appear never to have reread their untidy outpourings, the manuscripts of most good authors look like battlegrounds. The moral is plain: if mature writers find rigorous disciplining of first drafts necessary, immature writers must learn that it is indispensable. It is true that as writers increase in skill they learn to do much of their disciplining simultaneously with the initial expression, even automatically. We would hardly expect the professional writer to leave such gross matters as agreement of subject and verb, capitalization, and reference of pronouns unconsidered until the final draft; the mature writer's later disciplining consists of finding the more precise word, the more revealing detail, the more potent image, the more effective order of elements in the sentence. But immature writers need to discipline their expression consciously even at the level of subject-verb agreement and pronoun-antecedent relationship. They do not automatically spell correctly, punctuate consistently, properly attach their modifiers, or keep elements parallel. Because they do not do these things automatically, they cannot do them simultaneously with writing the first draft without diverting much of their mental energy from idea to mere mechanics. The more regularly they write, the greater the number of mechanical problems they will become capable of solving automatically. But the process cannot be rushed. It is useless for the teacher to admonish, "Now, this time, solve all your mechanical problems as you write."

Rather, we suggest that the teacher should regularly advise, "Get your thought down somehow, anyhow, without diverting energy to the mechanics. Once you have it down, discipline it." This is the principle that underlies the following treatment of Mechanics.

THE MECHANICS OF THE WHOLE

The standard device for disciplining the whole composition has been long in use and is well known. It is the outline. Textbooks mark the following steps:

1. Select a topic.
2. Narrow the topic.
3. Gather the materials.
4. Outline.
5. Write the paper.
6. Revise and rewrite.

We suggest, instead, the following steps:

1. Select a topic.
2. Study the details related to the topic until a developable idea about them is formed.

3. Phrase the idea pointedly as a thesis statement, or write a tentative first paragraph ending in a thesis statement.
4. Resurvey the material, this time with the thesis in mind, and jot down relevant details.
5. Write the first draft as rapidly as possible.
6. Outline the paper as it stands.
7. Correct the outline, re-ordering points as necessary, and resurveying the material to add developmental detail.
8. Rewrite the paper from the corrected outline.
9. Proofread, checking all details and rewriting where necessary.

Most differences in these two sets of steps are superficial, but one is basic: the first set requires application of mechanical discipline (the outline) *before* the first draft is written, whereas the second does it afterward. It should be added that when the textbooks say "outline" they mean no informal jotting of random notes, but a formal device elaborately developed to represent details. It is possible that human beings exist who can write effective prose by expanding the main, sub-, and sub-sub-points of a detailed outline; it may also be that some topics lend themselves better to this approach than others do.

But for most people, and for most subjects, this approach is ruinous. At best it produces a woodenly correct performance that exposes all too conspicuously the outline that dictated every step; at worst it results in a lifelong aversion to writing. With his outline before him, the student scratches his head for something to say beyond the fact itself, which is already expressed in the outline. The wells of his imagination dry up. After writing out in sentence form what was represented by a word or a phrase in the outline, he finds that he has exhausted *that* point. He would like to start a new paragraph and go on to the next point, but he dares not: one-sentence paragraphs are bad. He finds a way, ultimately, to restate the substance of the first sentence so as to make a second sentence. Relieved, he then proceeds to the next point.

When he reaches the bottom of the outline, he knows that he has written dully and painfully. Later the teacher will praise his "clear organization," but will give him a C "because you seemed to have nothing to say."

At any cost the wellsprings must be kept flowing. If waiting until after the first draft before making a formal outline helps in that respect, the writer should wait.

But is he to have no guidance in selecting and organizing his material? On the contrary, he is to have a better guide than an outline. Step number two of our approach to composition calls for students to ponder their materials until they get an *idea* about them and then to phrase that idea as a thesis statement. It is this that will control the selection and tentative arrangement of details.

The difference between "writing on a topic"—which one does in following an outline—and "developing an idea"—which one cannot do until he *has* an idea—is a crucial one. Given an idea, one no longer has only "a topic to write about"; he has a *subject to develop.* We can illustrate the difference by referring to a writing argument suggested in an earlier chapter. Students have been reading *Hamlet,* and one of them becomes especially interested in its imagery. He advises the teacher that he will write on "Imagery in *Hamlet.*" The teacher approves his topic and directs him to take the next step: an outline. Confident that he is doing right, he proceeds as follows, listing examples under each capital letter in parts I and II:

    I. Kinds of Imagery in *Hamlet*
       A. Metaphor
       B. Simile
       C. Personification
       D. Synecdoche
       E. Metonymy
       F. Others
   II. Imagery Used by the Main Characters
       A. Hamlet
       B. Claudius
       C. Polonius
       D. Gertrude

E. Ophelia
F. Laertes
G. Horatio
III. Conclusion
    A. Abundance of Imagery
    B. Varieties
    C. Used by all Characters

With this outline before him, the student assumes that he is ready for the biggest step of all: the actual writing. He sets out bravely and in due time produces 1,000 words, all faithful to the outline. It has been laborious work, and somehow, along the way, he has lost his interest in imagery. But he has followed instructions and therefore supposes that his effort has produced a good essay. But of course it has not. The "essay" is part survey, part catalogue. Most of his paragraphs are only a few sentences in length and consist of a quoted example or two, followed by a gratuitous comment: that images are "especially interesting" or that they "make the speaker's point very effectively." As composition the paper is a total loss. There is no coherence, no emphasis; the only unity is that of topic: everything included is about "Imagery in *Hamlet*." What is much more unfortunate is that the student has learned nothing at all about composition; he has written, but not composed. Worse still, he does not guess that there *is* a difference between writing and composing.

With a different kind of instruction, the student can have a meaningful experience. When he decides to write on "Imagery in *Hamlet*," the teacher does not say, "All right, make an outline," but "All right; now, what do you have to say about the imagery of *Hamlet*?" "Well," says the student, "I just want to write about it. That's my topic." "You can write about it," replies the teacher, "as soon as you find what it is that you want to say about it. Study the play until you find what you think is true and what you can demonstrate."

For all students who previously have jumped directly from topic to outline to writing, the change is drastic. What the new step involves is thinking: not "topic to outline to writing," but "topic to idea to composing." Ultimately, thoughtful study of the text yields an idea about imagery in *Hamlet*. "I believe," says the student, "that in *Hamlet* Shakespeare makes the images appropriate to each of the main speakers. Gertrude's images are different from Ophelia's, and Hamlet's are different from Claudius'." "Now," says the teacher, "you are on the edge of having something to say about imagery in *Hamlet*. Keep trying to phrase your idea exactly as you want it, and keep testing it by examining the text." Eventually the student is ready with a thesis statement: "The imagery in *Hamlet*, because it is appropriate to each speaker, helps to define character."

Proceeding to write, the student now has direction for the selection and ordering of detail. If he adheres to his own thesis, he will not say random things about certain images being "interesting" and others being "effective." He is not merely "writing about imagery"; he is demonstrating how imagery defines and differentiates character.

No formula for composition will produce a flawless result on the first try, nor will the student's problems of achieving unity, coherence, and emphasis be solved forevermore: each new composition will mean a new problem. But this approach has the merit of giving the student a chance to *compose*, because he now knows what he is doing. When he jumps directly from topic to outline to writing, he cannot know what he is doing—he is merely doing. He cannot achieve a "whole" if he does not know what the whole is; and the topic and outline together fail to suggest even that he ought to try to achieve one. Without *idea*, there can be no "whole" to strive for.

The foregoing example calls for a long essay on a complex subject. But the principle is the same as that involved in writing a single paragraph from a given topic sentence. If the teacher assigns a paragraph on "Hamlet and Laertes as Avengers," he gives a mere topic. Given this topic, students will aimlessly set down all they can think of about it; they will try to "cover" the topic with random details. But if they are given a topic sentence—"Hamlet (Laertes) is better qualified than Laertes (Hamlet) to undertake revenge"—they start off with an *idea* that controls selection and arrangement. The topic sentence dictates what is relevant and what is not, whereas the topic invites mere rambling.

In earlier chapters, wherever a brief writing assignment has been suggested as illustration, we have expressed it in the form of a topic sentence for a paragraph or a similar, positive assertion for a longer paper. It is recommended that most writing assignments take this form instead of the traditional "topic." Working regularly from a topic sentence, students come naturally to think of writing as a process of developing an idea; they form a habit of composing rather than a habit of merely writing. The latter habit is hard to break; it is better never to let it be formed.

But as a check teachers should occasionally start students off with a bare topic: "The Moon in *A Midsummer Night's Dream.*" Having written a series of paragraphs and longer compositions for which topic or thesis sentences were given, will they now study the text and evolve an *idea* before starting to write? Or will they set down the topic as title, blithely overleap idea, and fill up their pages with random comments and undeveloped paragraphs about moon imagery, the moon at beginning and end of the play, the "Pyramus and Thisbe" moon? Chances are that 90 per cent of the class will do just this. But two or three students, deliberately or by happy accident, may make an *assertion* about the moon and then stick to the demonstration of their assertion. The difference between these papers and all the others can be pointed out, and the next time perhaps half the class will compose rather than write. That is excellent progress.

Nevertheless, the habit of writing from a thesis is not easily formed, and careful control of the first few assignments in the semester will save many hours of student anguish in front of blank paper and as many hours of teacher anguish over poor writing. Use of a simple mimeographed form, to be filled in and approved by the teacher before actual writing of the composition, may at first seem like busywork but will, in fact, make the writing process more meaningful and easier. The form should include the following items: (1) topic; (2) thesis sentence; (3) tentative topic sentences for each paragraph; (4) concluding sentence; (5) title. This form avoids the dangers of the conventional outline, which, in inexperienced hands, tends to promote only a frantic searching for an item B to match an item A, accompanied by gnawing fears that item I is less important than either item A or B under it.

This composition plan, if carefully constructed and revised under direction by the teacher, reveals automatically several principles of composition that students tend to ignore: (1) the distinction between topic and thesis is predication, an assertion about the topic; (2) paragraphs must be ordered according to a principle; (3) no paragraph should appear that does not have a relationship to the thesis sentence; (4) the conclusion, the most emphatic part of the composition, should follow from what precedes.

Like any other tool, this plan has a limited usefulness, and when that usefulness is outlived, it should be abandoned. Once students have grasped the principles it embodies, they no longer need it and should not be obliged to use it mechanically. When that time arrives—and for some students it never does arrive—the plan becomes as unnecessary as parsing each sentence to be certain that subject and verb agree. However, when compositions of a class show weaknesses in organization and unity, the plan should be revived. It can also provide an excellent framework for revision.

THE MECHANICS OF THE SENTENCE

Our use of the term "mechanics" in the title of this chapter implies an attitude toward the large body of materials broadly classified as "grammar." The implication is that grammar is not an end in itself, but a means, and therefore should be studied not as an end, but as a means. We do not disbelieve in grammatical knowledge, for without it students are helpless to resolve a large number of mechanical problems that inevitably arise in the course of expressing themselves. In using the term "mechanics," we mean to underscore the idea of functional or, better, *focused* grammar. In disciplining the paper that he has written, the student applies whatever elements of grammatical knowledge are relevant to a particular problem—such as a dangling modifier. Mechanics is thus not grammatical knowledge in general, a body of forms and uses learned by the student; it is grammatical knowledge focused on a particular problem of expression.

Our conception differs markedly from the traditional one of "formal grammar." It was this traditional conception that led to the enormous "grammar and composition" textbooks, filled with countless pages of definitions, examples, rules, and exercise sentences, and to the practice of allowing approximately one semester each year for the isolated study of "grammar"—which meant identifying gerund phrases, naming parts of speech, underscoring subjects, verbs, modifiers, all, presumably, with no real purpose except acquisition of knowledge of these elements. Not only did this traditional form of study make no connection of "grammar study" with the study of literature, it also made virtually no connection between grammar study and the practice of composition. It has proved wasteful and all but totally ineffectual.

Our conception differs even more drastically from that of the "New English," in which one or another strain of "linguistic science" plays so large a part. The materials of traditional grammar, if they are taught specifically toward the end of equipping students to discipline their own writing, contain the potential for doing just that; they have largely failed because they have not been taught toward that end but toward their own end. But the materials, methods, emphases, and purposes of "linguistic science" appear to contain no such potential and could not be brought to bear on specific mechanical problems even if that were made a deliberate intent; indeed, the term "linguistic science" would then prove a misnomer. The purpose of "linguistic science" is descriptive only and is inevitably irrelevant to and incompatible with the application of mechanics as a means of disciplining expression. Conceivably "linguistic science" should be represented by its own course in high schools; or it might be made a formal part of the social science program at the twelfth grade level. But it is distinct from, and should be kept carefully separated from, the English program of literature and composition.

Let us now see what implications our conception of "mechanics" has for procedure. We have earlier stated as a principle that students should discipline their writing *after* the first draft has been completed, rather than try to discipline it as they go and thus divert energy from thought to mechanics. But in a literature-centered program, when and how are they to get the knowledge needed for disciplining sentences? And what knowledge *is* it they need? Should the literature book be laid aside one semester each year and the grammar book taken up? If so, there will be nothing to discipline, hence no apparent need for the knowledge. Disciplining textbook sentences—other people's sentences—is a mere exercise, and concentration on mere exercises is wasteful. It is their own sentences that students need to discipline, and if they are to have sentences of their own, they must write; and if they are to write something other than exercise-paragraphs "developed by comparison and contrast" and exercise-themes about their favorite uncles, they must read. The literature-centered program has no beginning or end, but continually revolves. Literature feeds composition, composition involves sentences, sentences require disciplining, and disciplining demands knowledge of mechanics.

By the beginning of the ninth grade, students should have surveyed the parts of speech, the elements of the sentence, the conventions of punctuation and capitalization. They should have learned to spell the words of their own vocabularies and should know the principal parts of verbs. As all experienced teachers know, few students at this level have mastered these mechanics. But they should have surveyed everything, and a surprising amount of what they have learned to do has become automatic. Though they are capable of botching sentences in many ways, of punctuating and spelling badly, they do have an acquaintance with subjects and predicates, with adapting verb forms as needed, and with writing in general. They can write, and what they now require is not the formal repetition of basic instruction—the resurveying of parts of speech, elements of the sentence, principal parts of verbs, and so on—but rather a steady practice of writing and of disciplining their writing.

Throughout the high school years the teacher should rely on students' own writing to furnish the basis for operations, *with a single handbook for reference use all four years.* The main responsibility for disciplining the writing of students, and ultimately the only responsibility that counts, is the students' own.

Does this method relieve the teacher of responsibility for dealing with grammar and other mechanics? On the contrary, the teacher must work harder than ever, but not in the traditional way. The usual way has been to teach exactly the same items, year after year: the parts of speech, the elements of the sentence, punctuation, spelling, principal parts of verbs—over and over again. If from all this tedium emerged a worthy result—the ability of students to discipline their own writing—we should never question its appropriateness. But student papers reveal that countless hours given to work of this kind is largely wasted. And because the aimless repetition of it turns students against the very thing they are supposedly working to perfect, we must conclude that the labor is worse than wasteful; it is harmful.

The hours saved from endless meddling with textbook exercises are better spent in writing and in disciplining writing. Let us assume that ninth grade students, reading *Julius Caesar,* have written a paragraph in the last fifteen minutes of the hour, developing this topic sentence: "Cassius works in various ways to turn Brutus against Caesar." Having written without a thought to mechanics, being intent only on getting everything down that is relevant, they are instructed to take their paragraphs home and, by class time next day, to put them into the best possible form. They are to inspect each sentence individually, to check punctuation and spelling, using the dictionary to correct both spelling and word choice. They are to read and reread what they have written, preferably aloud, improving transitions, pruning here and there, making sure at last that their writing says exactly what they want it to say in the best way possible. Some teachers tell their students to "edit" their writing as though it were to stand in print for all time.

Next day in class the teacher has three or four paragraphs read aloud and briefly discussed. And precisely here is a crucial point: they should be read aloud by the writers and discussed by the class, not as "exercises in the paragraph," but for what they have to say about one of the most important stages in the development of *Julius Caesar*, the winning of Brutus to the conspiracy. As soon as the paragraphs have been collected, teacher and class should go right on with the text of the play. At all cost, the teacher should preserve the students' sense of the purpose of writing, not as exercise but as illumination of a subject. If this sense is lost, the class may as well have written an exercise in "developing a paragraph by means of examples."

The students have now done their best to discipline their writing; the teacher's turn is next. The earliest papers in the ninth grade will reveal troubles in every department of mechanics. Some students will have run sentences together and will also have punctuated subordinate elements as if they were sentences. There will be dangling and misplaced modifiers, faults in agreement of subject and verb, shifts in tense, errors in the principal parts of verbs, faulty parallelism, misspelling, eccentric punctuation, improperly indicated quotations, wrong words, ambiguous reference of pronouns.

At this point the teacher will be tempted to put *Julius Caesar* aside, suspend further writing, and start a six-week review: parts of speech, sentence elements, punctuation, spelling. He should not do so. He should mark the paragraphs as clearly as possible, return them to students to rewrite and place in their notebooks (both copies, the original and the rewritten version), and, next day, assign a new paragraph: "Brutus finally decides to join the conspiracy, not merely because of Cassius' prompting, but as a result of decisions dictated by his own character." This set should be treated as was the previous set. Many teachers use the highly effective device of the "composition notebook," which at the end of the year includes all that the student has written and rewritten. Review of this folder during conferences can be extraordinarily useful.

But now we must concern ourselves with a very difficult problem: What if, when their marked papers are returned, students cannot understand what the teacher's correction symbols mean and therefore are helpless to rewrite? The problem is difficult because of the number and variety of risks involved. Suppose that on returning the first set of papers the teacher undertakes to run through the full list of "errors" contributed by the class as a whole, explaining what "dangling modifier" means and what grammatical information is needed to prevent it; what "agreement" means and what knowledge is needed to prevent errors in it; perhaps forty categories of error need to be treated. A thoroughgoing analysis of the faults and their remedies will require laborious classwork over a period of two to three weeks. The reading of *Julius Caesar* and further writing experiences are suspended while this remedial work is going on. The program is interrupted and probably ruined. Furthermore, the weight of emphasis suddenly shifted to the correction of mechanical matters will inevitably produce exactly the misconception that should be avoided, the notion that writing is "exercise" in which one strives to avoid errors. Finally, the chances are excellent that, no matter how thoroughly the teacher has tried to explain everything, the next set of papers will again run the gamut of errors.

The necessity is to keep the main program of reading and writing going forward with a minimum of interruption and at the same time to equip students with the mechanical knowledge needed in their continuing task of disciplining what they have written and are now to revise finally. Here the handbook is indispensable. Teachers should select a handbook that covers the mechanics clearly and succinctly. It should include—as good ones do—a table of "correction symbols," keyed to specific sections in the volume. To spare himself and the students needless difficulty, the teacher should adhere faithfully to these symbols in marking papers or make perfectly clear any variations he finds useful.

If the student finds "dm" written in his margin next to the sentence, "Finding letters that had been thrown in through the window, it was Brutus's final decision to kill Caesar," he can check the table of correction symbols, turn to the appropriate section in the handbook, and eventually correct his sentence. A handbook, like a dictionary, is a reference book to which one goes for a definite kind of help needed to solve a particular problem. It is not a classroom textbook to be "taught out of" with the expectation that specific bits of the broadside of information will chance to hit the mark. The handbook should be at the student's elbow while he is revising and especially when he is remedying the faults identified by the teacher.

This use of the handbook places the responsibility for mechanics where it should be: on the individual student. It also focuses handbook information where it should be focused: on the precise spots at which the student needs help.

Do we really mean that teacher and class should not spend hours, weeks, months each year repeating the "grand tour" of parts of speech, elements of the sentence, capitalization, punctuation, spelling? Do we really mean that they should abandon the grammar-composition textbook series and the workbook series, with their endless rounds of definitions, examples, and exercises? We do indeed. From the ninth grade on, mechanics should not be permitted to claim half of total class time as though they were the *positive* subject matter of the course. They are only negative and should be kept in their place, which is, so to speak, in the kitchen.

Removal of mechanics from a position as positive subject matter in the classroom frees an additional semester each year for the reading of literature and the oral and written discussion of ideas that emerge from reading. The gain is enormous. At the same time, placing responsibility for mechanics on the individual student through his need to discipline what he has written results in more significant improvement in writing than the traditional method has accomplished. Removal of broadside instruction and repeated drill from the classroom implies no lessening of the teacher's concern for students' handling of mechanics. On the contrary, if the teacher is to succeed in getting students to accept personal responsibility for disciplining their writing, he must make his concern unmistakable. Mainly, he does so through the marking of papers.

Two basic questions need discussion here: (1) Should he, from the outset, mark all errors, or should he first concentrate on a few major flaws, turning attention to others only after these have been eliminated? (2) What weight should he give mechanical errors in determining the grade on a paper? Let us say that a ninth grader developing a one-page paragraph from the topic sentence, "Titania fully deserves (does not deserve) the cruel trick played on her by Oberon," misspells eight words, mispunctuates at ten points, dangles two participles, commits four faults in grammatical parallelism, runs two sentences together, writes two incomplete sentences, omits three apostrophes, makes three errors in subject-verb agreement, misplaces a modifier, shifts twice from active to passive voice, uses the wrong case form twice, uses pronouns twice without clear antecedents, writes three sentences in which the meaning is ambiguous.

Abundant as they are, all these errors should be marked even in the student's first composition of the semester. With the exception of the "unclear" sentences, all can be remedied by reference to handbook or dictionary. In marking some errors, the teacher will need to do more than merely place a correction symbol in the margin. Though dangling modifiers can be underlined, misspellings circled, and faulty parallelism noted, comma punctuation requires something more explicit. In the case of an omission, it is advisable both to underline the point at which the comma should be placed and to identify the rule by citing the number assigned it in the handbook. So much is easy. But what of overpunctuation—often more common than underpunctuation? If the teacher simply draws a line through the inappropriate comma and records in the margin "no p.," little is accomplished; the student has nothing to look up in the handbook, and presumably he will continue using unnecessary commas in future compositions. Though some handbooks and textbooks include, along with their rules for the use of commas, a list of "do not's," a full list of "do not's" would be virtually endless. Students must master the relatively short list of "do's" for commas and be instructed to use *no* commas besides those authorized by the list.

There is an even greater value in rigorously limiting students to the use of a standard set of comma rules. The practice of patching up clumsy sentences with extra commas in order to make them intelligible, instead of reconstructing them, is well known to all teachers. A final comma rule in some textbooks states: "Use commas where they are needed to make the meaning clear." This vicious rule actively promotes bad writing by authorizing the use of commas to make the otherwise unintelligible intelligible. By insisting that students use no unauthorized commas, the teacher can use the set of comma rules like a lever to enforce improvement of structure. But how induce them to stay within bounds? At least one teacher is known to have had a rubber stamp made up with this injunction: "Use no unauthorized commas. Check the list." A few applications of this stamp to comma-cluttered papers make the point. A more common device is to prepare a comma sheet for pasting inside the front cover of students' notebooks. This sheet is useful not only because it is there when needed but also because it reduces the ten or fifteen pages given to comma punctuation in textbooks to a single page that can be scanned with a sweep of the eye.

Some comma rules are more difficult than others. The difference between restrictive and non-restrictive clauses eludes many students all the way through college. When a student proves his inability to cope with this problem without more aid than the handbook supplies, he should have a private conference with the teacher. If half the class have persistent trouble with this or any other tricky matter of mechanics, the teacher should collect examples from their papers and discuss these with the whole class. But such sessions must be brief and to the point, or the principle of keeping mechanics from becoming positive subject matter is endangered.

Many teachers use a chart, also kept in students' notebooks, on which students check the mechanical errors marked by the teacher on successive papers. This chart becomes one basis for discussion when student and teacher have a conference. If the student has dangled modifiers in seven consecutive writing assignments, or has blundered repeatedly in grammatical parallelism, the focal point for the conference is obvious.

Conference time is indispensable for the efficient teaching of composition, not only for remedying mechanical defects but also for discussing style, organization, and development of ideas with the student's own composition as the basis for discussion. Unfortunately, the moments that can be seized before and after school are inadequate. If conference time can be made an accepted part of the English teacher's day, the composition program will improve dramatically. In some schools experiments with team-teaching and flexible programming have already made such conference time available, but the practice is by no means general. Such conference time is universally considered necessary at the college level, but it is clearly even more useful at the high school level, when students are developing their basic habits of writing and composing.

GRADING MECHANICAL ERRORS

We turn next to the question of the appropriate weight to be assigned mechanical errors in determining grades. Let us take as our example the paragraph earlier cited, which includes serious mechanical faults in great abundance. But let us now describe the paper somewhat more fully. Marred by mechanical faults though it is, this paper has much to commend it. The writer has written a full page, whereas some students managed less than half a page. He has stayed well within the bounds set by the topic sentence and has argued cogently on the side of Oberon, insisting on the appropriateness of the lesson taught Titania. He has reviewed the origin of the quarrel between the couple and has carefully assessed Titania's conduct that caused Oberon's wrath. He has quoted aptly from the play to make his points. Above all, the paper evinces that this writing was no mere exercise in paragraph-writing for the student; it has the ring of conviction.

On all counts, as a ninth grade effort, the paragraph deserves the grade of "A"—except for the abundance of gross mechanical faults. For these, it deserves an unqualified "F." The teacher has three obvious choices:

1. to give it an A.
2. to give it an F.
3. to average the good and the bad and give it a C.

The first choice will show that the teacher values the positive qualities of the paper and will encourage the student to "keep up the good work." He will attack his next assignment with zeal and confidence. But the grade of A will also deceive him, for the paper is not *actually* an A paper; it is only *potentially* an A paper. Even though the teacher adds a strong comment urging him to remedy his technical troubles, the student will plainly see that the only thing that "counts" is the grade itself. He will correct his paper routinely, file it in his notebook, and repeat the same errors next time.

The second choice also has its points. The grade of F expresses what the paper is *actually* worth. And even though the teacher strongly commends his thought and the other values of the paper, the student will recognize that what *really* counts is to avoid errors, for these earned him his F. He will dig into his handbook in a panic—and the next time he writes, most of his mind will be pre-occupied with spelling, punctuation, and sentence structure; his paper will be better mechanically, but it will have lost its fire. If he and the teacher persist, he will eventually write correctly and inanely.

The third choice—the most common one in use—has

no points at all in its favor. The grade of C does not accurately reflect either the *potentiality* (A) or the *actuality* (F) of the paper. Both the degree of reward and the degree of penalty are false. Neither the "pull" (the grade of A for the potentiality) nor the "push" (the grade of F for actuality) is asserted strongly enough by the compromising C. This grade is guaranteed to foster mediocrity.

None of these choices is either accurate or effective. But there is a fourth choice—the split grade, which in this case would be A/F. The A gives "pull," incentive to keep up the good work, and the F gives "push," incentive to get rid of the mechanical defects. This method of grading often produces dramatic results.

There are two ways of using the split grade, one effective, the other much less so. The ineffective way—the one in common use—involves eventual averaging of the upper and lower grades; say, for example, that a student has received the following composition grades during a semester:

A/F A/F A/D B/D A/F B/D A/D B/F A/D:
final grade C.

Here the teacher has merely postponed the averaging, and might as well have averaged each time. The split grade has been, after all, only an illusion. The more effective way requires an initial explanation by the teacher of what the upper and lower grades mean, together with a statement that they will *not* be averaged at the end of the grading period. Suppose the student has the following record:

A/F A/F A/D A/C A/B A/B A A A: final grade A.

This student has demonstrated convincingly that he has eliminated the mechanical troubles that beset him earlier. The lower grades on all his papers are accordingly forgiven; he is awarded the upper grade not only for the later papers but for all. It should be noted that the final three grades are unqualified A; hence no split grade is indicated. The designation A/A would be meaningless. On the other hand, suppose the student's grades are as follows:

A/F A/D A/F A/D A/F A/F A/F A/F A/F:
final grade F.

Here the student's performance never wins for him the "potential" indicated by the upper grade; he is entitled, at the end, only to the "actual." The teacher should make clear that the upper grade never means "content" and the lower "form," but that the upper means "potential" and the lower "actual." The "potential" is what the paper *would be* except for the mechanical execution.

It should be noted, finally, that the second grade is always lower than the first; logically there can be no grades like C/B, D/A, F/A—which would assert that the actual performance was superior to the potential; the grade F/A would mean that the student said nothing, but said it flawlessly. It would assign *positive* value to the avoidance of errors, whereas in fact the avoidance of errors is purely negative, as we have emphasized throughout by insisting that study of mechanics be kept, as it were, in the kitchen.

The split grade frees the teacher to reward generously, even lavishly, to nurture imagination and honest effort. At the same time, it allows him to penalize more candidly than he would otherwise do. It is painful for any teacher to give a single grade of F to a mechanically wretched paper that contains a spark of originality or a sign of promise that he wants desperately to encourage; hence he gives such a paper a C, which is unjust both ways. The split grade lets the student see truly how good and how bad his performance is.

Appendix

The following works have been selected and placed for grades nine through twelve according to the principles formulated in Chapter 2. They are not arranged, however, except alphabetically by genre. As Chapters 3 and 4 make clear, the individual teacher should devise the specific arrangement best suited to his purpose.

The lists include primarily works that need intensive classroom teaching; outside reading is not included, though many works not chosen for actual teaching in the earlier years can be offered for outside reading in later years. The list for each grade includes more titles than could possibly be taught in any one year; the individual teacher should make the final choices.

Although no series of anthologies in print contains all these selections in this sequence, the lists should be useful in making text selection purposeful, and the wealth of paperbacks available should make much of the program feasible even now.

NINTH GRADE

Novels
   Brontë, Charlotte   *Jane Eyre*
   Dickens, Charles   *David Copperfield*
   ———— *Great Expectations*
   Twain, Mark   *The Adventures of Huckleberry Finn*
Short Novels
   Crane, Stephen   *The Red Badge of Courage*
   Wharton, Edith   *Ethan Frome*
Plays
   Shakespeare, William   *Julius Caesar*
   ———— *A Midsummer Night's Dream*
   ———— *The Taming of the Shrew*
Short Stories
   Benét, Stephen V.   *By the Waters of Babylon*
   ———— *The Devil and Daniel Webster*
   Chekhov, Anton   *On the Road*
   ———— *A Trifling Occurrence*
   ———— *Vanka*

TENTH GRADE

Plays
   Goldsmith, Oliver   *She Stoops to Conquer*
   Shakespeare, William   *As You Like It*
   ———   *The Merchant of Venice*
   ———   *Romeo and Juliet*

Short Stories
   Anderson, Sherwood   Death in the Woods
   Bierce, Ambrose   Chickamauga
   ———   A Horseman in the Sky
   ———   An Occurrence at Owl Creek Bridge
   Cather, Willa   Neighbor Rosicky
   Chekhov, Anton   The Chorus Girl
   ———   A Day in the Country
   ———   An Upheaval
   France, Anatole   Putois
   Gogol, Nikolay   The Cloak
   Hawthorne, Nathaniel   Ethan Brand
   ———   Rappaccini's Daughter
   ———   Wakefield
   ———   Young Goodman Brown
   Hemingway, Ernest   The Killers
   ———   The Snows of Kilimanjaro
   Irving, Washington   The Devil and Tom Walker
   Lardner, Ring   Haircut
   Maugham, Somerset   The Letter
   ———   Rain
   ———   Red
   ———   A String of Beads
   Maupassant, Guy de   Hautot Father and Son
   ———   Looking Back
   ———   The Story of a Farm Girl
   ———   Two Little Soldiers
   O'Connor, Frank   Guests of the Nation
   ———   My Oedipus Complex
   ———   The Storyteller
   Poe, Edgar Allan   The Cask of Amontillado
   Pushkin, Alexander   The Queen of Spades
   Saroyan, William   The Summer of the Beautiful White Horse
   Steinbeck, John   The Leader of the People
   Stevenson, Robert L.   A Lodging for the Night
   Tolstoy, Leo   God Sees the Truth but Waits
   ———   Three Deaths
   Turgenev, Ivan   Byezhin Meadow
   ———   The District Doctor

Essays
   Addison, Joseph   Tulips

——— It Is a Beauteous Evening
——— Lines Written in Early Spring
——— The World Is Too Much with Us

Poetry—American

Bryant, William Cullen   Thanatopsis
cummings, e. e.   next to of course god america i
Dickinson, Emily   Bring Me the Sunset in a Cup
——— The Heart Asks Pleasure First
——— I Taste a Liquor
——— The Soul Selects
Frost, Robert   The Death of the Hired Man
——— Mending Wall
——— The Road Not Taken
Longfellow, Henry Wadsworth   The Day Is Done
——— Hymn to the Night
——— My Lost Youth
——— The Tide Rises
Lowell, James R.   Rhoecus
Markham, Edwin   The Man with the Hoe
Millay, Edna St. Vincent   I Shall Go Back Again
——— Pity Me Not Because the Light of Day
Poe, Edgar Allan   The Haunted Palace
——— Israfel
——— To One in Paradise
Pound, Ezra   Commission
Reed, Henry   Naming of Parts
Robinson, E. A.   Ben Jonson Entertains a Man from Stratford
——— How Anandale Went Out
——— Luke Havergal
——— Miniver Cheevy
——— Richard Cory
Teasdale, Sara   I Shall Not Care
——— Let It Be Forgotten
——— The Long Hill
Whitman, Walt   One's Self I Sing

ELEVENTH GRADE

Novels

Austen, Jane   *Emma*
——— *Pride and Prejudice*
Balzac, Honoré de   *Père Goriot*
Brontë, Emily   *Wuthering Heights*
Flaubert, Gustave   *Madame Bovary*
Hardy, Thomas   *The Return of the Native*
——— *Tess of the D'Urbervilles*

Kafka, Franz   *The Trial*
Tolstoy, Leo   *Anna Karenina*

Short Novels
Conrad, Joseph   *The Heart of Darkness*
James, Henry   *The Turn of the Screw*
Melville, Herman   *Billy Budd*
Porter, Katherine Anne   *Noon Wine*
———   *Pale Horse Pale Rider*

Epics
Homer   *Odyssey*
———   *Iliad*

Plays
Ibsen, Henrik   *A Doll's House*
———   *Hedda Gabler*
Shakespeare, William   *Henry IV, Part 1*
———   *Henry V*
———   *Macbeth*
———   *Twelfth Night*
Shaw, George Bernard   *Pygmalion*
Sheridan, Richard B.   *The School for Scandal*
Wilde, Oscar   *The Importance of Being Earnest*

Short Stories
Aiken, Conrad   *Impulse*
Cather, Willa   *Paul's Case*
Conrad, Joseph   *An Outpost of Progress*
———   *The Tale*
Crane, Stephen   *The Blue Hotel*
———   *The Bride Comes to Yellow Sky*
———   *The Pace of Youth*
Faulkner, William   *Spotted Horses*
———   *That Evening Sun*
Joyce, James   *Araby*
Mansfield, Katherine   *At the Bay*
———   *The Daughters of the Late Colonel*
———   *The Doll's House*
———   *The Garden Party*
———   *Je ne Parle pas Français*
———   *The Life of Ma Parker*
———   *Marriage à la Mode*
Parker, Dorothy   *Big Blonde*
Porter, Katherine Anne   *Flowering Judas*
———   *He*
———   *Old Mortality*
———   *Theft*
———   *The Witness*
Salinger, J. D.   *For Esmé—with Love and Squalor*

——— Trainor the Druggist
Millay, Edna St. Vincent   Sonnet to Gath
——— What Lips My Lips Have Kissed
Poe, Edgar Allan   To Helen
Whitman, Walt   A Noiseless Patient Spider
——— When Lilacs Last in the Dooryard Bloomed
Williams, William Carlos   This Is Just to Say

TWELFTH GRADE

Novels
  Dickens, Charles   Bleak House
  Dostoevsky, Fyodor   Crime and Punishment
  James, Henry   Portrait of a Lady
  ——— Washington Square
  Melville, Herman   Moby Dick
  Stendhal   The Red and the Black
  Thackeray, William M.   Vanity Fair
Short Novels
  James, Henry   The Aspern Papers
  ——— The Beast in the Jungle
  ——— Daisy Miller
  ——— The Spoils of Poynton
  Joyce, James   The Dead
  Mann, Thomas   Death in Venice
  ——— Tonio Kröger
Other Long Works
  Cervantes, Miguel de   Don Quixote
  Dante   The Divine Comedy
  Swift, Jonathan   Gulliver's Travels
  Thoreau, Henry David   Walden
  Virgil   The Aeneid
Plays
  Shakespeare, William   Hamlet
  ——— King Lear
  ——— The Tempest
  ——— The Winter's Tale
  Shaw, George Bernard   Man and Superman
  Sophocles   Antigone
  ——— Oedipus Rex
Short Stories
  Aiken, Conrad   Silent Snow, Secret Snow
  Crane, Stephen   The Open Boat
  Huxley, Aldous   The Gioconda Smile
  James, Henry   The Altar of the Dead
  ——— Brooksmith

Index